Early Framers of Tourism Knowledge, Volume I

T0313180

This book emphasises the work, the remarkable contributions, and the lifetime achievements of internationally respected scholars who have made lifelong contributions to advancing tourism studies and the dissemination of tourism-based knowledge and education across the world.

Strengthening a field and its ability to form its own traditions is undoubtedly possible with a bridge to be established between the past, present, and future. The capacity of research carried out today and in the future is built on the outputs of education and research completed in the past, adding new links to the chain. The history of tourism studies and education dates to the early years of the 20th century and began recording a momentum in its second half. There is, therefore, a lot more to do in terms of the institutionalisation of such a young and dynamic field and this book aims to introduce tourism scholars with their widest geographical representation, dating from the first years of tourism research back in the early 1900s.

Volume I of IV includes tributes to 20 scholars who have defined tourism as an object of academic study, established its foundations and organisations, and widened its scope to encompass thousands of empirical studies. Each of these volumes contains different profiles thereby bringing 80 of the pioneers in tourism more vividly to life.

This book was originally published as a special issue of *Anatolia: An International Journal of Tourism and Hospitality Research*.

Metin Kozak is Professor in the School of Communication, Kadir Has University, Turkey. He holds both Master's and Ph.D. degrees in tourism. His research focuses on consumer behaviour, tourism marketing, public health, and sustainability.

Nazmi Kozak, Retired Professor, School of Tourism, Anadolu University, Turkey. He gained both his Master's and Ph.D. degrees in tourism. His research activities focus on tourism marketing, history of tourism, and bibliometrics.

Early Framers of Tourism Knowledge, Volume I

Edited by
Metin Kozak and Nazmi Kozak

Routledge
Taylor & Francis Group

LONDON AND NEW YORK

First published 2023
by Routledge
4 Park Square, Milton Park, Abingdon, Oxon OX14 4RN

and by Routledge
605 Third Avenue, New York, NY 10158

Routledge is an imprint of the Taylor & Francis Group, an informa business

Introduction © 2023 Metin Kozak and Nazmi Kozak
Chapters 1–20 © 2023 Taylor & Francis

British Library Cataloguing in Publication Data
A catalogue record for this book is available from the British Library

ISBN13: 978-1-032-01476-0 (hbk)
ISBN13: 978-1-032-01480-7 (pbk)
ISBN13: 978-1-003-17880-4 (ebk)

DOI: 10.4324/9781003178804

Typeset in Minion Pro
by Newgen Publishing UK

Publisher's Note
The publisher accepts responsibility for any inconsistencies that may have arisen during the conversion of this book from journal articles to book chapters, namely the inclusion of journal terminology.

Disclaimer
Every effort has been made to contact copyright holders for their permission to reprint material in this book. The publishers would be grateful to hear from any copyright holder who is not here acknowledged and will undertake to rectify any errors or omissions in future editions of this book.

Contents

Citation Information

The following chapters were originally published in various volumes and issues of the journal *Anatolia*. When citing this material, please use the original page numbering for each article, as follows:

Chapter 16

Charles R. (Chuck) Goeldner: a profile of service and contribution to the tourism research community
Richard R. Perdue
Anatolia, volume 26, issue 1 (2015), pp. 137–142

Chapter 17

A portrait of Chris Cooper
Noel Scott
Anatolia, volume 26, issue 1 (2015), pp. 122–128

Chapter 18

Clare Gunn: pioneer, maverick and "founding father" of academic tourism in the USA
John L. Crompton
Anatolia, volume 26, issue 1 (2015), pp. 165–170

Chapter 19

Claude Kaspar: a life devoted to tourism and transport –moving theory into practice
Norbert Vanhove
Anatolia, volume 26, issue 3 (2015), pp. 493–500

Chapter 20

Daniel R. Fesenmaier: an accidental, colourful and quintessential scholar
Dan Wang and Bing Pan
Anatolia, volume 29, issue 2 (2018), pp. 311–318

For any permission-related enquiries please visit:
www.tandfonline.com/page/help/permissions

Notes on Contributors

David Airey, School of Hospitality and Tourism Management, University of Surrey, Guildford, Surrey, UK.

Nevenka Čavlek, Faculty of Economics & Business, University of Zagreb, Zagreb, Croatia.

David C. W. Chin, School of Hotel and Tourism Management, The Hong Kong Polytechnic University, Hong Kong S. A. R., P. R. China.

John L. Crompton, Department of Recreation, Park and Tourism Sciences, Texas A&M University, College Station, TX, USA.

John C. Crotts, College of Charleston, Charleston, SC, USA.

Simon Hudson, College of Hospitality, Retail and Sport Management, University of South Carolina, Columbia, USA.

Ana Inácio, Centre for Geographical Studies, University of Lisbon, Lisbon, Portugal; Estoril Higher Institute for Tourism and Hotel Studies, Estoril, Portugal.

Metin Kozak, School of Communication, Kadir Has University, İstanbul, Turkey.

Nazmi Kozak, School of Tourism, Anadolu University, Eskisehir, Turkey.

Mimi Li, School of Hotel and Tourism Management, The Hong Kong Polytechnic University, Hong Kong S. A. R., P. R. China.

Xiang (Robert) Li, Department of Tourism and Hospitality Management, Temple University, Philadelphia, PA, USA.

Victor T.C. Middleton, Independent Management Consultant, Academic and Author, UK.

Alastair M. Morrison, School of Hospitality and Tourism Management, Purdue University, West Lafayette, IN, USA.

Ghazali Musa, Faculty of Business and Accountancy, University Malaya, Kuala Lumpur, Malaysia.

Bing Pan, Department of Recreation, Park, and Tourism Management, Penn State University, University Park, PA, USA.

Richard R. Perdue, Pamplin College of Business, Virginia Tech, Blacksburg, VA, USA.

Arie Reichel, Guilford Glazer Faculty of Business and Management, Ben-Gurion University of the Negev, Be'er Sheva, Israel.

João Sarmento, Geography Department, University of Minho, Guimarães, Portugal; Centre for Geographical Studies, University of Lisbon, Lisbon, Portugal.

Noel Scott, UQ Business School, University of Queensland, St Lucia, Australia.

Gareth Shaw, Department of Management Studies, University of Exeter Business School, Exeter, UK.

Svetlana Stepchenkova, Department of Tourism, Recreation, & Sport Management, College of Health and Human Performance, University of Florida, Gainesville, FL, USA.

Natan Uriely, Guilford Glazer Faculty of Business and Management, Ben-Gurion University of the Negev, Be'er Sheva, Israel.

Norbert Vanhove, Former Vice-President AIEST, Honorary President TRC, Member Board of Directors WES, Bruges, Belgium.

Dan Wang, School of Hotel & Tourism Management, The Hong Kong Polytechnic University, Kowloon, Hong Kong.

Roy C. Wood, Academy of Hotel and Facility Management, NHTV Breda University of Applied Sciences, Breda, The Netherlands.

Introduction[1]

Early framers of tourism knowledge landscape

Metin Kozak and Nazmi Kozak

Although tourism has gained its independence in terms of educational bureaucracy and taxonomy, the debate regarding its scientific position still persists. At the heart of this debate is the fact that many disciplines in the social sciences play a significant role in the production of knowledge in tourism studies (Jafari, 1990; Tribe & Xiao, 2011; Wen, Kozak, & Jiang, 2022). Jafari claims that tourism has developed by importing knowledge from other fields and through the formation of a synthesised body of knowledge that should now be 'exported' back to other disciplines. Historical analysis suggests that such a process of importation has lasted for almost three quarters of a century, helping the field to become more mature and perhaps generating knowledge that could feed back into other fields. As a result, these volumes have looked at the pioneers of tourism studies and acknowledged their contribution, in the context of the development and history of tourism knowledge. From a generic perspective, nested as a very minor subject field more than a century ago, tourism was fertilised primarily by non-tourism scholars, and in today's academic world has become a mature field of research and education.

Historically, tourism emerged as a field of academic research and education during the interwar years. During this period, as well as following the Second World War, when it was necessary to rebuild cities and infrastructure decimated by conflict, regimes from across the political spectrum utilised tourism for various ideological and economic ends (Zuelow, 2016). Consequently, academics, primarily economists, paid increased attention to tourism as an emerging field of study. Tourism research in this period focused mainly on the macro-level impacts of tourism as a financial activity at the national level, such as the contribution of leisure travel to the balance of payments. Scholars from Germany and Switzerland were at the forefront of promoting this approach. From the 1950s onwards, academics from other disciplines such as sociology and geography turned their attention to tourism. This trend broadened in the 1960s to include academics affiliated with psychology, anthropology, and business management. Through the rapid liberalisation of the world economy and the widening impacts of international tourist movements, the geopolitical distribution of tourism scholars became more internationally diversified, representing countries in the Americas, Europe, Africa, Asia, and Australia.

Such developments have, over the last century, played a role in the creation of a new field of research and education called 'tourism studies'. Because this subject is interconnected with major fields such as economics/business, sociology, geography, psychology, history, anthropology, architecture, and literary studies, it is self-consciously interdisciplinary. While tourism studies were

1 This text has been edited from the article formerly published as: Kozak, M., & Kozak, N. (2016). Institutionalisation of tourism research and education: From the early 1900s to 2000s. *Journal of Tourism History*, 8(3), 275–299.

perpetuated by awarding a large number of postgraduate degrees during the past three decades, it also accommodates non-tourism scholars, as listed in this series, who prefer to conduct empirical research and who consider tourism the best platform for this purpose.

While the field of tourism studies first emerged in the early 1900s, and was developed in the 1940s by scholars with a background in economics, such as Hunziker, Krapf, and Kaspar, since the 1980s it has evolved to become more management oriented (Xiao & Smith, 2006). This has opened new avenues with a more professional focus on tourism education at the institutional level, and the development of many training programmes at the business or organisational level. The reason for this change is quite simple. Following World War II, tourism was considered to be the primary and most convenient way of supporting the economic development of nations as more visitors became involved in tourism activities and more destinations were introduced to meet the increased demand. As a result, it became clear that the lack of managerial skill was an issue that needed to be dealt with firmly and professionally.

German culture had a considerable influence on the evolution of tourism as an academic field from the 1920s onwards. German culture was also influential in terms of debates concerning the scientific credentials of tourism research. In the 1930s, tourism and science came together in German academic circles. In 1942, in the midst of World War II, both Hunziker and Krapf, pioneers of academic tourism, proposed rules in relation to tourism education at the scientific level and they defined tourism as a science. In 1955 both continued to believe that the study of tourism was scientific in nature. Yet soon afterward, in 1960, Krapf changed his tune. In a presentation delivered at the University of Bern, Switzerland, he suggested there was little scientific about this branch of scholarship. René Baretje-Keller recalls the discussion:

> Fifty-two years ago, Professor Kurt Krapf, University of Bern, Switzerland, explained to me that tourism is not and will never be a science, but is rather an activity like agriculture, industry, or transport, which needs to use all the methods, techniques and models of other disciplines systematically.

Debate among pioneering scholars helps to understand the geographic distribution of academic tourism studies from the 1910s onwards. Representing Germany, Glücksmann was an active personality in the development of tourism as an academic activity from the 1910s to the 1930s. His Swiss–German counterparts succeeded him: such men as Hunziker and Krapf in the 1940s and 1950s. They were followed in the 1950s by Kaspar and Bernecker who retained German language dominance. From the 1960s, a series of tourism scholars emerged representing a wider geographical distribution, such as Archer, Baretje-Keller, Burkart, Cohen, Crompton, Goeldner, Gunn, Jafari, Krippendorf, Mazanec, Medlik, Olali, Pizam, Wahab, and Woodside, among others. In addition to those in the U.S. and the U.K., other scholars became very active in the field and were pioneers in introducing tourism education and studies and in advancing standards in their own countries. As in the first period of academic tourism studies, the majority of those scholars affiliated with the second period were trained in economics. Today, as the founders of tourism studies, all these names have become benchmarks in their countries of origin.

Among the applauses to their contributions is a series dedicated to releasing tributes to internationally renowned tourism scholars. This series was first introduced by the journal *Anatolia* in 2013 with the aim of introducing two or three scholars in each issue. Dating back to the early period of the emergence of tourism studies, for instance, the 1920s and 1930s, this series emphasises the work, the remarkable contributions, and the lifetime achievements of the pioneers who have played a key role in building the field of tourism studies and the dissemination of tourism-based knowledge and education. These pioneers defined tourism as an object of academic study, established its foundations and organisations, and widened its scope to encompass thousands of empirical studies, as well as contributing to the education of millions of younger researchers and practitioners. Tributes published to date include those dedicated to 80 scholars in four volumes, containing the history of those from the early 1900s until the 1990s. Each profile has been contributed either by their close colleagues or former students.

The tourism studies literature has also expanded to encompass a series of special book editions, published under the leadership of Jafar Jafari as series editor. This series, which began in the mid-2000s, introduces a number of renowned scholars across various disciplines, via their own reflections on how to study tourism and how to contribute to the tourism literature. Three books in this series have already been released, each dedicated to a tourism-related field of academic research, e.g., the pioneers of the sociology and anthropology of tourism (Nash, 2005), the pioneers of the psychology of tourism (Pearce, 2011), and the pioneers of tourism economics (Dwyer, 2011). However, this series has in large part been limited to exploring the work of second-generation scholars who are still active in research and teaching, rather than the first-generation pioneers.

The purpose of these volumes is therefore to present the formation of a body of knowledge concerning the evolution of the tourism field and its scholars beginning in the early 20th century. An overview of secondary sources illustrates the *institutionalisation* of tourism research and education as well as how it gained momentum, eventually reaching its present status as a field of study. The type of development described in these volumes refers to the exchange and communication of the scholarly research in tourism. The data sources include books, journals, reports, theses, dissertations, events, and personal experiences and observations. Academics who had personal communications with the first generation of pioneers in tourism research, or who had personal experience of the transformation of tourism as an academic discipline from its junior (prior to the 1960s) to its mature stages (after the 1990s) offered us a richer database.

As the volume editors, we are thankful to those who have devoted much time in completing each profile and those who have agreed to be involved in the series. Without their patience, eagerness, punctuality, and faith, this series may not have been on your desk. Furthermore, Jafar Jafari helped us in finding the right title to better reflect the mission of these volumes. Lastly, we would also like to extend our appreciation to Taylor & Francis that agreed to firstly include these portraits as a part of special series in *Anatolia* and in a book form subsequently. In doing so, Taylor & Francis plays another leading role in launching a new series named as the portraits of pioneers in tourism research and education that aims to introduce tourism scholars with their widest geographical representation, dating the first years of tourism research back to the early 1900s, represented by Professor Glücksmann and so on.

As simply indicated in these volumes and eagerly emphasised by Jafari, Rome is not built in one day, but we still have more to accomplish to strengthen its conceptual and methodological structure for future generations of the academia.

References

Dwyer, L. (ed., 2011). *The Discovery of Tourism Economics, Tourism Social Science Series*, Volume 16, Bingley: Emerald.

Jafari, J. (1990). Research and scholarship: The basis of tourism education. *Journal of Tourism Studies*, 1(1), 33–41.

Kozak, M., & Kozak, N. (2016). Institutionalisation of tourism research and education: From the early 1900s to 2000s. *Journal of Tourism History*, 8(3), 275–299.

Nash, D. (ed., 2005). *The Study of Tourism: Anthropological and Sociological Beginnings*, Bingley: Emerald.

Pearce, P.L. (2011). *The Study of Tourism – Foundations from Psychology*, Bingley: Emerald.

Tribe, T., & Xiao, H. (2011). Development in tourism social science. *Annals of Tourism Research*, 38(1), 7–26.

Wen, J., Kozak, M., & Jiang, Y. (2022). Beyond sightseeing: How can tourism affect public/global health in modern society? *Journal of Global Health*, 12, 03035.

Xiao, H., & Smith, S.L.J. (2006). The making of tourism research: Insights from a social science. *Annals of Tourism Research*, 33(2), 490–507.

Zuelow, E.G.E. (2016). *A History of Modern Tourism*, New York and London: Palgrave.

Abraham Pizam: an academic visionary and entrepreneur

Arie Reichel

Introduction

I am honoured by Dr Kozak suggestion that I write a portrait about Prof. Abraham Pizam (a.k.a. "Abe"). I have known Prof. Pizam for almost 40 years. I needed to calculate the number of years' time again because it is hard to believe that so many years have gone by. Abe is the founding and current dean of the Rosen College of Hospitality Management at the University of Central Florida in Orlando. He is definitely one of the world's leaders in the field of hospitality and tourism management. Since 2006 he serves as Editor-in-Chief of the *International Journal of Hospitality Management.* In addition, he is a member of countless advisory and scientific boards and frequently appears on national TV, newspapers, and radio networks on current tourism issues.

If one has to summarize Abe's academic persona, it means endless curiosity in countless fields of human behaviour and a notable ability to combine scientific, theory-based research with an applied approach. He has always kept his scientific integrity and does not let his personal opinions interfere with the analysis and conclusions of his work. He is humane towards his subjects, yet does not preach about a new source of "light" he discovered, that will make our world a perfect place to live in. Nor does he believe that tourism is the panacea for the world's problems. He is a remarkable model of a mentor who defies all theories about the presumably unavoidable inherent "terminating" conflict in mentor–protégé relationships. This is compatible with being a *mensch, a* person of integrity and honour (*Yiddish*, human being, from *Middle High German*).

As a scholar, he has laid the foundation for several research issues that mainly deal with the organization or the hospitality and tourism industry, and its effects on the environment, be it social, cultural, or economic. Prof. Pizam's books include the *International Encyclopedia of Hospitality Management*, 2nd ed. (2010); *International Dictionary of Hospitality* (2008) Ed. with J. Holcomb; *Tourism, Security and Safety: From Theory to Practice* (2005) Ed. with Y. Mansfeld; *Consumer Behavior in Travel and Tourism* (1999) Ed. with Y. Mansfeld and Tourism; and *Crime and International Security Issues* (1995) Ed. with Y. Mansfeld. Altogether, Prof. Pizam is active on 23 scientific journals' editorial boards and received numerous awards and honours for his scholarship and leadership. He is soon to get a special recognition award for his contribution from the forthcoming World Conference for Graduate Research in Tourism, Hospitality, and Leisure in Istanbul, Turkey. His more than 150 publications appeared in such journals as *Annals of Tourism Research, Cornell Hospitality Quarterly, Hospitality Education and Research Journal, Journal of Hospitality and Leisure Marketing, Journal of Travel*

Research, Tourism Management, and many others. As will be noted later, Prof. Pizam has had considerable impact on the development of the field of hospitality and tourism management, and has a firm view of the directions that research should be aimed at.

I have first met Prof. Pizam in the summer of 1974. I was a graduate student at Tel-Aviv University, looking for a research assistant job. Enquiring about this possibility with the students' secretary, I was advised to try to contact Prof. Pizam for a possible job. Those were the days of knocking on doors, rather than sending emails or other communication means. Sure enough, he was in his office, and in 20 min a mutual decision has been made. I can declare that this decision has changed my life. Prof. Pizam has become my mentor, my friend, and my family away from home when I resided in the USA. During the 40 years of acquaintance, I saw Abe developing from a humble, hardworking lecturer to a world-renowned scholar in the field of hospitality and tourism management, and I am astounded by the fact that he keeps working on research and supervises graduate students while functioning as dean of a large college.

Prof. Pizam was born in Romania and was educated in Israel and the USA. He graduated with a BA degree in Sociology and Political Science from the Hebrew University in Jerusalem in 1962. He then obtained two graduate degrees in top USA universities: an MPA degree from Graduate School of Public Administration, New York University, NY, in 1964, and a Ph.D. from Graduate School of Business Administration, Cornell University in Ithaca, NY, in 1970. After a period as Chair of the Hotel & Tourism Administration Department at the University of Haifa, he moved to the USA and worked as a faculty member at the University of Massachusetts before taking a position at the University of Central Florida as the founding of the Department of Hospitality Management. At present, he holds the position of Eminent Scholar Chair and Dean of the University of Central Florida's Rosen College of Hospitality Management.

Influential areas of research

Prof. Pizam's considerable contribution to tourism and hospitality theory and practice focuses on several subjects that were central to his research throughout the years. I will try to outline some of the most noted issues, illustrated with some references.

First, it is clear that Abe pays much attention to the nature of the impact of tourism on a destination. As early as the late 1970s, Prof. Pizam investigated the nature of the relationship between tourism and the host environment. Among these studies, most frequently items are as follows: *Dimensions of tourist satisfaction with a destination area* (1978); *Tourism's impacts: The social costs to the destination community as perceived by its residents* (1978); *The social impacts of tourism in Central Florida* (1988); *The perceived impacts of casino gambling on a community* (1985); *Social impact of tourism: Host perceptions* (Fiji) (1993); *Perceived impact of tourism: The role of tourists' familiarity with a destination* (1995); *The case of Samos* (1996); and *Tourism impacts on the Island of Mykonos* (1999).

Second, over the years, he published a stream of studies related to culture and consumer (tourist) behaviour. In them, the role of culture on (tourist) consumer behaviour is highlighted. Among his many studies are such classics as *How nationality affect tourist behavior* (1995); *Customer satisfaction and its measurement in hospitality enterprises* (1999); *Predicting satisfaction among first time visitors to a destination by using the expectancy confirmatory theory* (1993); *Cross-cultural tourist behavior: Perception of Korean tour-guides* (1996); *Israeli tour-guides* (1996); *Dutch tour-guides* (1997); *Tourists' attitude change: U.S. students visiting the USSR* (1991), etc.

Third, Prof. Pizam is noted in studying the employees of the hospitality and tourism industry. Whether he did it out of concern for our graduates, humane interest, or out of sheer academic interest, it is difficult to say but what we know is that before starting his academic career Prof. Pizam served as a human resource executive (and gained experience into the work conditions and life of employees. Examples of this realm of research include the *Perceptions of tourism employees and their families towards tourism* (1994); *Tourism manpower: The state of the art* (1982); *Emotional labor ("Are hospitality employees equipped to hide their feelings?")* (2004); *Absenteeism and voluntary turnover in central Florida hotels* (2000); and more recent concerns such as alcoholism, drug abuse, obesity, divorce rates, and fatal accidents, among hospitality rank and file employees.

Fourth, one cannot overestimate Prof. Pizam's contribution to two phenomena that have a considerable impact of life in the twenty-first century: terror and crime. Often, tourists seem to be the perfect target as they are most vulnerable, easy to detect, and generate media attention. As early as 1982, Prof. Pizam wrote about tourism and crime – a subject that probably raised some eyebrows. Later on, Prof. Pizam and his colleague Y. Mansfeld edited the landmark book on the effects of the absence of safety, security, and peace on domestic and international tourism in *Tourism, crime and international security issues* (1996). He also wrote about *Classifying act of crime and violence at a tourism destination* (1999); *Severity versus frequency of acts of terrorism* (2002); *A quantitative analysis of major terrorist acts and their impact on tourism destinations* (2000); and *Whose responsibility is it to make tourists feel safe* (1997).

It should be noted that the above analysis leaves out numerous papers, editorials, and books. There is no question that Prof. Pizam is one of the most prolific researchers in our field. When asked by Prof. Philip Pearce to participate in the book on the study of tourism, Abe wrote a fascinating account that he entitled "This I believe". This is a summary of a set of beliefs of a person who has been to more than 100 countries, has written more than 150 articles, supervised countless graduate students, and always fought for his integrity, ready to incur the costs of independence and resistance.

"This I believe"

A thorough look at Abe's scientific experience and approach to hospitality research and education is provided by his own account in a set of beliefs titled "This I believe" (Pizam, 2011). In this paper published in Pearce's (2011) edited book on the study of tourism, with an emphasis on the foundations from psychology, Prof. Pizam relates to his strong and consolidated beliefs that were formed during the decades of his vast experience and enquiry into the nature of the hospitality and tourism industry. Having said that, I clearly misrepresent Prof. Pizam's important distinction between various industrial settings. His first deep perception of our "field" is that the Travel, Tourism, and Hospitality industries are not one and the same:

> ... the travel industry is made up of all those businesses that move people (passengers) from one place to another via various modes of transportation. The tourism industry is made up of all businesses that provide goods and services to tourists ... the hospitality industry is an industry that is made up of businesses that provide accommodation, food and beverage and meetings to tourists, travelers and local residents.

Clearly, Prof. Pizam approach is reflected by his own research, teaching, and the *IJHM* (*International Journal of Hospitality Management*) and can be considered as "functional" in nature.

Second, Prof. Pizam believes that academic programmes of study in hospitality and tourism should focus mainly on the micro levels, rather than the macro levels. "The main focus of our research and teaching should be on the management of hospitality and tourism organizations, be they in the private or public sectors ...." I find it quite interesting that given Prof. Pizam approach, he is nevertheless included in the aforementioned Philip L. Pearce book that deals with "foundation from psychology". However, the answer is rather simple: in spite of Abe's declared conviction about the nature of research and education in hospitality and tourism, he is fully aware of the significant role of consumer behaviour. While shunning away from broad brush works of "culture", he is well aware of its macro role in shaping the tourist experience (see, for example, the aforementioned studies on the effect of culture and terror). It seems that his argument that hospitality and tourism management education should apply business curricula is rooted in two tenets: first, his fear of the "liberalization" of hospitality management education from its vocational and management orientation (Morrison & O'Mahony, 2003). Second, his belief that our role as educators is to prepare highly skilled, sophisticated managers, who fit modern organizational settings (Pizam, 2008). So, while there is definitely a room for discussions on macro issues such as the social and economic impacts of tourism on the society, the majority of the curriculum should be devoted to such subjects as the operation, marketing, human resources, accounting, and finance of hospitality or tourism organizations. Examining Prof. Pizam's research along the 40 years indicates a personal openness to both micro and macro issues, so he clearly has gained the "privilege" to form his view on his present preference for the direction of tourism and hospitality curricula.

The third assertion of Prof. Pizam deals with research issues. Abe does not hesitate to explicitly state his reservation about tourism scholars whose research focuses on themselves and/or their institutions. Indeed, this approach is manifested in the nature of research published in the *IJHM*. This is hardly the home for a paper that describes the internal trials and tribulations of a researcher during his/her data collection and analysis processes or a comparative study on curricula development. Some may take issue with this approach; however, it is clearly stated in Prof. Pizam's editorials, academic talks, and mentoring graduate students, "... Let's leave the study of pedagogy and educational institutions to our colleagues in schools of education and concentrate our research on the hospitality and tourism industries that is our 'reason dêtre'" (Pizam, 2003). Similarly, Prof. Pizam objects to the growing trend in using students as proxy for real tourists or consumers of hospitality products and services. In his fifth statement he writes:

> This practice is so prevalent that in some courses the instructors incorporate the collection of data from students as an integral part of their curriculum. This is done not because the instructors/researchers believe that students in hospitality or tourism programs are true representatives of real tourists or customers, but mostly because it is convenient and cheap to use them. (Pizam, 2011, p. 70)

The fourth belief deals with the rift between academe and the workplace ("shop"). He found out that that too much scientific and lengthy writing style and jargon deter practitioners from reading our research. Hence, he advocates mutual listening. Indeed, as dean, Prof. Pizam is deeply involved with practitioners and leads the Rosen College in this direction. However, I beg to differ with Prof. Pizam on the ability or willingness of researchers to change their writing style for academic journal articles. In spite of the "respect" gain (see Pizam, 2003), our field still thrive to be recognize as a "serious" disciple or a combination of disciples. I believe that given the dozens of new tourism and hospitality journals, there is a room for one journal whose main role is to disseminate knowledge in a clear, succinct style that every manager will be ready to read, enjoy, and adopt some useful new ideas. Clearly, this idea required joint efforts on the side of researchers and administrators to fully recognize publications in this outlet.

The sixth principle refers to tourism and hospitality research coming of age. No longer just a descriptive, case oriented, and other disciplines borrowed methodologies, current hospitality and tourism research has advanced to the level of respectability. In one of the funniest editorial ever, Abe wrote: no more Rodney Dangerfield "no respect "skit" (Pizam, 2003). Indeed, many modern tourism and hospitality researchers have made successful attempts to develop completely new theories that apply to not only hospitality or tourism enterprises but also other service organizations such as hospitals and religious and voluntary service organizations. Indeed, this approach has been recently aired by editors of top journals in the field, including Prof. Jafari, who encouraged us to penetrate the generic management, marketing, and other disciplines, rather than focusing only on hospitality and tourism outlets, in order to disseminate out knowledge and enable its adoption by other disciplines.

It is especially interesting to relate to Prof. Pizam's approach to the never ending discussion in our literature: who is a tourist? " ... I believe that in some aspects all tourists are alike; in others they are similar to some groups but different than others, and in a few aspects tourists are unique individuals". Relating to the work of Prof. Cohen (1972, 1979) and other social anthropologists, Abe agrees that " ... tourists, and especially leisure tourists share common beliefs, values, attitudes, meanings, motives and knowledge which means that they possess a common 'tourist culture' which affects their cognition and behavior while on trips" (Pizam, 2011, pp. 72 and 73). Yet, they can be segmented according to various criteria, thus products or services can be specifically designed to satisfy their needs. Also, every tourist is like no other tourists in the sense that his/her physical and psychological characteristics, personality, upbringing, heritage, life, and travel experiences, as well as numerous other factors, make him/her a unique individual. Given these statements, it is clear that Prof. Pizam does not advocate the post-modern approach, which attempts to construct and de-construct the concept of the tourist and ask time again what distinguishes the tourism experience from our daily real of life. From Prof. Pizam's perspective, as I interpret, this line of enquiry is redundant.

Another strong conviction held by Prof. Pizam involves the participation of residents in tourism development planning. Abe admits investigating this subject (which, indeed, he has done much since the late 1970s), but scorns himself for remaining passive. Nowadays he strongly proposes that the academic tourism community become a strong advocate for participatory tourism development not just by talking about it but by action research, demonstration projects, and training of citizens. Another process that has become prevalent among tourism and hospitality organization is social responsibilities. According to Prof. Pizam, in spite of the fact that many hospitality/tourism firms join this trend in order to gain competitive advantages, there are those who practice it because it is "the right thing to do": feeling good about themselves, but also good for business purposes. It is interesting to analyse this 10th belief of Prof. Pizam vis-à-vis his 9th observation that is substantiated by his countless visits in hospitality and tourism organizations where he observed that:

> many ... low-skilled or semi-skilled employees work in unpleasant physical surroundings such as hot, noisy and poorly ventilated areas, standing on their feet eight hours or more a day. They have inconvenient working hours such as nightshifts, weekends and holidays, work under constant pressure and in many instances have to satisfy the whims of hard to please customers. For many of them there are very few if any career progression opportunities and in a majority of cases their wages are low and significantly below those in other industries.

> On top of these hardships, employees are required to hide their true feelings of frustration and anger and instructed to manage these emotions so that they are consistent with their job rules ... called emotional labor. (Pizam, 2011, p. 74)

Clearly, his observation complies with other scholars. The first that come to mind are Riley (1996) and Baum (1996). The question that I would like to pose to Abe's realistic, humane, and kind observation is related to social responsibility. Should not we all believe that "charity begins at home", and take care of our employees before we dwell in more luminous pastures of popular and populist social responsibility? I certainly believe that Prof. Pizam will agree with that.

Moving back to the arena of education, Prof. Pizam's 11th belief calls for integrating "professional attitudes" in the curriculum. Indeed, given the aforementioned working conditions and attitudes towards employees and the prevailing attitudes of university administrators to students as "clients" (see the following section), the sense of professionalism, if exists at all, often evaporates as quickly as one starts working in an entry-level position. He defines professionalism as an acculturation process adopted from law and medicine, often ignored in higher education altogether that includes the following components:

- An array of appearances and behaviours such as neatness, good grooming, good manners, good taste, civility, proper speech, etc.
- An assortment of technical and conceptual skills and a commitment to maintaining competence in a given body of knowledge.
- A set of internalized character strengths, values, and attitudes directed towards high-quality service to others, such as ethical and moral conduct, concerns for others, honesty, integrity, fairness, sound judgement, respect for the rule of law, commitment to excellence, etc.

Thus, Prof. Pizam "... strongly advocate that we revise our curricula and incorporate in them a healthy dose of professionalism that at the same time ought to be practiced and formally assessed while in school or in internships" (Pizam, 2007, 2011).

Finally, Prof. Pizam's 12th belief brings us back to our everyday reality at school. He laments the consumerism and entitlement approach that became prevalent among students. Giving into these demands will actually betray our commitment to "the two industries and society at large". As a former dean of The Guilford Glazer School of Management in Ben-Gurion University of the Negev in Israel, I could not agree more with Abe's assertion that "... all students should possess all the rights that every citizen possesses in a democratic society". But these rights should not be confused with consumer rights that exists between sellers and buyers. As I often tell my students, a tourist's ticket entitles him or her to occupy a seat on a flight to Paris, but not ownership of either the plane or the airline.

After presenting Prof. Pizam's belief system, I would like to suggest a 13th principle, not accentuated thus far by Prof. Pizam: mentoring graduate students. I have heard about very few veteran professors whose former Ph.D. students admire their mentoring, the way Prof. Pizam's former students do. In the years 1976–1979, I spent at the University of Massachusetts at Amherst, I was lucky to have Abe as one of my two mentors. I remember clearly the many hours he taught me about academe in his old office in Flint lab, and at his home, which became my second home. Following me was Prof. Ady Milman and later on in Florida were Dr Manuel Rivera, Dr Amir Shani, Dr Ernest Lasten, and Dr Judy Holcomb. Given Abe's personality and geographical transitions (was also visiting professor in numerous countries) during the years, he has become a great believer in cultural diversity and true liberalism. A cursory examination of the faculty and student body at Rosen College is a testimony to his open non-prejudice approach, which is appreciated by so many representatives of numerous nations. I am tempted here to go back to Dangerfield's wit: representative of cultures and countries that "no one would give them the time of day" are welcome and thrive in Rosen College accepting environment.

I started my account of Prof. Pizam with a personal note. I would like to take the liberty to close the circle with a personal observation: the strong woman behind him, Esther. Esther has always been a real pillar of support. In order to achieve Abe's incredible performance, it is clear that the family becomes an integral part of the process. Esther has always been a guide, an advisor, a source of wisdom and vitalization, and most helpful to Abe's protégés.

References

Baum, T. (1996). Unskilled work and the hospitality industry: Myth or reality? *International Journal of Hospitality Management, 15*, 207–210.

Cohen, E. (1972). Toward a sociology of international tourism. *Social Research, 39*, 164–182.

Cohen, E. (1979). A phenomenology of tourism experiences. *Sociology, 13*, 179–201.

Haralambopoulos, N., & Pizam, A. (1996). Tourism's perceived social impacts: The case of Samos. *Annals of Tourism Research, 23*, 503–526.

King, B., Pizam, A., & Milman, A. (1993). The social impacts of tourism on Nadi, Fiji, as perceived by its residents. *Annals of Tourism Research, 20*, 650–665.

Milman, A., & Pizam, A. (1988). Social impacts of tourism in Central Florida. *Annals of Tourism Research, 15*, 191–204.

Milman, A., & Pizam, A. (1995). The role of awareness and familiarity with a destination: The Central Florida case. *Journal of Travel Research, 33*, 21–27.

Pearce, P. L. (2011). *The study of tourism: Foundations from psychology*. Tourism social science series, Vol. 15, Bingley: Emerald.

Pizam, A. (1978). Tourism's impacts: The social costs to the community as perceived by its residents. *Journal of Travel Research, 16*, 8–12.

Pizam, A. (1982). Tourism manpower: The state of the art. *Journal of Travel Research, 21*, 587–620.

Pizam, A. (1999). A comprehensive approach to classifying acts of crime and violence at tourism destinations and analyzing their differential effects on tourism demand. *Journal of Travel Research, 38*, 5–12.

Pizam, A. (2003). What should be our field of study? *International Journal of Hospitality Management, 22*, 339.

Pizam, A. (2004). Are hospitality employees equipped to hide their feelings? (An editorial). *International Journal of Hospitality Management, 23*, 315–316.

Pizam, A. (2007). Educating the next generation of hospitality professionals. *International Journal of Hospitality Management, 26*, 1–3.

Pizam, A. (2011). This I believe. In P. L. Pearce (Ed.), *The study of tourism: Foundations from psychology* Tourism social science series (Vol. 15, pp. 63–78). Bingley: Emerald.

Pizam, A., & Ellis, T. (1999). Customer satisfaction and its measurement in hospitality enterprises. *International Journal of Contemporary Hospitality Management, 11*, 326–339.

Pizam, A., & Fleischer, A. (2002). Severity, vs. frequency of acts of terrorism: Which has a larger impact on tourism demand? *Journal of Travel Research, 40*, 337–339.

Pizam, A., Jafari, J., & Milman, A. (1991). Tourists' attitude change: U.S. students visiting the USSR. *Tourism Management, 12*, 47–54.

Pizam, A., Jansen-Verbeke, M., & Steel, L. (1997). Are all tourists alike regardless of nationality? The perceptions of Dutch tour-guides. *Journal of International Hospitality, Leisure & Tourism Management, 1*, 19–40.

Pizam, A., & Jeong, G.-H. (1996). Cross-cultural tourist behavior: Perceptions of Korean tour-guides. *International Journal of Tourism Management, 17*, 277–286.

Pizam, A., & Mansfeld, Y. (Eds.). (1995). *Tourism, crime and international security issues*. New York, NY; London: Wiley.

Pizam, A., & Milman, A. (1993). Predicting satisfaction among first-time visitors to a destination by using the expectancy disconfirmation theory. *International Journal of Hospitality Management*, *12*, 197–209.

Pizam, A., Milman, A., & King, B. (1994). The perceptions of tourism employees and their families towards tourism: A cross-cultural comparison. *Tourism Management*, *15*, 53–61.

Pizam, A., Neumann, Y., & Reichel, A. (1978). Dimensions of tourist satisfaction with a destination area. *Annals of Tourism Research*, *5*, 314–332.

Pizam, A., & Pokela, J. (1985). Perceived impacts of casino gambling on a destination community. *Annals of Tourism Research*, *12*, 147–165.

Pizam, A., & Smith, J. (2000). Tourism and terrorism: A historical analysis of major terrorism acts and their impact on tourism destinations. *Tourism Economics*, *6*, 123–138.

Pizam, A., & Sussman, S. (1995). Does nationality affect tourist behavior? *Annals of Tourism Research*, *22*, 901–917.

Pizam, A., Tarlow, P., & Bloom, J. (1997). Making tourists feel safe: Whose responsibility is it? *Journal of Travel Research*, *36*, 23–28.

Riley, M. (1996). *Human resource management in the hospitality and tourism industry* (2nd ed.). Oxford: Butterworth-Heinemann.

Abdul Kadir Haji Din: an academic biography

Ghazali Musa

Introduction

When I returned to Malaysia from New Zealand in 2003, after completing studies at Otago University, I was eager to communicate and meet up with Professor Kadir Din. During my five-years study in New Zealand (1997–2002), he was the only Malaysian featured in several publications of the prestigious *Annals of Tourism Research*. Reading the depth of his philosophy, especially on Islam and tourism, he became my inspiration, the scholarship to benchmark my academic career. Din was the person who invited me to Universiti Utara Malaysia (UUM) to deliver my first public lecture in the country. He gave me the impression of a gentle person, steeped in tourism knowledge and a great listener. Another Malaysian scholar who speaks highly of Din is Professsor Amran Hamzah. Amran is currently the most active academic scholar who works on tourism consultancy research, contributing the most to the formulation of various Malaysian tourism strategies and policies. When asked to summarize about Din he wrote:

> Long before the emergence of a thriving tourism research fraternity in Malaysia, Kadir Din was the path breaker; in a way a lone ranger in producing research and publications on tourism in Malaysia. Always ready to lend a helping hand to budding local researchers, he was Malaysia's sole flag bearer on the international stage, and his body of work, especially on Islamic tourism is unrivalled in terms of its intellectual rigour and scholarship, providing deep insights into the Other and streets ahead of the current neo-positivistic research on the subject being churned out in journals.

It is a pleasure to be asked to summarize the illustrious academic biography of Din. He has contributed substantially to tourism knowledge, especially on the Islamic perspectives and social impacts of tourism. His research interests cover tourism planning and policy formulation, Islamic tourism and pilgrimages, economic, environmental and social impact assessments, heritage management, and border tourism. Din has co-edited three collections on tourism and has published several research papers for several distinguished journals among which are *Annals of Tourism Research, Akademika* and *Contemporary Southeast Asia*. He was on the editorial boards of *Annals of Tourism Research, Asia Pacific Journal of Tourism Research, Tourism, Culture and Communication,* and *Pacific Tourism Review,* and served as the editor-in-chief of the *Malaysian Management Journal* and the Malaysian Social Science Journal (*Ilmu Masyarakat*). He played an active role in the tourism industry by being a member of the board of directors of the Islamic Tourism Centre under the Malaysian Ministry of Tourism, board of directors of UTTSB, Universiti Utara Malaysia, and the chairman of Hospitality, Tourism and Consultancy Expert Group in UUM. Having established himself as the founding Dean of the UUM School of Tourism Management, Din worked closely with Pradeep Nair (now DVC of Taylors University) in 2001 to form an academic association which he coined TEAM (Tourism Educator's Association of Malaysia). Today, the TEAM fraternity is a mature professional body which runs its own journal and provides a firm platform for public discourses on tourism and hospitality.

Din was born on 5 July 1949 in Kampung Kunluang, Asun, Kedah near the Malaysian–Thai border. He was brought up in the era before Malaysia's independence from the British and received his elementary education at Sekolah Melayu Binjal. Initially, his academic career was a second option, for like many of his Malay school mates, he had chosen to become an air force officer. However, he changed his life course to pursue an opportunity to be a graduate teacher in geography, following an offer to go for further studies in Australia through the Colombo Plan Teaching scholarship. He completed a Bachelor of Arts in Geography from Monash University (Melbourne) (1970–1973) and was in the first batch of students in Masters of Environmental Science (1974–1976) to graduate from Monash University, for which he wrote a thesis on "Users' attitudes to ionizing radiation in the Melbourne Metropolitan Area". Din's Ph.D. degree was awarded by the Department of Geography, University of Hawaii (1982–1989) with a thesis titled "Bumiputra entrepreneurship in the tourist industry in the Penang-Langkawi Region".

Academic career background

Upon his return to Malaysia (1977), Din began his academic career with a teaching position at the National University of Malaysia (UKM), where he taught human geography and environmental studies. He also taught historical geography and tourism geography at UKM for two years before moving on to help develop the tourism and hospitality programme at Universiti Utara Malaysia (UUM). At UKM, Din continued his studies in Hawaii and his scholarly contribution on local entrepreneurship in tourism earned him a Ph.D. in geography. In 1989, Din was promoted to Associate Professor while heading the geography department. In that year, he was a visiting assistant professor for the department of geography at the University of Hawaii for the summer, and three years later (1992), he took sabbatical as an adjunct professor for the department of Hotel, Restaurant and Tourism Administration at the University of Massachusetts, Amherst.

In 1994, Din was the founding director (dean) of the Centre for General Studies at UKM. Outside the university, he was nominated as the Deputy President of the Malaysian Social Science Association, while contributing as the Chief Editor of its journal Ilmu Masyarakat for two years (1996–1997), before taking a sabbatical leave at the University of Southampton during which he was also a visiting scholar at the University of Bournemouth and a guest lecturer at the University of Surrey. Returning from the UK (1998), Din was appointed as the deputy dean at the faculty of social science and humanities in UKM. Intellectually able and destined for a leadership role, within the same year, he was appointed as the founding dean of the school of tourism management in UUM, the position which he held for three years, before moving on to take up the Tun Razak Distinguished Chair at the Center for Southeast Asian Studies, Ohio University.

Utilizing his skills and knowledge, Din also served actively the tourism industry organisations both in Malaysia and internationally. He worked on various committees including as the protem chairman for TEAM and a member of the Natural Resource Committee of the Malaysia Academy of Science from 2000 until 2003. He was inducted through vote, as a member of the International Academy for the Study of Tourism (IAST), 1989–2004 when he wrote to the then President (Richard Purdue), for permission to suspend his membership so that he could leave tourism to concentrate on his new job as a senior professor in Southeast Asian studies. As a pioneer in tourism studies, Din's academic journey may be described as peripatetic – from human geography under David Mercer's tutelege, to environmental science, to history and general studies, then tourism management and area studies, religion and at this juncture he is reading on the social anthropology of *balik kampung,* which is about the universal practice of returning home, either to retire, to search for roots or to pursue nostalgia or utopia. Like many colleagues in his generation, going back to his birthplace where he will be buried, is a preferred end of the journey. Kadir has built a new home in his village of origin and spends much of his time fishing and tending to his fruit orchard.

Din has been described as an open-minded and sociable person. Indeed, he is less comfortable with attending ceremony and perfunctory acts. Apart from that, being raised in a poor family of a village community has built his character as a helpful person and he continues to be so by helping the poor people around him. His nature of work as an academician was the reason for him to be alone most of the time, despite which on certain occasions, he would engage in serious discussion with a few of his academic colleagues. He is also a friendly person and easy to get along with, but dislikes academic dishonesty, a trait which he discusses at length in his Academic Writing class which he teaches at the graduate level.

When teaching, Din is taken seriously by the students, and he prefers to inculcate some moral values in his classes. He loves to help the students under him as much as possible and wants the students to excel in their academic studies. Din expresses his concern about the attitude of the young generation towards learning. He dislikes the undisciplined students and strives to live by his own example, like being early to the class. It is also disturbing for him to see some students who put minimal effort into the assignments given, resulting in inferior academic quality. He said,

> Students here are usually very passive; they don't ask questions and rarely make comments during lectures or class presentations. This tires me sometimes for having to do most of the talking. Worse still some do not even have the basic courtesy to listen, preferring instead to chat away at the back, or fiddle with their smart phones. Fortunately, the reluctant learners are a minority.

He believes that mediocrity and corner-cutting are also an issue prevalent among graduate students, who display minimal critical thinking, and are unable to participate or contribute constructive comments on colleagues' work. Some of the students, however, are more articulate and biddable. They would take the trouble to get to know the APA format without being pressured to do so. Din has successfully supervised 8 Ph.D. students to completion.

Lately, with advancing age, Din prefers to spend quality time on being with family, reading, watching TV, gardening, and talking with close friends. During his younger days, he fancied fishing, travelling and playing sports such as ping pong, takraw (rattan ball), and badminton. He neither watches soccer on TV nor celebrates his own birthday.

Academic development

Growing up in Asun 40 years ago, his family established a close relationship with local Thais and the Chinese community. He speaks local Thai and had hard time at a Malay school in the beginning due to little exposure to the Malay language. Influenced by difficult childhood experiences at school, he saw a literacy gap in understanding the differences between the Malays and other ethnic individuals. Spurred by a subconscious desire to know others and to be accepted by his own people, he developed an academic interest in how others see Islam, and whether tourism has any impact on inter-ethnic relations. Throughout his academic journey, Din's interests have gradually expanded to relate his tourism knowledge with peace, justice, heritage, environment, and ethnic relations. He recalled with a tinge of sadness when he was deprived of a request for airfare to go and present a paper at a conference in Montreal (1988) on the theme *Tourism: A Vital Force for Peace?* organized by D'Amore in collaboration with Jafar Jafari. The organizers accepted his paper and published it in the proceedings. As a junior lecturer, a single income breadwinner, he could hardly pay for accommodation, let alone the airfare. Fortunately, a young lady (now Professor Norain Othman of UITM), who attended the conference was able to bring home a copy of the proceedings which Jafar had kindly sent him.

Kadir's interest in promoting cross-cultural understanding through tourism is a reaction to the clash of civilization thesis and the stereotypes being profiled about Muslims. He also recalled the day when his Jewish foster parents took him into their home a week after arrival in Australia in 1970, and the friendship and help he had received from his non-Muslim classmates while struggling with English during undergraduate days. The experience was one of full mutual acceptances of the other irrespective of creed or social background. At this late stage in life, one of the few wishes he has is that Muslims embrace cultural diversity and are equally accepted by others. To get to that stage, Muslims must know the others as much as others must know them. As the Malay adage goes, "Tak kenal maka tak cinta" (you can't possibly love a person if you don't know him/her). Of course "nor would one hate the other without knowing him/her". If the world can accept Yoga, karate, taekwondo, kosher, and Sufi practices, tourism scholars can promote Islamophilia rather than Islamopobia through their writing. In this way as Jafar Jafari, Noel Scott and many others have done, we have to promote ethnic literacy of others as well as our own heterogenous identities, no matter which group we belong to.

His sources of inspiration as an academic scholar came from Kamal Salih and David Mercer. Kamal was four years his senior, a man with a brilliant mind, a winner of the Commandant Award at the Malaysian Royal Military College, and a top student at Monash University. Kamal's thesis was published in an international journal – *Regional Science*-during his undergraduate days. These achievements had motivated Din to excel in his own studies. David Mercer was another figure who had been influential to Din. Mercer was an inspiring lecturer who taught recreational geography. His observation on religious ceremony as a tourist attraction in Bali had attracted Din to develop an interest in tourism geography and the *National Geographic's* places of interest.

Din's interest in tourism was driven by his passion for travel. He participated in hitchhiking activities from the time he was in secondary school. He continued to develop his interest as an undergraduate when he travelled to New Zealand at the end of his studies. Furthermore, he was attracted to analysing the tourism resources from the ideas that he had gained in recreational geography on travel motivation and perception of places or tourist destinations. However, his involvement as a tourism scholar came from the opportunity to further his studies. At first, he was offered a place in Chicago which he believed had the best geography programme in the 1980s. However, the Chicago winter would have been too cold for his wife who was asthmatic. When he was assigned by UKM to do further studies in Hawaii, it was a double blessing for him and his wife, since the weather in Hawaii is not only milder but almost consistently pleasant. In Hawaii, he decided to conduct a study on tourism entrepreneurship, and later he developed an interest in pilgrimage and tourism. He was supervised by Donald W. Fryer, a traditional geography scholar who although never having produced an academic paper related to tourism, nevertheless helped him by instilling passion and a drive to venture into tourism as an emerging area in geographic studies.

Din's academic background was in environmental science. Therefore, he saw human activities and tourism in a much broader perspective. He took initiatives through an independent study which enabled him to build his own corpus of references. At the same time, he was very fortunate to have the opportunity to learn from many scholars who came for short visitorships in Honolulu. Among the American visiting scholars who contributed to his doctoral studies were Sam Hilliard, Turgut Var, Lisle Mitchell, Norton Ginsberg, and Linda Richter. Din was grateful to many of his former resident professors at the University of Hawaii, especially Brian Murton, the Chair of the Department, who seems to be a typical jovial Kiwi, who would welcome him and wife at the airport and then invited them to stay for a week before they could find their own accommodation. Din also worked with academicians from several non-American universities such as Chong Tong-Wu (Sydney), David Wu (Taiwan), Tan Chwee Huat, and Stephen Yeh (Singapore). He took classes with many fellow graduate students from Korea, Japan, Nepal, Malaysia, Indonesia, Pacific Islands, the UK, and the United States. He built good relations with two of his graduate students, Antonia Hussey and Charles Johnston, who had an interest in tourism studies. They both hosted Din in their homes, helping him learnt a great deal about tourism from foreign perspectives. The graduate program in University of Hawaii allowed students to take independent studies or directed research under the guidance from many visiting professors. The mode of learning allowed students to read extensively for their research papers. At the end of the second year, Din managed to publish two of such papers in international journals. His pro-active work gained him an invitation to review papers for *Annals of Tourism Research*. Two years later, he was invited to become a member of the editorial board. Needless to say, Din's entry into the tourism field had been gradual, following autonomous learning mostly through desk work and peer support.

Before embarking on his doctoral program Din taught Geography of the Third World which led him to organize a seminar on the subject. While reading on development issues of the so-called Third World he came across Jafar Jafari's master's thesis entitled *Role of tourism in the socio-economic transformation of the developing countries*. Din wrote to Jafar and was eventually invited to review papers and to join the *Annals of Tourism Research* as a resource editor. This connection with Jafar was probably one of the major factors that facilitated him to a future career in tourism studies.

Tourism research interests and selected publications

As stated earlier by Amran Hamzah, Din is the Malaysian pioneer, a sole flag bearer in the international circle of tourism research and publication. The refereed paper "Tourism in Malaysia: competing needs in a plural society" published in 1982 by the *Annals of Tourism Research* is the first scholarly article on tourism published by a Malaysian. The paper "Economic implications of Muslim pilgrimage from Malaysia" published in the same year in *Contemporary Southeast Asia*, was also the first social science article on the subject in the country.

According to Din, back in the 1970s, it was a taboo to discuss ethnic perspectives or religion unless one was an anthropologist conducting ethnological work. The situation had made him reluctant to seek reasons for the absence of Malay or Indian entrepreneurs in the tourism industry during that period although he was wondering whether the non-halal and permissive practices in the hotel sector (alcohol, sex, unkoshered food etc.) had posed cultural obstacles to Malay participation in the business. He was also wondering why there were no Indian hotels either. Was it discrimination, structural impediments of sorts or what? However, a decade later, he wrote a paper on "Islam and tourism", examining some ideological issues centred on the fundamental belief system of the Islamic religion. He discovered that personal attributes rooted in ethnic identity and religion does have an impact on the extent to which individuals are predisposed to certain patterns of tourism engagement. Unfortunately, his ideas failed to attract social science audience both in Malaysia and Indonesia. As part of his interest in understanding the religious motivated tourism subject, his research scope included studying Muslim pilgrimage which shed much light on issues of poor pilgrims performing *Hajj* in Mecca as one of the causes of Malay poverty. He was also keen on exploring old travelogues, history and spiritual quest through the evolutionary perspectives on tourism.

Din is of the opinion that religious travel by definition is clearly ethnic-based, with every religious group having their own "centre out there" (see an encyclopaedia chapter titled "Religious Tourism" (Khan, Olsen, & Var, 1993, pp. 822–829) in VNR's *Encyclopedia of Hospitality and Tourism*. New York: Van Nostrand Reinhold. In a chapter in Stoddard and Morinis (eds) (1997), *Sacred Places, Sacred Places: Geography of Pilgrimages*, Din described the evolution of Muslim pilgrimage from Malaysia with a focus on transportation and administration. At the time of writing, two decades ago, Islamic pilgrimage was less subject to market-driven imperatives but more influenced by a greater degree of piety and abstinence. Din examined the corporeal mobility and socio-cultural mobility of pilgrims. This interest in pilgrimage and outdoor recreational mobility led him to explore Islam and tourism which required exegesis of the Quran and *hadith*. Up to that point, he had not seen any work that tried to use content analysis of religious text as a source of data in tourism publications.

One of the topics that captured Din's long held interest was to understand the reasons why there was not a single Malay-owned hotel in a country whereby the majority of the population are Malays. This was addressed in the paper titled, "Still in search of more equitable mode of tourism development" which was also raised in his earlier (1982) paper "Tourism in Malaysia: Competing needs in a plural society" published in *Annals of Tourism Research*.

Din felt that colonial monetisation of the economy gradually marginalized the *Bumiputera* (autoch-thon to the Malay Archipelago) group in the urban economy where tourism started, especially in Penang, Kuala Lumpur and in all state capitals. In the article "Differential ethnic involvement in the Penang tourist industry: Some policy implications" in *Akademika* 29, pp. 3–20, 1986, he described the pattern of ethnic dominance in the accommodation industry leaving the Malays being completely marginalized in ownership. He asserted that a serious scholar cannot be oblivious to the ethnic fac-tor in explaining tourism development. In a fugitive occasional paper series (UKM), he presented a contrasting situation compared to the urban pattern of ownership; that low-capitalized involvement in both Cherating and Pulau Tioman and possibly rural resource-based locations led to a complete Malay monopoly in this relatively more dispersed activity.

He considered the Malays as having the least understanding of other cultures – Chinese and Indian – compared with the understanding of these two races about the Malays. He described; "Many are almost illiterate about Chinese culture let alone language which is more difficult to acquire compared to Bahasa Melayu". Furthermore, Malays probably have less networks in their professions, leading to a lack of connectivity and mobility. He was convinced that there are examples of well-connected Malay professionals, who may identify themselves as Malaysian and Islamic specialists, without knowing much about neighbouring countries of Thailand, Indonesia and Singapore. In his opinion, Malaysian Malays rarely ventured to "know the other" due to certain restrictions within the ethnic circle and products. He also felt that researchers rarely addressed ethnic competition and discrimination in tourism development and ignored the religious factor as an important issue to be addressed. He argued that there is a disconnect between what is imagined and what is in the real world and believed that these factors always exist and are visible in the media along with the development of the current global tendencies such as Islamophobia, Iraq–Afghan–Syria war and almost crusadic media presidential campaign of Donald Trump.

Regarding Islam and tourism, Din did not see a noticeable conflict except for the proscription on sexual encounters, dress code, food and beverage, gaming, and finance. He believed that the Islamic-Arabic ambiance seems exotic enough to tourists in Egypt and Morocco and the Gulf Arab states, and Islamic precepts certainly enjoins friendly if not favoured treatment of visitors due to the religious call to provide good treatment to travellers. However, a study conducted by Norbert Hoffmann in 1979 concluded that Islam was not marketable and as Din wrote in 1989, Islamic precepts still did not have much influence on the way tourism was planned and promoted, notwithstanding a stronger resolve to promote the halal brand as a ready commodity in the Malaysian market. In the present situation, there is more evidence of commoditized Islam, which is made visible and promoted. Unfortunately, he claimed that the concept can be misleading whereby the Arab Street in Brickfields (Malaysia) is mistakenly regarded as a sign of Islamic tourism. Pertaining to Islamic tourism potential in the world market, he argued that there are obstacles on the subject due to signs of Islamophobia which were less evident in the past.

Din also wrote a paper on tourism governance related to policy and administration. Among his interests was to investigate the "so-what" questions regarding any difference academic researches made to policy and host-guest behaviour or whether they were more of a depoliticising tool. Related to this topic, the issue of ideals against realities was reflected in the chapter titled "Dialogue with the hosts: Educational strategy towards sustainable development". In an effort to encourage critical writing in tourism, he also worked with a colleague from Universiti Sains Malaysia, editing a collection of academic papers with a title "Tourism Research in Malaysia: What, Which Way and So what?" It attracted 19 publishable contributions from tourism scholars. However, he found that the majority failed to address the "so what questions" which was meant to encourage some reflections on the policy implications of their research findings.

Being regarded as a senior academic with an interest in tourism, he was invited to join several editorial boards, acting as a resource editor on several occasions and also as chief editor. From the editorial experiences, he argued that there has never been a sustained discourse on tourism-related issues in the country, let alone academic contribution to public discourse on the subject. Therefore, he wrote his opinions in newspapers such as *New Straits Times, Watan, Berita Harian, Utusan Malaysia, Dewan Budaya* and *Dewan Masyarakat* intended to share his many concerns about tourism. Two newspaper commentaries titled "Academic neglect of tourism" and "Reasons for the obsession to develop Langkawi", claimed that the tourist industry and the government have been equally negligent of the academia.

Remarkable and significant contributions to tourism

In terms of major achievements, Din has contributed to a diverse range of important tourism agenda in his research. As mentioned earlier, he has published analyses on a wide range of topics in *Annals of Tourism Research, Akademika* and *Contemporary Southeast Asia*. He conducted more than 20 research and consultancy projects in the tourism field, which helped the dynamic understanding of the then new industry in Malaysia. Din also wrote papers for roughly more than 30 local and international seminars and conferences where his experience and insights were clearly recognized in both the tourism sector and the academia. He was a pioneer in many ways and helped the world understand better the religious, economic, social and environmental impacts, many of which have not been thoroughly studied even at the current stage. For example, in the 1982 paper, he raised questions on the possibility of an ethnic multiplier which may bring negative impacts on society even though the aggregate economic impacts (*ceteris paribus*!) are clearly positive. Similarly, his hypothesis on a triangular relationship between hosts and guests mediated by a third role (the intermediary broker), may result in international understanding, or it may leave the opposite consequences, depending on the role of the tourist who he predicts can easily become a "confidante" in a divided plural society, such as in most of the Muslim world today, especially in Syria, Egypt, Libya, Tunisia, Yemen, Iraq, Afghanistan, and Nigeria.

Din was engaged in a number of consultancy projects with UNDP, Asian Development Bank, Institute of Strategic and International Studies, Malaysian Institute of Economic Research and the UKM Bureau of Research and Consultancy. The experience led him to co-mingle and discuss survey data, mostly for environmental impact assessment and strategic studies reports. It gave him enough confidence to address the better exposed and perhaps better read colleagues from Western universities in a short keynote address presented in Rotorua, New Zealand on "The indigenization of tourism development", published in M. Oppermann (Ed) *Pacific Rim Tourism*. Wallingford, CABI, 1997, pp. 76–81. His argument was that many of the ideas informing tourism development were western inspired, either through consultancy services which were mostly done by foreign consultants, or through the western training which Malaysian scholars obtain abroad. Because of this the religious and ethnic factors rarely surface in final reports, partly at least, because it was not considered "objective" to address those issues. Given this orientation it was not surprising that issues of religious and ethnic sensitivities, including language, were rarely included in the Malaysian tourism research agenda.

Din's consultancy assignments provided technical reports in studies completed for the Ministry of Rural Development which initiated rural tourism programmes, namely the homestay enterprise. His involvement with Asian Development Bank and ISIS yielded technical reports on the tourist sector for the Melaka state government, the IMT-GT and the BIMP-EAGA growth triangle initiatives. Through the UKM Research and Consultancy bureau, he contributed technical reports for several projects which included the Proposed Oil Refinery Project in Terengganu; the Ulu Muda Dam Project; *Rakan Kembara* (youth travel fraternity) and the Sarawak Mendamit Dam Project. The Sarawak state government also invited him to study the impact of tourism on the longhouse communities which resulted in two publications covering the socio-economic dimensions of rural tourism. Before involvement in tourism he helped an NGO, Environmental Protection Society of Malaysia, which had requested him to investigate the plight of villagers in the face of environmental problems caused by a palm oil refinery in Kg Medan, Kelang. An article titled "Villagers' perception of environmental pollution in Kampung Medan, Kelang, Malaysia" was singled out as "first class" by Professor T. G. McGee of the University of British Columbia, Vancouver, in a book review published in the American geography journal, *Professional Geographer*. Din was also the principal investigator for the socio-economic section of the Malaysian Tourism Policy Study (1992).

Delivering speeches at seminars and conferences were among the significant contribution of Din in the tourism sector. Two of his notable participations were to deliver a keynote address for the IAHA (2015) and two years ago, to deliver an invited paper at the Malaysian Historical Association Summit in Kuala Lumpur pertaining to his tourism quest. Among other involvements, he was a consultant to the Ministry of Tourism Malaysia in a consulting project completed in November 2008, which sought to evaluate the effectiveness of the *Visit Malaysia Year 2007* promotional campaign. In 2009, he was appointed with Amran Hamzah as an academic representative of the board of trustees of the Islamic Tourism Centre under the Ministry of Tourism. Through this position, he was able to encourage two Chinese female students, a Muslim and a Non-Muslim, to seek industrial attachment at the centre with a view of exploring the perspective of the other (non-Muslims). He adopted the same approach in his classes, encouraging students to do assignments that involve research on groups other than your own co-religionists. His students seem to be excited about such exercises although, like the stereotype of the African-American students who would prefer to sit around with their own kind in the school canteen or classroom, in-group preference prevails. Din believes that it is the duty of educators to promote cross-cultural understanding as an essential element that should be embedded in all courses. It is only through such contact that we can achieve cross-cultural literacy and hence the international understanding that tourism purports to propagate in this glocalized world.

Din translated Mathieson, A. and G. Wall's (1982) *Tourism: Economic, Physical and Social Impacts.* New York: Longman Scientific and Technical, following which he was invited to present three papers in seminars organized by the Dewan Bahasa & Pustaka (DBP): "Impacts of tourism on the Malay language", "Forest as a key resource in the development of the Malay language", and "The relationships of history and tourism". At present, he chairs a committee on Malay terminology in tourism, hospitality, and culinary arts, for the DBP, the Malaysian National Language Agency.

Conclusion

Kadir Din has successfully laid a foundation of theory and practice pertaining to religion and social impact on the dynamic character of tourism. Through his in-depth knowledge in the subject, he was able to raise issues among academicians and established institutions, including the government, to provide a bridge between the disconnected reality within tourism, in which he lived and contributed to so much. His personality and long experience at the senior level, has given him the much needed credibility to serve and influence the decision makers in the government, tourism businesses and academia. Recognizing his monumental contribution to social science and tourism, Din was conferred as an Emeritus Professorship in 2012 by Universiti Utara Malaysia.

In terms of present contributions, Din said he has retired from active work and prefers to read the work of others. However, he still writes on the subjects which interest him or by request. This year he wrote a paper for a conference pertaining to "ethnic literacy", the topic which has been given a lack of attention in the literature. He also co-authored a paper on "understanding learning in context" for a conference in Penang and wrote a commemoration chapter in honour of a Malaysian Literary Laureate (*Sasterawan Negara*) Muhammad Haji Salleh. Finally, he has also edited a collection and contributed a chapter to commemorate UUM's 30th anniversary. In addition to being a caring husband and father, Din has devoted his entire self to teaching his students. His academic contributions leave a pioneering legacy in tourism research and teaching which will live on for many years to come.

Disclosure statement

No potential conflict of interest was reported by the author.

Funding

This work was supported by the Universiti Malaya.

Selected Publications

Biodun, A., Din, K. H., & Abdullateef, A. (2013). The relationship between tourist expectation, perceived quality and satisfaction with tourism products. *International Business Management, 7*, 158–169.

Biodun, A. B., & Din, K. H. (2012). Post choice satisfaction among Nigerian students studying in Malaysian universities: A pilot study. *International Journal of Education, 4*(2), 1–16.

Din, K. H. (1982). Tourism in Malaysia: Competing needs in a plural society. *Annals of Tourism Research, 9*, 453–480.

Din, K. H. (1982). Economic implications of Moslem pilgrimage from Malaysia. *Contemporary Southeast Asia, 4*, 58–75.

Din, K. H. (1986). Differential ethnic involvement in the Penang tourist industry: Some policy implications. *Akademika, 29*, 3–20.

Din, K. H. (1987). Tourism in Muslim countries: Patterns, issues and options. *Akademika, 31*, 15–40.

Din, K. H. (1987). Upland tourism and its socio-ecological consequences. In Y. Hadi (Ed.), *Impact of man's activities on tropical upland ecosystems* (pp. 387–406). Serdang: UPM Press.

Din, K. H. (1988). Towards an integrated approach to tourism development. In H. L. Theuns, T. V. Singh, & F. M. Go (Eds.), *Towards appropriate tourism: The case of the developing countries* (pp. 181–204). Amsterdam: Peter Lang.

Din, K. H. (1988). Social and cultural impacts of tourism. *Annals of Tourism Research, 15*, 563–566.

Din, K. H. (1990). The relevance of tourism to socioeconomic development in Sarawak. In V. King (Ed.), *Tourism in Borneo: Issues and perspectives* (pp. 327–355). Hull: Borneo Research Council Proceedings Series.

Din, K. H. (1992). Dialogue with the hosts: An educational strategy towards sustainable development. In M. Hitchcock, V. King, & M. Parnwell (Eds.), *Tourism in Southeast Asia* (pp. 327–355). London: Routledge.

Din, K. H. (1996). Impacts of tourism on local population. *Jurnal Angkatan Zaman Mansang (Kuching), 12*, 71–78.

Din, K. H. (1997). Still in search of a more equitable mode of tourism development. In C. Cooper (Ed.), *Tourism development: Environment and community issues* (pp. 104–118). Chichester: Wiley.

Din, K. H. (1997). Tourism and cultural development in Malaysia: Issues for a new agenda. In S. Yamashita, K. H. Din, & J. E. Eades (Eds.), *Tourism and cultural development in Asia and Oceania* (pp. 104–118). Bangi: UKM Press.

Din, K. H. (2004). Strategic issues in the tourism-agriculture linkage. In H. M. Dahlan (Ed.), *ASEAN in the global system* (pp. 275–282). Bangi: UKM Press.

Din, K. H. (1997). Indigenization of tourism development. In M. Oppermann (Ed.), *Pacific Rim Tourism* (pp. 76–81). Wallingford: CABI.

Din, K. H. (2006). Contributed four entries for the *Encyclopedia of world geography*. New York, NY: Golson Books.

Din, K. H. (2008). Contributed four entries for the *Encyclopedia of recreation and tourism in marine environments*. New York, NY: CABI.

Din, K. H. (2008). The fishing community and tourism development in Pulau Mabul (co-author J. Mapjabil). In Y. Ibrahim, S. Mohamad, & H. Ahmad (Eds.), *Pelancongan di Malaysia: Isu pembangunan, budaya, komuniti dan persetempatan* (pp. 195–206). Sintok: UUM Press.

Din, K. H. (2010). *Tourism research in Malaysia: What, which way and so what*. Sintok: UUM Press (co-editor of a 26 chapters' collection with Jabil Mapjabil of Universiti Sains Malaysia).

Din, K. H. (2012). *Tourism in Malaysia: Selected research issues* (in Malay) (co-editor: J. Mapjabil). Sintok: UUM Press.

Din, K. H., Owoyemi, M., & Zaharuddin, S. (2012). Nigerians in diaspora: Local community perceptions in Indonesia and Malaysia (in Malay). In R. A. Ghani (Ed.), *Indonesia-Malaysia: Pelbagai sudut pandang* (pp. 202–239). Sintok: UUM Press.

Din, K. H. (2013). Book review of selling destinations by Marc Mancini. *Malaysian Management Journal, 16*, 72–75.

Arthur John Burkart: pioneer scholar in tourism studies

Victor T. C. Middleton

Introduction

I was pleased to be asked to write an appreciation of the academic contribution of the late Arthur John Burkart. Appointed by Professor S. Medlik (1970), a year or so ahead of myself, John and I were the first full-time tourism university academics in England to develop the teaching of tourism with Rik and other colleagues at the University of Surrey, UK. The first full-time dedicated one year university degree course (Postgraduate Diploma in Tourism) was launched in 1972/73 with the option for a Master's Degree to be taken part-time in the following year.

Regrettably, John was not a man to record his own achievements and much of the key records of his life and contribution did not survive his death (1998). Combined with the fact that his academic contribution did not commence until he had already reached his late 40s and was effectively over due to ill health by his early 60s, this appreciation is shorter than other profiles of the pioneer contributors to tourism in this series. In writing it I wish to acknowledge the supporting evidence provided by Professor David Airey and information from Burkart's daughter Caroline.

Forty-five years ago in the UK it was not possible to target and recruit suitably qualified tourism academics. No such people existed. Practitioners with research interests in the field were the logical source. Of course some geographers, some economists, hospitality academics and others involved in higher education were certainly covering aspects of spatial relationships, economic development, transport economics, tour operation, and hospitality that are part of tourism. But there were no degree level courses at the time that set out to provide a balanced synthesis between theory and practice within a holistic framework that could be developed to reflect and explain an emerging body of knowledge about the dynamic nature and structure of the domestic and especially the international tourism phenomenon that had emerged in the twentieth century with the rapid growth of affordable motor car and air transport since the 1950s. The pioneer scholars had a mountain to climb in establishing tourism as a proper subject for study to rank with other subjects within higher education.

As recorded in David Airey's appreciation (Airey, 2014), Medlik had obtained a scholarship to travel around Europe and assess the forms of tourism teaching that then existed in the realms of higher education (1968). His report led to the design and academic acceptance of the first postgraduate course in England in 1972/73 at the University of Surrey and he, with John Burkart, took the leading role in that pioneering process. When I joined them in 1972, Burkart and Medlik were completing *Tourism Past Present and Future* (Burkart & Medlik, 1974a) and I was involved as the Reader for that book, which became the first published textbook in tourism in the UK. It also served as the structural foundation for what was subsequently known as the "Body of Knowledge" about tourism. Of course, that body of knowledge has developed and broadened extensively in recent decades but the original text in 1972 provided the first systematic, integrated approach for teaching of the subject at degree level.

Burkart and Medlik knew exactly what they were aiming to achieve with that first text. In the preface to *Tourism Past Present and Future* they stated (1974a, p. vi):

This [book] is different in its structure and approach [from other earlier books on tourism] in attempting to draw a synthesis between theory and practice and to reflect the dynamic nature of tourism in the second half of the twentieth century.

The need is for a systematic framework to explain the tourism phenomenon in its various manifestations .... Two alternative approaches may be distinguished. One is to use a basic discipline as a starting point; thus we may study the economics of tourism, the geography of tourism, the sociology of tourism. The other is to conceive of tourism as study of its own in which a body of knowledge is formulated and examined systematically, with its own boundaries and relationships. This book endeavours the latter approach.

To get an understanding of John's contribution and the research focus, he chose to pursue it is first necessary to have some understanding of the career background that led him to the University of Surrey (1970).

John Burkart – the businessman background

From the current viewpoint and hindsight of those teaching and researching aspects of tourism in the twenty-first century, John Burkart must now appear a most unlikely figure as a pioneer contributor. Of course hindsight usually brings distortions of fact but he was born in 1921 to middle-class parents who were brought up at the end of the Victorian era. He was educated at a traditional English public school before the Second World War where he gained awards for academic achievement and then at Keble College at Oxford University. He first went up to Oxford in 1941 but left to serve in the British Army until 1945. Thus, the war interrupted his studies at Oxford. He was commissioned as an officer in The Royal Artillery serving in France and Germany and promoted to the rank of Captain before he was able to return and finish his degree in Philosophy, Politics, and Economics as a mature student in 1947. Oxford University, then crowded with returning war-time veterans still in their early twenties, would have been a fascinating experience.

In the 1940s, Oxford Graduates were a rare commodity and had a status that was attractive to businesses and the public sector seeking management recruits. Intellectually able and clearly headed for a senior management role, John's career began with publishing in the 1940s before becoming a Director for Development of new business for the London Press Exchange, a national advertizing Agency. In 1957, he had switched to airlines becoming Advertizing Manager for British European Airways where he was responsible for advertizing worldwide, consumer marketing research, which included analysis of passenger transport patterns and the expected effect of those on the airline's services. He was also responsible for industrial design of the airline. This was followed by a senior management role as Commercial and Sales Director for the Cunard Shipping Company based in Southampton. His time at Cunard in the years 1966/67 was actually very short but it must have been traumatic. The company when he joined it was in crisis and being forced to come to terms with unsustainable losses deriving from the rapid and terminal decline of long haul transatlantic passenger travel by ocean liners as airlines took over the market. There was massive and growing over capacity for traditional shipping companies. In his time, total reorganization of Cunard led to the closure of the Head Office in Liverpool and its transfer to Southampton. Within months, a further re-organization was implemented in which John was directly involved. To survive, the Company was forced to impose major staff redundancies, many handled personally by John at the time. To anyone who has worked at senior level in such a crisis the mental pressure on the Directors In such turmoil can be imagined. In the starkest of ways he would have had to come to terms with the reality of air transport competitors enjoying the key marketing advantages of price, speed, and convenience offered by the rapidly expanding jet aircraft fleets of the 1960s. John absorbed the reality of international transport economics at first hand.

Then, in his late 40s, already a senior management figure in the transport sector, John switched his focus from a business career to research and academic pursuits that led him in due course to Medlik and an academic career at the University of Surrey. It is this author's speculation, which unfortunately cannot now be confirmed by available evidence, that John's experiences at Cunard had a massive personal impact on his view of life and what he wanted to achieve and contribute to. It may, perhaps, have contributed to his later health problems. What is known is that he decided to leave the Company after a short tenure and opted to undertake research in aspects of industrial economics becoming an honorary research fellow at Lancaster University working within a research framework developed by the eminent economist P.W.S. Andrews and Elizabeth Brunner, whom he had known in his Oxford days. Professor Elizabeth Brunner at that time was editor of the Journal of Industrial Economics and had published a pioneering study in the 1940s into what were then known as the holiday trades (Brunner, 1945). Her work was prescient and one can clearly see in it a very early analysis and grasp of what would come to be defined as the multiplier effect of tourism development that attracted so much attention later from tourism scholars.

Thus in his early fifties, face to face with the first generation of students wearing jeans and T shirts who were brought up with the Beatles and related popular culture, John would have appeared unusual to put it mildly to his first students in the early 1970s. Softly spoken, always courteous but reserved by nature, formally dressed wearing a tie with a three-piece suit complete with a fob watch chain in his waistcoat pocket – John must have seemed a very austere figure who was out of his era. He looked and conducted himself as a distinguished Edwardian gentleman might, possibly reflecting his experiences of tutors at Oxford and the senior management styles of post-war Britain. As one of the early postgrad tourism students, subsequently a tourism academic in Scotland put it:

> Known to his students as Mr. Burkart, never John, he was very formal in his dealings with students but he encouraged us to pursue our chosen careers with enthusiasm and in this sense he was not only an adviser he was also a wise leader. (Brian Hay, Herriot-Watt University)

As so often in life first appearances are deceptive. Beneath the old-fashioned exterior that John projected lay a keen analytical brain and a fascination with the intricacies of tourism that he had chosen to teach. He was especially focused on researching the remarkable and far-reaching developments in air transport and tour operation that were revolutionizing international tourism in the 1970s and 1980s.

John's remarkable decade of significant academic contribution

From the late 1960s to the mid-1980s, John's contribution as a scholar to the study of tourism was actually short but very significant. David Airey, whose early career overlapped at Surrey with John's time there, writes that:

> I always considered John Burkart to be one of the real founders of the serious study of tourism which began in the mid-1960s and is still continuing. He drew upon a distinguished career with two of the leading international companies in the tourism sector but his real contribution to our field came from his academic publications in books and journals; his work in establishing, and for some years editing, what is now one of the leading journals (Tourism Management); his chairmanship of one of the very first academic associations (Association of Teachers of Tourism) and his scholarly work as a teacher. In the 1970s John's work provided a high benchmark for the role of an academic in tourism and I consider myself fortunate to have benefitted from his guidance and support. (David Airey, Emeritus Professor, University of Surrey, UK)

He was also contributing to transport staff college seminars where his insight and experience were clearly recognized in the travel sector and participating in international conferences of tourism academics.

John's research interests in tourism were wide as can be seen in the selected publications included in this tribute. Combined, however, with his understanding of consumer changes his key focus was on the economics of public transport operation and especially the effects and complex relationships of government shifts in regulation on the airline sector. His research took place at the time when the then traditional close inter-Governmental regulation of airlines was shifting and dissolving. At that time, such regulation was a matter of bi-lateral agreements between countries covering all international air routes, capacity offered, fares charged, and control over which airlines were allowed to operate where and when. The first charter flights operated by tour operators and charter airlines were emerging to challenge, compete with, and begin to drive some traditional airlines out of business. The rise and subsequent collapse of Freddie Laker's transatlantic Sky Train development in the 1970s and 1980s

(Baker, 1982) is an appropriate illustration of the issues commanding John's research attention and teaching. Combined with growing economic prosperity in the developed world the shifts in regulation reflected a saga of profound changes that underlay the growth of international tourism in the 60s and 70s and 80s, and were then at the leading edge of how global tourism would develop further with budget airlines by the 1990s. It's history now and the outcome is clear. It wasn't at the time. The changes were driven by the very rapid growth of international tour operation in which the British were pre-eminent in Europe and for John, the two research interests coincided at that time and underpinned his academic contribution and his teaching at Surrey.

John Burkart as colleagues and former students saw him

As an internationally known leading transport industry practitioner and writer on the impact of regulation and competition on international air transport noted for this article:

> I knew John Burkart from his earlier career with what was then British European Airways. John brought to the development of tourism studies and his teaching at the University of Surrey a combination of business experience in transport and tourism at senior level and a deep personal commitment to tourism research and education. That combination, reflected in the books and many articles that he wrote or co-authored, provided very valuable pioneering insights in the 1970s and 1980s that have stood the test of time. (Stephen F. Wheatcroft, a former Director of British Airways and later Emeritus Governor of the London School of Economics)

In terms of published work in the late 1960s to early 1980s, John's contributions included 19 books and articles in Journals, 15 editorials in Tourism Management, and 10 conference papers (see abridged list). His main pioneering contribution was to the first British text book *Tourism: Past, Present and Future,* in which he co-wrote and developed the themes with Rik Medlik. Sadly, after little more than a decade John's teaching role was increasingly hampered by the onset and development of Parkinson's disease which influenced his speech and made it more and more difficult for him to be understood by students. Notwithstanding these difficulties, however, he was always held in high regard by his students. As one commented:

> John Burkart was a key figure for our cohort of international postgraduate students of Tourism Management at the University of Surrey in 1976 by whom he is remembered with affection and respect. With his quiet scholarly and gentlemanly air, often to be seen smoking a pipe, he seemed to us old-fashioned, old-school but rather charming. His textbook co-authored with Professor Medlik was our "bible" for the course and his lectures drew on years of first-hand experience in the travel industry and links with the advertising industry. He encouraged us to think critically about the travel business and had strong views expressed at the time in a series of articles in the Tourism media. He was also my personal tutor and proved himself to be sympathetic and supportive, wanting us to do well and making the overseas students feel welcome. He even managed to organize bursaries for buying textbooks and participating on field trips for a few of us who did not have financial grants for the course. I recollect that he and his wife invited us all to their house in Guildford in the summer semester for sherry in the garden. (Brenda Birmingham, postgraduate student and later travel writer and publisher)

Another British Professor of Tourism who was a junior manager in sales and marketing for Cunard in New York in the 1960s saw John from two very different viewpoints and contexts. He recalls John:

> As a man who projected two personas – that of the director/manager for Cunard in the crisis times of the 1960s and that of the academic in the 1970s. As a senior Director dealing with junior executives John came across as distant and austere, rather abrupt and seemingly disinterested in what the staff had to communicate. At that time, John's strengths did not extend to good human relations, which were not helpful as at the time he was responsible for closing down Departments and dealing personally, which he chose to do, with widespread redundancies. In the 1970s, as an academic I found a man seemingly totally transformed – thoughtful, listening, friendly and helpful. Also encouraging and supportive, the contrast with the man I knew earlier could not have been greater. (Chris Holloway, Former professor of tourism management at the University of West of England)

Collaborative activities in tourism

Over the relatively few years of his academic involvement in tourism, John was actively engaged in a number of collaborative activities. These included his role as editor of the International Journal of

Tourism Management (subsequently Tourism Management) between 1980 and 1986; industry contributions as a Director of HTS Management Consultants Ltd in 1970; and as a Council Member of the Tourism Society launched in 1977. Other academic support activities included his role as Chair of the Association of Teachers of Tourism (now ATHE); and international involvement as an elected professorial member of AIEST (1970). In recognition of his contribution, he was elected a Companion of the Royal Aeronautical Society (1970).

Conclusion

Looking back to the 1970s and early 1980s, I shared just over a decade with John Burkart as a personal friend as well as a valued colleague. This was the short but highly productive period in which he established his contribution and reputation in tourism studies before illness shortened his career. I found his commitment to tourism studies and his deep knowledge inspiring, thought provoking and often challenging and I was fortunate to enjoy many shared hours debating issues generally and in tourism marketing in particular, a subject in which our different experiences and backgrounds found so much of common interest. To those who knew him well, his sense of humour and fun far outweighed any earlier impressions of his somewhat austere demeanour. He was an excellent companion.

As a pioneer contributor in his research and teaching I consider John succeeded in the aim stated in *Tourism: Past, Present and Future* to provide a synthesis of theory and practice in the dynamic character of tourism as he knew it. Through the depth of his knowledge of the subject, the natural authority of his personality and the stature he reflected through his long experience at senior level, he gave much needed credibility to tourism studies in its emerging decades. His credibility served to influence decision-makers in government and tourism businesses as well as academia. In the process, John's contribution also helped to provide a bridge between the two halves of twentieth-century tourism through which he lived and contributed so much. He was, as Professor Airey noted in his contribution to this article, both a scholar and a gentleman.

Selected list of publications

Burkart, A. J., & Medlik, S. (1974). *Tourism: Past, present and future*. London: Heinemann.
Burkart, A. J. (1974). The regulation of non-scheduled air services in the UK 1960–1972. *Journal of Industrial Economics*, 23(1), 51–64.
Burkart, A. J. (1974). Why tour operators collapse. *Tourism International*, 18(74).
Burkart. A. J. (1975). Sto Donosi tour operator, Kreativne Komunikacije, 36(37).
Burkart, A. J., & Medlik, S. (1975). *The management of tourism*. London: Heinemann.
Burkart, A. J. (1977). Car ferries between Western Europe and the UK. *International Tourism Quarterly,* 1, 44–55.
Burkart, A. J. (1977). Trends in tourism – Investment in industry. *Investors Chronicle*, 18–24th March. vii–x.
Burkart, A. J. (1980). Tourism. In P. Johnson (Ed). *The structure of British industry* (pp. 3577–359). London: Crosby Lockwood.
Burkart, A. J. (1982). Tourism- Key Issues for the 1980s. *Long Range Planning*, 15(4), 91–97.
Burkart, A. J. (1983). Trends in UK Business Travel Overseas. *Tourism Management*, 4(1), 54–57.
Burkart, A. J. (1984). Marketing Package Holidays. *Services Industries Journal*, 4(3), 187–192.
Burkart, A. J., & Medlik, S. (1990). *Historical development of tourism*. Centre des Hautes Etudes Touristiques. Aix-en-Provence. 54 pages.
Burkart, A. J. (1970). *Principles of marketing*. Royal Aeronautical Society Air Transport Course. Oxford.
Burkart, A. J. (1973). Seminar on tourism. British Transport Staff College. Woking.
Burkart, A. J. (1974). Seminar of tourism. British Airways Staff College. East Burnham.
Burkart, A. J. (1975). *A review of research into the industrial economics of tourism: 1950–1975*. 25th Congress of AIEST. Belgrade.

Selected editorials in Tourism Management

Burkart, A. J. (1980). Lawlessness in Tourism, 1(2), 74–75.

Burkart, A. J. (1980). The impact of politics, 1(1), 3–4.

Burkart, A. J. (1981). Tourism – a service Industry? 2(1), 2–3.

Burkart, A. J.(1981). Are air fares too low? The case for widening the debate, 2(2), 81–82.

Burkart, A. J. (1981). How far is tourism a trade or industry? 2(4), 146.

Burkart, A. J. (1982). Co-operation and competition in tourism, 3(2), 70.

References

Airey, D. (2014). Profile of Rik Medlik. *Anatolia: An International Journal of Tourism and Hospitality Research, 25*, 492–498. doi: http://dx.doi.org/10.1080/13032917.2014905134

Baker, A. (1982). *The rise and fall of Freddie Laker*. London: Faber and Faber.

Brunner, E. (1945). *Holiday making and the holiday trades*. London: Oxford University Press.

Burkart, A. J., & Medlik, S. (1974a). *Tourism: Past, present and future*. London: Heinemann.

Burkart, A. J., & Medlik, S. (1974b). *Tourism: Past, present and future*. London: Heinemann.

Allan M. Williams: a life course perspective

Gareth Shaw

Introduction

Writing about the achievements of a good friend and close colleague, such as Allan Williams, is always going to be a pleasurable task. Allan's autobiographical account has already appeared under the title "An Accidental Tourism Researcher? People, Places and Turning Points" (Williams, 2010) in Stephen Smith's *The Discovery of Tourism* published in 2010. This presents his journey towards tourism and the twists and turns in that journey. Whilst I will draw on parts of this personal and reflective account; my main aim is to highlight the significant contributions. Allan has made to various aspects of tourism studies, and to bring that earlier account fully up to date. I also want to give particular attention to some of the key points in his career set within the context of his academic life course.

An academic life course uncovered

Allan began his academic career as an undergraduate at University College Swansea where he studied Economics and Geography (1969–1972). He was born in a small village, near Swansea (1951). He grew up and spent his childhood in a Welsh coal mining community and has always been proud of his Welsh heritage – which he constantly reminds me of even now, particularly if Wales and England are playing rugby. After graduating, he went to the London School of Economics (LSE) to undertake a Ph.D. in the urban social geography of the nineteenth Century city (1973). His move to London was centred, it would seem, on two motives; the first to be based at LSE due to its reputation as a high quality research institution and the second to experience London Life. As he admits both these motives were fulfilled by undertaking a Ph.D. However, the excitement of being based at the LSE was somewhat dampened by the actual Ph.D. topic which certainly failed to fire his academic curiosity; this was at a time when greater strides were being made to understand the geographies of the Victorian City.

Having decided he was working in what was for him "the wrong area" of human geography he duly decided to change his research field. He, therefore, took up a temporary lectureship in geography at the University of Durham (1976) after obtaining his Ph.D., and this was more opportunistic rather than planned but it gave him the means of changing his research direction. In large part, this was facilitated by meeting two human geographers, Ray Hudson and Jim Lewis who were to become life-long colleagues and friends, and influence him to embark on the changed pathway for his research interests. Both Hudson and Lewis at that time were part of group of young geographers working on uneven regional development from a Marxist perspective. Allan soon became drawn into this area of economic geography and felt entirely at home in this new area of study; to which over the years, he has made important contributions as we shall discuss later.

A further opportunistic development was being offered by the chance to go with other staff from Durham on a field class to Portugal. This sparked an enduring interest in that country and one that also led to a number of influential studies. In this context, Allan and Jim Lewis collaborated on a number of projects relating to aspects of uneven development and urban geography (see for example, Lewis & Williams, 1981, 1985, 1987, 1988, 1991). To a large extent, tourism as an economic activity, did not figure much in these studies until the book chapter published in 1988 under the title of "Portugal: market segmentation and regional specialisation"; although about tourism, that activity did not figure in the actual title of the paper. This lack of interest in tourism in the earlier stages of his career was also reflected in the book he edited somewhat earlier on southern Europe (Williams, 1984). Clearly these publications highlighted both his growing interest in regional economic development and more especially within the domain of southern Europe, along with increased recognition of his expertise in this area of research.

In everyone's academic life course, there are critical turning points and in Allan's case the move to Durham was one such key point. Following on from this and, representing another turning point, was his collaboration with Russell King and Tony Warnes which led to a plethora of significant publications on aspects of retirement migration (King, Warnes, & Williams, 2000; Williams, King, & Warnes, 1997), and these in part also linked to aspects of tourism (Williams, King, & Warnes, 2004). More generally this was to move him into, and contribute to, research on mobilities which was then a new and expanding area of study. This was to become another enduring area of work in which Allan acquired a strong international reputation. Moreover, his skills and contribution to regional economic geography were being increasingly strengthened and his love of Portugal also increased leading him to struggle fitfully to become, if not fluent then, at least conversant in Portuguese at this time. This in turn opened up strong contacts with geographers at the University of Lisbon, where he became a regular visitor and remains so today.

It was during this very productive period, when he first started to reorientate his research that he made the move from Durham to Exeter, where he took up a permanent position as Lecturer in Geography (1978). Indeed, it was this established position that provided the platform for much of the research activity in the geographies of southern Europe and the development of the mobilities research. This was the catalyst for him to finally move away from his thesis into these newer areas, which was enabled by his appointment to more secure academic position. It was also another period of experimentation and he started to work with another newly arrived geographer at Exeter, David Phillips. This was a short lived collaboration, which on reflection was seemingly more opportunistic compared with his work in economic and regional geography. For a short time, he turned to social and rural geography (Phillips & Williams, 1984). These early points in his life course were to be key foundations for further major contributions to come, particularly in tourism studies.

Travelling into tourism geography

Another critical turning point in Allan's academic life course came during his time at Exeter and yet again occurred much more by chance than design. This was the start of his journey towards tourism research and the significant contributions he has made in this area. Together with myself, we had been asked by our head of department to develop research projects in the University of Exeter's Institute of Cornish studies based in Cornwall. The initially funded project was on branch factory locations and inward investment on industrial estates or parks. On one of the many journeys to Cornwall for this research, which neither of us were inspired by, Allan and I decided to switch our attention to tourism as an economic sector within Cornwall. His travel into tourism research started in 1986 when funding was gained to undertake a Cornwall wide study of the tourism economy of the county, where tourism was the major economic sector. Small firms became a natural focus given their numerical dominance and related publications followed. The importance of entrepreneurial backgrounds was clearly identified, including the ability to draw on different types of capital and also revealing a link between tourists and entrepreneurs usually through pathways of wanting to follow different lifestyles by moving from being a tourist to an entrepreneur within the tourism industry.

Taken together some of these publications help map the changes in research towards SMEs in tourism as well as charting Allan's contributions (Shaw & Williams, 1990; Williams, Shaw, & Greenwood, 1989). This was a time of an increasing range of work on many aspects of tourism. The study on Cornwall was in three large sections, the entrepreneurial part which contributed to an understanding of entrepreneurial types, a very large-scale survey of visitors and a section on those employed in tourism. The second became an annual visitor survey but sadly the final part was something of a failure. The bulk of the survey work was driven by Justin Greenwood our research fellow who was such an effective field worker. From this point, Allan established a consultancy group with myself and Justin that become focused on tourism – producing many reports on the local economy in south-west England. In the current way of thinking, this would be valued as "impact" which has become significant across U.K. universities, but then in the late 1980s, it was considered as somewhat an oddity within a very traditional Geography Department.

During this early stage of tourism research Allan also decided that the group at Exeter would hold a conference on Tourism in western Europe – bringing into play his interests on Europe and economic development. This was successful and led to an edited book which subsequently went into three editions (Williams & Shaw, 1988). It was also a time when his research on tourism, which in large part had been developed in the study of Cornwall, was broadening out by using different conceptual frameworks and research themes. For example, the research on SMEs was developed into more general frameworks linked to entrepreneurial types (Shaw & Williams, 1998). A larger break-through came with the publication of *Critical Issues in Tourism: A Geographical Perspective* (1994). This started as an attempt to merge tourism geography with aspects of leisure but it proved difficult to capture the diverse range of approaches in context of a textbook. As more fruitful alternative, the text became more focused on the production and consumption elements of tourism set within a geographical framework.

Allan had and has an excellent talent for writing textbooks and the success of *Critical Issues* is a testament to that and I learned a good deal from him in this project. Its success as a textbook came swiftly and led Allan to explore other perspectives on tourism, all the time being influenced by the work of the late John Urry a sociologist, along with approaches by such people as Samuel Briton, whose work focused more on a political economy approach. In his own autobiography (Williams, 2010), Allan describes the writing of *Critical Issues* as audacious given our limited knowledge of tourism and in one sense it was, yet its success came from taking a different approach even if that was enforced by a patchy knowledge, which meant we had fewer preconceived ideas. He puts in more succinctly "if the book has any claims to originality, it lies in our ignorance" (Williams, 2010, p. 101).

As his reputation grew within tourism studies he became more recognized international scholar much in demand. This represented another key point in his academic life course as he started to work with Michael Hall and Alan Lew. Hall was instrumental in getting him to join the Commission for the International Geographical Union of Tourism Study Group, from which collaboration a number of jointly produced volumes emerged. Two of these were on tourism and migration (Hall & Williams, 2002; Williams & Hall, 2002). A third volume was published on tourism and innovation (Hall & Williams, 2008). All three were to be ground breaking in different ways and to lead to other research projects. The theme of innovation and migration was also to form a further strand of research in a project on innovation and migration in the hotel sector funded by the U.K.'s Economic and Social Research Council (ESRC), which Allan and I worked on between 2006 and 2008. It brought together for him the dual interests of migration and innovation but within a framework of the hotel sector which neither of us had a great deal of experience in at that particular time. The project also was to hold greater significance to Allan's future career as I will explain later.

During this phase in the early part of this century Allan was in increasing demand as an international keynote speaker and as a co-author. He had already assisted in the creation of the journal *Tourism Geographies* by Alan Lew which was to become a major outlet for the many geographers interested in tourism. This relationship with Lew and Hall was to result in a major edited text *A Companion to Tourism* under Blackwell's Companion to Geography series (Hall, Williams, & Lew, 2004). As the editors wrote in the preface of the book; "it was initially conceived as an exploration and review of the contributions of geographers and geography to our understanding of tourism" (p. xvii). In essence the volume, whilst reflecting their aim, also highlighted the inter-disciplinary nature of tourism. For Allan, it also seemed to help bridge his own wider interests both as a geographer and increasingly within the wider domain of tourism studies, as well as his continued interests in regional economic development. Indeed, his own chapter in the book was on the *Political Economy of Tourism*, bringing together his early interests.

As we have seen Allan's academic life course has comprised some key turning points – some by chance others more due to talent and hard work. Another key chance encounter was to set in motion a very significant research partnership. This was with an academic from Slovakia, Vlado Baláž who wrote to him wanting to visit Exeter on a British Academy funded visit. This was the start of another productive collaboration and lasting friendship that flourished with a research project on the role of tourism in the transition economies of central Europe (Williams & Baláž, 2000). As this partnership developed it produced numerous key academic papers and also moved into different pathways, including cross-border mobility along with studies of the associations between knowledge transfer and international migration (Williams & Baláž, 2001; Williams, Baláž, & Bodnarova, 2001; Williams, Baláž, & Kollar, 2001). In 2008, two texts were produced that highlighted these interests, the first with Baláž (Williams & Baláž, 2008) the second I discussed earlier was with Hall on innovation. The migration theme is a re-occurring one that has been the foundation of a good deal of Allan's research, from his early days at Durham and his work is located as much in migration studies as in tourism studies.

During this extremely busy and productive period Allan made a decision to leave Exeter after 28 years, during which time he has moved from Lecturer to Professor and a leading researcher. In addition, he had built up a strong reputation as a good teacher and, although it was never something he himself highlighted, he was extremely popular with the students both at undergraduate and postgraduate level. I know his move was not an easy decision from conversations we had at the time. However, it was a bold move that saw him move to London Metropolitan University (2006). Unfashionable as this University was, it offered him greater freedom to work in an interdisciplinary environment. This was reflected in the chair he held which was in two different institutes within the University, namely: the Institute for the Study of European Transformations and the Working Lives Research Institute. It was at this time that Allan and I received an ESRC grant to research innovation in the hotel sector which was discussed earlier. This was significant for another reason in that it made us both innovation fellows of the ESRC's Advanced Institute of Management based in London. Given Allan's inter-disciplinary interests and his background in economic geography, he was immediately at home in this environment. The learning curve from mixing with some top academics from Management was steep but productive for him providing fresh insights into ideas of innovation and knowledge management, along with the mobility of hotel workers in the knowledge transfer process.

It wasn't too long before Allan was on the more again this time to the University of Surrey which he joined as Professor of Tourism and Mobility studies (2011). Since joining there his research has continued to flourish and in terms of gaining further research grants on worker performance in the hotel sector and a series of European funded fellowships brining academics from across Europe to work with him in Surrey on two year fellowships. His impact on the research environment there has been extremely strong as reflected in the research projects established. These include a major ESRC funded project on International migration and flexible working and productivity in hotels, and an Horizon 2020 project on International mobility in transition from youth to adulthood (Janta, Cohen, & Williams, 2015) Again these have been supported by a considerable number of high quality research papers including an important strand of research on the behavioural and evolutionary economics of mobility (Williams, 2013; Williams & Baláž, 2014).

In addition to all his other achievements his academic contribution has also been recognized by being made an academician of the prestigious Academy of Social Science in the U.K. He is also a fellow of the International Academy of for the Study of Tourism and an elected member of the Tourism

Research Centre. He has served on a number of national grant awarding bodies in the U.K. and also holds the post of adjunct professor in the National Centre for Research on Europe at the University of Canterbury in New Zealand. Moreover, as a productive and experienced supervisor with an interdisciplinary focus, his more than 50 doctoral students have included Andy Pratt (Professor of Cultural Economy, City University, U.K.), Stephen Syrett (Professor of Local Economic Development, Middlesex University, U.K.), Sheela Agarwal (Professor of Tourism, University of Plymouth, U.K.), Christian Schott (Victoria University, NZ), Neil Carr (Professor, Otago University, NZ), and Adi Weidenfeld (Coventry University, U.K.).

Conclusion

Allan's academic life course has been characterized by chance encounters but each key point has also been significant. Significant in two ways, first by the establishment of a number of strong collaborative partnerships and more importantly by being extremely productive. In his autobiography (Williams, 2010), he concluded by stating: "I can only hope that, along the way, I have made a useful contribution". From this account we can safely say he has made an extremely significant contribution to tourism studies in a variety of ways and from a number of perspectives. He is a prolific writer and the contributions discussed here are only a small part of his outputs. Of equal importance is that Allan has forged many good friendships throughout his career and as I can testify it has been a joy to work alongside him.

Disclosure statement

No potential conflict of interest was reported by the author.

References

Hall, C. M. & Williams, A. M. (Eds.). (2002). *Tourism and migration: New relationships between production and consumption*. Dordrecht: Kluwer.

Hall, C. M., Williams, A. M., & Lew, A. A. (2004). Tourism: Conceptualizations, institutions, and issues. *A companion to tourism*, 3–21.

Hall, C. M., & Williams, A. M. (2008). *Tourism and Innovation*. London: Routledge.

Janta, H., Cohen, S. A., & Williams, A. M. (2015). Rethinking visiting friends and relatives mobilities. *Population, Space and Place, 21*, 585–598.

King, R., Warnes, A. M., & Williams, A. M. (2000). *Sunset lines: British retirement in southern europe*. Oxford: Berg.

Lewis, J. R., & Williams, A. M. (1981). Regional uneven development on the European periphery: The case of Portugal, 1950–1978. *Tijdschrift voor Economische en Social Geografie, 72*, 81–98.

Lewis, J. R., & Williams, A. M. (1985). Portugal: The decade of return. *Geography, 70*, 178–182.

Lewis, J. R., & Williams, A. M. (1987). Productive decentralisation or indigenous growth? *Small manufacturing enterprises and regional development in central Portugal, Regional Studies, 21*, 343–361.

Lewis, J. R., & Williams, A .M. (1988). Portugal: Market segmentation and regional specialisation. In A. M. Williams & G. Shaw (Eds.), *Tourism and Economic Development: West European Experiences* (pp. 101–122). London: Frances Pinter.

Lewis, J., & Williams, A.M. (1991). *Portugal: Market segmentation and regional specialisation* (2nd ed., pp. 107–129). Retrieved from Cabdirect.org

Phillips, D., & Williams, A. M. (1984). *Rural social geography*. Oxford: Blackwell.

Shaw, G., & Williams, A. M. (1990). Tourism, economic development and the role of entrepreneurial activity. *Progress in Tourism, Recreation and Hospitality Management, 2*, 67–81.

Shaw, G., & Williams, A. M. (1994). *Critical issues in tourism: A geographical perspective*. Oxford: Blackwell.

Shaw, G., & Williams, A. M. (1998). Entrepreneurship, small business culture and tourism development. In D. Ioannides & K. D. Debbage (Eds.), *The economic geography of the tourism industry* (pp. 235–255). London: Routledge.

Williams, A. M. (1984). *Southern Europe transformed: Political and economic change in Greece, Italy, Portugal and Spain*. London: Longman Higher Education.

Williams, A. M. (2010). An accidental tourism researcher? People, places and turning points. In S. Smith (Ed.), *The Discovery of Tourism* (pp. 93–106). Emerald: Bingley.

Williams, A. M. (2013). Mobilities and sustainable tourism: Path-creating or path-dependent relationships?. *Journal of Sustainable Tourism, 21*, 511–531.

Williams, A. M., & Baláž, V. (2000). *Tourism in transition: Economic change in central Europe*. London: I.B. Tauris.

Williams, A. M., & Baláž, V. (2008). *International migration and knowledge*. London: Routledge.

Williams, A. M., & Baláž, V. (2014). Mobility, risk tolerance and competence to manage risks. *Journal of Risk Research, 17*, 1066–1088.

Williams, A. M., & Baláž, V. (2001). From collective provision to commodification of tourism? *Annals of Tourism Research, 28*, 27–49.

Williams, A. M., Baláž, V. I., & Bodnarova, B. (2001). Border regions and trans-border mobility: Slovakia in economic transition. *Regional Studies, 35*, 831–846.

Williams, A. M., Baláž, V., & Kollár, D. (2001). Coming and going in Slovakia: International labour mobility in the central European 'buffer zone'. *Environment and Planning A, 33*, 1101–1123.

Williams, A. M., & Hall, C. M. (2002). Tourism, migration, circulation and mobility: The contingencies of time and place. In C. M. Hall & A. M. Williams (Eds.), *Tourism and migration: New relationships between production and consumption* (pp. 1–52). Dordrecht: Kluwer.

Williams, A. M., King, R., & Warnes, T. (1997). A place in the sun: International retirement migration from northern to southern Europe. *European Urban and Regional Studies, 4*, 115–134.

Williams, A. M., King, R., & Warnes, T. (2004). British second homes in Southern Europe: Shifting nodes and flows of migration and tourism. M. Hall & D. Muller (Eds.), *Tourism mobility and second homes: Between elite landscape and common ground* (pp. 97–112). Clevedon: Channel View Publications.

Williams, A. M., & Shaw, G. (1988). *Tourism and economic development: Western European experiences*. London: Frances Pinter.

Williams, A. M., Shaw, G., & Greenwood, J. (1989). From tourist to tourism entrepreneur, from consumption to production: Evidence from Cornwall, England. *Environment and Planning A, 21*, 1639–1653.

Alastair Morrison: people, partnerships, packaging, and programming (4Ps to success)

Svetlana Stepchenkova

Introduction

When the Fall-2013 academic semester was in full swing, I was contacted by Metin Kozak, Editor-in-Chief of *Anatolia: An International Journal of Tourism and Hospitality Research*, to write a portrait of Dr Alastair Morrison. The *Anatolia*'s editorial team had just launched a new journal section that would introduce an internationally recognized scholar in each issue, and Dr Alastair Morrison, a distinguished Professor Emeritus at Purdue University, USA, who specializes in tourism and hospitality planning, development, and marketing, and a UNWTO consultant who has provided advice for the World Bank, Pacific Asia Travel Association, European Union, U.S. Agency for International Development, and other multinational organizations, was one of their first choices.

I always wondered how such choices are being made. We can obtain various ratings and debate whether numerical indicators reflect productivity and impact. But when one is asked who the most influential person in the field is, "holistic" perceptions are very accurate. Alastair Morrison is a pillar in contemporary tourism and hospitality marketing, and this is simply common knowledge. The list of Alastair's distinctions and recognitions is very long. To date, he has published more than 200 academic articles and conference proceedings, as well as over 50 research monographs related to marketing and tourism. He has been elected as a Fellow of the world's most elite organization of tourism scholars, the International Academy for the Study of Tourism. Alastair is an Editorial Board Member of several major hospitality and tourism academic research journals. The International Society of Travel and Tourism Educators selected Alastair as the Year 1998 recipient of the Lifetime Achievement Award for his contributions to tourism education, and his name is in Purdue's Book of Great Teachers. Alastair is currently the CEO of Belle Tourism International Consulting (BTI) and the Director for International Research and Communication at the International Center for Recreation and Tourism Research at Peking University. He serves as the President of the International Tourism Studies Association (ITSA) and is the Co-Editor of the *International Journal of Tourism Cities*.

Despite all these recognitions, I have always known him as Alastair. He was my mentor when I was a master student at Purdue University and the only professor whom I called by first name and was comfortable with it. In 2002 my family came to the USA, and we settled in West Lafayette, Indiana, as my husband was a researcher at Purdue. Our two daughters entered the university and a local high school, while I was staying home and desperately wanted to do something with my life. On one sunny day I was strolling Purdue campus where on the main square a Study Abroad Fair was taking place. I talked to a person at the Department of Tourism and Hospitality Management booth and he gave me his card. It was Alastair. We met several weeks later discussing the Hospitality and Tourism Management (HTM) programme, and when I entered the programme, it was a start of the most fulfilling period in my life. We published several articles together, I was also involved in two industry-related projects which were led by Alastair, and we have been keeping in touch since he went to China in 2006. Thus, I agreed to write about Alastair with a great pleasure, as I have always felt that he was probably the most influential person in my transition from a housewife to a tourism researcher.

Academic development and scholarship

Alastair was born in Johnstone, Scotland. He became an academic after working for several years as a management consultant in hospitality and tourism. His interest in teaching students and further developing his research skills were the main reasons for moving from consulting to academia. Alastair had been involved in tourism and hotels from an early age, so the move into tourism research was a natural progression for him. Family members, especially Alastair's mother, Jessie Morrison, were his greatest source of inspiration to succeed in academics. Alastair credits Emeritus Professor Jim Russell of Purdue University for his solid grounding in teaching and instruction and counts Professors Joe O'Leary and Philip Pearce as his most important research mentors and colleagues. Alastair attributes his success to following two schools of thought: the "school of hard work" and the "school of practical experience". Alastair has several favorite quotes: "there is no substitute for hard work" (his mother); "preparedness is the key to success and victory" (General Douglas MacArthur); and "failing to plan is planning to fail" (Winston Churchill).

Professor Joseph O'Leary, who has known Alastair for a long time as a colleague, recalled that they first met when Alastair, after having been involved in consulting for a number of years, joined Purdue University in 1985 as a faculty member in the department that was then called "Restaurant, Hotel, and Institutional Management".

> My first images of him seem to include a smiling, cordial, very personable colleague who always seemed to be carrying a book with him. Of course the book was his marketing text and I think I regularly gave him grief about always 'selling'. And it was always fun when that Scottish accent he brought with him was used as a way to describe that you could probably tell he came from some place a little east of Lafayette! His pleasant demeanor and Pied Piper synthesis of ideas captured the interests and imagination of students, other faculty and people from outside the university community.

When Alastair first came to Purdue he did not have a Ph.D. and in his "spare time" he began and completed this effort. Very soon he became an important part of student committees, as graduate students wanted to take advantage of his marketing expertise in their theses and dissertations: Alastair was able to make excellent real world suggestions about ideas, and because of his consulting background was especially talented at the translational aspect of research – so what does it mean? At those times – 1990s and early 2000s – the department used to have monthly meetings to exchange ideas and facilitate research, which were open to graduate students and interested faculty from other schools as well. Because of their intensity, these meetings were known as "Projects from Hell", and Alastair is remembered as being especially good at organizing them: it usually took a table with bagels, cream cheese, and coffee to get it going. During his tenure at Purdue University, Alastair became the leader of a research team which included collaborators from other institutions, his Purdue colleagues, as well as his Ph.D. and Master's students.

It was an incredibly productive time, and much of the success that emerged was because of Alastair's enthusiasm and participation.

Today Professor Alastair Morrison is one of the most productive and cited authors in tourism and hospitality research. In an analysis by Ryan (2005), he was placed among the five most prolific contributors in the world to the academic journals in tourism management, and his name consistently appears in other lists of leading contributors as well (Jogaratham, Chon, McCleary, Mena, & Yoo, 2005; McKercher, 2008, 2014; Zhao & Ritchie, 2007). When asked about qualities that make Alastair a successful researcher, his colleagues cite excellent awareness of global trends in tourism marketing, ability to see the big picture, and to relate what is happening in the USA, Asia, Europe, and Oceania. As his colleague Dr Philip Pearce put it, "Alastair can often see what needs to be done or what is possible and can be done." His particular strength is having skills in bringing people together, strong abilities to foster and galvanize a team to complete work, high productivity, and a strong work ethic. His collaborators attest to Alastair being very focused and structured when working on a paper, leading the pace of paper development, and always questioning things to make sure that all issues had been investigated and always being open to suggestions and questioning.

There are several areas where Alastair's scholarly contributions are especially noteworthy: destination management and marketing, tourism Internet marketing, consumer behaviour, and market segmentation. He and his colleagues were among the first researchers who studied travel market segmentation and its practices and procedures in tourism and hospitality (e.g. Frochot & Morrison, 2000; Hsieh, O'Leary, & Morrison, 1992; Jang, Morrison, & O'Leary, 2002; Moscardo, Pearce, & Morrison, 2001). They evaluated various bases for market segmentation, including benefit segmentation, travel decision-making patterns and arrangements, household and trip characteristics, information source variables, travel activities, and geographic origin, and applied these segmentation approaches to various markets defined by location, trip purpose, gender, or special interest.

From its very inception, Alastair took web-based marketing very seriously, recognizing its potential for tourism and hospitality. The Internet era presented new challenges in studying consumer behaviour, and Alastair, together with his graduate students and university colleagues, contributed to understanding of online information search (Kim, Lehto, & Morrison, 2007; Letho, Kim, & Morrison, 2006), shopping motivations for travel products (Beldona, Morrison, & O'Leary, 2005), and travel booking (Morrison, Jing, O'Leary, & Cai, 2001). In addition, Alastair studied destination representations on the web (e.g. Choi, Lehto, & Morrison, 2007; Stepchenkova & Morrison, 2006), web-based permission marketing (Brey, So, Kim, & Morrison, 2007), and associated issues. He was especially concerned with less than rigorous adherence of Destination Marketing Organizations (DMOs) and Convention and Visitor Bureaus (CVBs) to best marketing practices in destination representation (Morrison, Taylor, & Douglas, 2004), and, together with his industry partner Don Anderson and Purdue colleague Dr Juline Mills, created WebEVAL, an evaluation tool to benchmark destination websites against the best industry practices.

Graduate students

The time and effort that Alastair was giving to training future tourism and hospitality scholars during his tenure at Purdue are remarkable. Alastair was a great mentor: he met with his students regularly, listened to them, provided feedback and encouragement: I remember leaving his office after these 30-min sessions with new ideas and a desire to test them in the laboratory immediately! He was gently pushing students to realize their potential but was always ready to provide support and help. Whenever a problem arose that was beyond the student's ability to overcome, Alastair stepped in – contacting his industry partners with request to assist in recruiting survey respondents, paying for the data, bringing to the project a person with a unique expertise, etc. He involved students in his research team effort early in their Master's and Ph.D. studies. One of Alastair's students, Dr Dae-Young Kim of the University of Missouri and now a productive tourism scholar with more than 40 publications to his name, worked under Alastair's supervision on travellers' information search behaviour and convention and meetings management. He describes Alastair's mentoring style as:

> [Alastair] is a great person and persistent go-getter. I had worked with him as a RA and TA for about 5 years, and I had learned from him a lot and was especially impressed by his relentless enthusiasm for research. His mentoring style was not directive, but inductive. That is, he always tried to induce ... research ideas through the discussions with his students ... He respected his students and treated his students as his colleagues in academia.

Alastair has a great ability to recognize and nurture talent, as he has done for my fellow Purdue classmate Dr Liang (Rebecca) Tang of Iowa State University, who is now a successful mentor herself. In 2002 being a student at Beijing International Studies University, she contacted Alastair with a detailed feedback on his newly published article about tourism in China, and he was impressed by her knowledge of the Chinese tourism market, firm grasp of the issues, and the sharpness of her conclusions and recommendations. Alastair felt that she was ready to contribute immediately to his team's research effort and awarded Rebecca with a research assistantship, which was a rare distinction for a first-year Master's student to get. For Rebecca, working with Alastair became the life changing experience:

> I always say to others that it is Professor Morrison who changed my fate and helped me achieve my dreams. I especially would like to stress his support and help after I started my career in Iowa State. He told me that graduation is not the ending, but the start of a new adventure. In my career, he has given me numerous opportunities and linkage that helps me to establish reputations in the area, such as serving in ITSA. He does not mentor students for a period of time (e.g. 3–5 years), but the whole life ... I follow his steps to do the same thing to my students.

Another Alastair's student, Dr Eric Brey of University Wisconsin-Stout, is now a prominent marketing scholar, speaker, and industry advisor who has been recognized as one of the most extraordinary minds in hospitality marketing by Hospitality and Sales Marketing Association International and who is regularly quoted in media outlets including Forbes, Business Week, China Post, USA Today, New York Post, Washington Post, and CBS. Eric spoke to me about Alastair's mentoring style, highlighting that Alastair was expecting a lot of him but was also very supportive. When Eric was working on his Ph.D., the two of them used to meet at breakfast regularly to discuss Eric's progress. The conversations, however, went far beyond discussing research. "Alastair taught me how to operate my own career and how to be successful, and this was probably the most important outcome of these meetings." From my own experience I can testify that Alastair takes a genuine interest in following careers of his former students, connecting people with one another, and introducing research opportunities to junior scholars. Through Alastair, I have formed a research partnership with Dr Xiang (Robert) Li of the University of South Carolina Columbia, and the common interest in destination branding has sustained our research partnership for 5 years by now. When I became a faculty member at the University of Florida, Alastair shared his unique experience and knowledge of destination marketing with students in my tourism and hospitality management classes. In our skype sessions he answered students' questions about the role of government in tourism development and DMOs models in different countries, and I played various segments of the skype video sessions in class.

Practitioner

Alastair's understanding of marketing and how it can be applied for the global tourism industry is unparalleled. To date he has provided tourism planning, development, and marketing advice in approximately 30 different countries, including Australia, Bahrain, China, Ghana, Honduras, Hong Kong SAR, India, Italy, Jamaica, Macau SAR, Malaysia, New Zealand, Poland, Russia, Scotland, Singapore, Slovenia, Sri Lanka, Thailand, Trinidad & Tobago, and Vietnam. For years, he has been sharing his scholarship, experience, and vision with tourism and hospitality practitioners through training of future industry leaders on topics related to tourism planning, development, and marketing. Prior to joining the Purdue faculty in 1985, Alastair worked in Canada as the President of The Economic Planning Group of Canada and as a hospitality and tourism management consultant. These experiences were foundational when he and his colleague Don Anderson from the University of Calgary organized and developed the Certified Destination Management Executive programme for Destination Marketing Association International, through which many destination management executives from North America and the Caribbean were trained. In addition, Alastair has developed and facilitated training programmes on behalf of the UN World Tourism Organization (UNWTO) for eight South Asian countries and the China–Tibet Tourism Bureau, European Union, and the U.S. Agency for International Development. He also assisted several agencies with marketing and other planning advice in preparation for the 2010 Shanghai World Expo and the 2015 Milan World Expo.

Serving as an Associate Dean for Learning at the Department of HTM in Purdue University, Alastair, together with Dr Liping Cai, established several study abroad and scholarship programmes, with one of them, a six-month sponsored internship in China, being especially popular among the students. Under Alastair's supervision, educational and research exchanges between HTM and universities in Asia brought together both students and scholars: I well remember attending insightful presentations of Drs Cathy Hsu and Haiyan Song of Hong Kong Polytechnic University. Dr Bihu "Tiger" Wu was another prominent Chinese scholar whose academic ties with U.S. researchers in general and Alastair in particular grew stronger with the passing years. Through exchange of ideas with colleagues on the other side of the world, Alastair was involved in a number of tourism projects: since 2000, he has completed more than 80 individual projects in China, including the *Strategic Marketing Plan for Jiangsu Province* and the *Marketing Strategies for Ningbo and Shaoxing* on behalf of the World Bank, with acting as the Team Leader for both projects. Today Alastair speaks fluent Mandarin, but how he could have competed multiple projects without speaking the language remains a mystery!

The day when Alastair announced his move to China, the country in which tourism future he believed so passionately, was a sad day for me: I had been just accepted into the HTM doctoral programme and hoped that Alastair would remain my academic advisor and mentor. Looking back, this was the point when I began to fully understand the strong impact that Alastair made in students' lives and how much he was respected by them. Several people expressed regret about the move but at the same time were happy for Alastair and wished him success in his new journey. As we continued our research collaboration, I started receiving emails from Shanghai with "Belle Regards" right above

Alastair's signature, referring to "Belle Tourism International" (BTI), the consulting company that he established in China. Belle Tourism was created as a tourism and hospitality advisory services company, with the mission of providing sound advice, research and practical solutions for governments, private-sector companies, and not-for-profit organizations located within Greater China or interested in the Chinese and Pan-Pacific markets. The services included establishing comprehensive tourism development and marketing strategies, conducting marketing research and feasibility studies, as well as other promotional solutions for destinations and businesses.

People who worked with Alastair characterize him as an active and dynamic person, who shows no signs of slowing down and who has exceptional time management skills. While being CEO for BTI, he, together with his long-time colleague and collaborator Dr Bihu Wu, established the International Tourism Studies Association (ITSA) with the purpose of building stronger bridges between academic and industry world and focusing on the collaboration between West and Asia and growth of tourism, especially in Asia. In 2010, Alastair joined Peking University as a visiting professor and moved to Beijing. There he once again immersed himself in academic research on a wide range of issues related to Chinese tourism, such as tourist experiences with wildlife (Cong, Wu, Morrison, Shu, & Wang, 2014), women's role in sustaining villages and rural tourism in China (Ling, Wu, Park, Shu, & Morrison, 2013), analysis of Golden Week policy reform in China (Wu, Xue, Morrison, & Leung, 2012), as well as tourism education in China (Wu, Morrison, Yang, Zhou, & Cong, 2014). At the same time, as the ITSA president, Alastair has been the driving force under ITSA conferences, such as those in Shanghai China, Malaysia, Bali Indonesia, and Perth, Australia, which is scheduled for November 2014. The academic and industry representation at ITSA conferences is international and extremely strong, they have current and relevant academic agenda, and are conducted in the partnerships with destination premier universities.

In 2013, together with Dr Wu, Alastair organized *The International Journal of Tourism Cities* (*IJTC*), with the first issue scheduled to launch at the end of 2014. In countries such as China, Russia, or India, large cities that receive a sizable share of overall tourist arrivals are not perceived as tourist destinations per se, but rather as commercial, industrial, or transportation hubs. For the DMOs, issues of marketing and branding this type of destinations, studying tourist mobility patterns, creating optimal tourism experiences, understanding tourism at the edge of cities, where urban and rural areas converge, are of utmost importance. Thus, *IJTC* is aimed to stimulate more interdisciplinary research on tourism in cities, with the emphasis on the integration of tourism and urban studies and sharing best practices in city tourism worldwide through in-depth analyses and the production of exemplary case studies.

Contributions

Alastair is the unique blend of an academic, a practitioner, and an educator. He used his rich experience to teach thousands of students through his texts on tourism and hospitality marketing and development. He has authored five tourism books: *Marketing and Managing Tourism Destinations* (Routledge, 2013); *Global Marketing of China Tourism* (China Architecture & Building Press, 2012); *Hospitality and Travel Marketing*, 4th edition (Cengage Learning, 2010); *The Tourism System*, 6th edition, (Kendall/Hunt Publishing, 2010); and *Tourism: Bridges across Continents* (McGraw-Hill Australia, 1998). On the large scale of things, the success of his work to date is probably most directly associated with his continuing ability to write fresh and up-to-date versions of his

Hospitality and Travel Marketing textbook, cementing his role as an integrator and conduit to students and the applied tourism marketing community. This classical textbook first appeared in 1989 and has enjoyed four editions to date. It is one of the favorite texts for both students and teachers of marketing.

The manner in which Alastair packages the ideas and learning materials is very accessible. As my colleague Dr Lori Pennington-Gray put it, framing the essence of marketing process as a series of questions "Where are we now?", "Where would we like to be?", "How do we get there?", "How do we make sure we get there?", and "How do we know if we get there?" is so intuitive and simple; however, this simplicity stems from in-depth understanding of the subject, the industry, and all its players. Such an approach allows seamless integration of various topics and firmly grounds them in respective stages of the marketing process. The subsequent editions make the text contemporary, provide numerous examples, updated online resources, and relevant case studies on practical aspects of the industry. Together with a web page where Alastair compiled many of the tourism and hospitality resources that students and professionals could use in learning, research, and engagement, this textbook had a big impact on the field as an important educational tool and resource.

I would like to conclude with a reference which I put in the title of this portrait. One of the most known concepts of marketing has probably been the concept of 4Ps, i.e. Product, Price, Place, and Promotion. In the context of destination marketing, Alastair recognized the vital importance of another 4Ps – People, Partnerships, Packaging, and Programming. He incorporated the updated concept into his textbooks and, as this portrait shows, in his own life. Alastair has always been successful in building partnerships with people and keeping these relationships alive through the years. While I was writing this piece, different people commented to me that they greatly benefited from such partnerships, both as individuals and as tourism professionals. Alastair's current location in China is a special and new contribution in connecting Asian scholars and Western researchers. Through the organization of ITSA and its activities he is facilitating new research partnerships, and his skill in being fluent in Mandarin is especially noteworthy in his current influence in linking communities of interest. "Finding out what people need and want and then assembling various services and facilities to match these needs," is packaging, and Alastair's life as a consultant really informed both the development of meaningful research questions and the translation of research results into practice. Finally, Alastair practices programming, i.e. thorough planning, time management, and relentless pursuit of what needs to be done in a systematic and organized way; it is no wonder that his favorite quote is "failing to plan is planning to fail." To support his academic and integrative roles, on top of all hard work and impressive accomplishments, Alastair is a very open and friendly individual with excellent abilities to get along well with people and be an interesting companion and fellow researcher.

Acknowledgements

I am thankful to Alastair's colleagues, collaborators, and fellow researchers Drs Joseph O'Leary, Philip Pearce, Bihu "Tiger" Wu, Isabelle Frochot, and SooCheong (Shawn) Jang, as well as his former graduate students Drs Eric Brey, Dae-Young Kim, and Liang (Rebecca) Tang for providing their perspectives to this portrait and, thus, helping me to "triangulate" Alastair's achievements and impact on the tourism field as a researcher, collaborator, practitioner, educator, and mentor.

References

Beldona, S., Morrison, A. M., & O'Leary, J. (2005). Online shopping motivations and pleasure travel products: A correspondence analysis. *Tourism Management, 26*, 561–570.

Brey, E. T., So, S.-I., Kim, D.-Y., & Morrison, A. M. (2007). Web-based permission marketing: Segmentation for the lodging industry. *Tourism Management, 28*, 1408–1416.

Choi, S., Lehto, X. Y., & Morrison, A. M. (2007). Destination image representation on the web: Content analysis of Macau travel related websites. *Tourism Management, 28*, 118–129.

Cong, L., Wu, B., Morrison, A. M., Shu, H., & Wang, M. (2014). Analysis of wildlife tourism experiences with endangered species: An exploratory study of encounters with giant pandas in Chengdu, China. *Tourism Management, 40*, 300–310.

Frochot, I., & Morrison, A. (2000). Benefit segmentation: A review of its applications to travel and tourism research. *Journal of Travel and Tourism Marketing, 9*, 21–45.

Hsieh, S., O'Leary, J. T., & Morrison, A. M. (1992). Segmenting the international travel market by activity. *Tourism Management, 13*, 209–223.

Jang, S. C., Morrison, A. M., & O'Leary, J. T. (2002). Benefit segmentation of Japanese pleasure travelers to the USA and Canada: Selecting target markets based on the profitability and risk of individual market segments. *Tourism Management, 23*, 367–378.

Jogaratham, G., Chon, K., McCleary, K., Mena, M., & Yoo, J. (2005). An analysis of institutional contributors to three major academic tourism journals: 1992–2001. *Tourism Management, 26*, 641–648.

Kim, D.-Y., Lehto, X. Y., & Morrison, A. M. (2007). Gender differences in online travel information search: Implications for marketing communications on the internet. *Tourism Management, 28*, 423–433.

Letho, X. R., Kim, D.-Y., & Morrison, A. M. (2006). The effect of prior destination experience on online information search behavior. *Tourism and Hospitality Research, 6*, 160–178.

Ling, R. S. J., Wu, B., Park, J., Shu, H., & Morrison, A. M. (2013). Women's role in sustaining villages and rural tourism in China. *Annals of Tourism Research, 43*, 634–638.

McKercher, B. (2008). A citation analysis of tourism scholars. *Tourism Management, 29*, 1226–1232.

McKercher, B. (2014). *A changing of the guard in tourism research leadership*. Retrieved from http://www.robiveltroni.it/wp-content/uploads/2014/02/changing-the-guard-2.pdf

Mill, R. C., & Morrison, A. M. (2012). *The tourism system* (7th ed.). Dubuque, IA: Kendall Hunting.

Morrison, A. M. (2010). *Hospitality and travel marketing* (4th ed.). Clifton Park, NY: Delmar Cengage Learning.

Morrison, A. M. (2012). *Global marketing of China tourism*. Beijing: China Architecture & Building Press.

Morrison, A. M. (2013). *Marketing and managing tourism destinations*. New York, NY: Routledge.

Morrison, A. M., Jing, S., O'Leary, J., & Cai, L. A. (2001). Predicting usage of the Internet for travel bookings: An exploratory study. *Information Technology and Tourism, 4*, 15–30.

Morrison, A. M., Taylor, J. S., & Douglas, A. (2004). Web site evaluation in hospitality and tourism: The art is not yet stated. *Journal of Travel & Tourism Marketing, 17*, 233–251.

Moscardo, G., Pearce, P. L., & Morrison, A. M. (2001). Evaluating different bases for market segmentation: A comparison of geographic origin versus activity participation for generating tourist market segments. *Journal of Travel and Tourism Marketing, 10*, 29–50.

Pearce, P. L., Morrison, A. M., & Rutledge, J. L. (1998). *Tourism: Bridges across continents*. Sydney: McGraw-Hill.

Ryan, C. (2005). The ranking and rating of academics and journals in tourism research. *Tourism Management, 26*, 657–662.

Stepchenkova, S., & Morrison, A. M. (2006). The destination image of Russia: From the online induced perspective. *Tourism Management, 27*, 943–956.

Wu, B., Morrison, A. M., Yang, J. K., Zhou, J. L., & Cong, L. L. (2014). Cracks in the ivory tower? A survey-based analysis of undergraduate tourism education and educators in China. *Journal of Hospitality, Leisure, Sport and Tourism Education, 14*, 26–38.

Wu, B., Xue, L., Morrison, A. M., & Leung, X. Y. (2012). Frame analysis on golden week policy reform in China. *Annals of Tourism Research, 39*, 842–862.

Zhao, W., & Ritchie, J. R. B. (2007). An investigation of academic leadership in tourism research: 1985–2004. *Tourism Management, 28*, 474–490.

Moving ahead while standing still: a tribute to Arch G. Woodside

John C. Crotts

When Metin Kozak asked me to write a tribute to Arch, I quickly accepted the opportunity to publicly acknowledge a colleague who has had such a profound impact on my life both professionally and personally. Once I accepted, I quickly realized how little I knew of his life story, for you see Arch is one of the most outwardly focused people I know. He is always looking ahead to his next project or demonstrating a willingness to help others, finding little need to seek praise or focus on his own life.

Hence, this project required me to dig deep into his record and reflect on my personal experiences with him. In addition, I also chose to reach out to some of his former PhD students and colleagues who know him quite well. What these efforts revealed to me is an extraordinary intellect who continues to evolve and develop. We scholars in the field of tourism, hospitality, and leisure research have truly been blessed to have such a colleague who focuses so much of his attention in our way.

Arch exposed me years ago to the storytelling method, which is based in grounded theory. Any good story is composed of chapters, which describes where the protagonist came from and what he or she has accomplished, to where life story is leading them (and us). I will draw upon this framework in describing Arch Woodside.

From then to now: the body of evidence

It came as a surprise to me that Arch after earning his PhD in Business Administration from Penn State University, enlisted and rose to the rank of Captain in the U.S. Army serving as a Research Psychologist during the height of the Vietnam conflict. Conducting research on what was at the time a needed but still unproven technology – night-vision goggles – involved him in research, measuring treatment effects and behavioural effectiveness, as well as the socio-psychological and environmental conditions that can moderate such effects. This focus on socio-psychological principles underlying human decision-making (risk-taking) served him well in his later development as a university researcher.

Moving on to the University of South Carolina, Arch advanced from Assistant to Associate Professor in 3 years; from Associate to Full Professor in three, and then on to the rare classification of Distinguished Professor of Marketing in two more years. No doubt this meteoric rise was quite the exception in this Division 1 business school, but supported by the quality and quantity of his scholarship (43 peer-reviewed journal articles, 6 books), quality teaching (several best teacher awards), and service (Programme Director of

Marketing). What is truly remarkable is after gaining the highest title a university can bestow on a faculty member, Arch went on to publish to date a total of 267 refereed journal articles in our best journals as well as 48 books. In addition, he established several journals and currently serves as the Editor-in-Chief of the *Journal of Business Research*. JBR currently ranks second among all marketing journals in terms of its h-5 impact factor even though it includes articles from all business disciplines – not just marketing journal per se. Equally impressive is the fact that the leading Academies and Associations in our field have bestowed on him their highest honours. They are:

- Fellow of the American Psychological Association (awarded 1980),
- Fellow of the Society for Marketing Advances (awarded 1994),
- Fellow of the Association for Psychological Science (awarded 1996),
- Fellow of the Royal Society of Canada (awarded 2000),
- Fellow of the International Academy for the Study of Tourism (awarded 2003),
- Fellow of the Global Academy of Information and Knowledge Academy (2012), and
- Honorary Doctorate Degree, University of Montreal (2013).

Arguably, the best body of evidence of Arch's impact comes from those he has mentored along the way. Though the list includes me, for reason of parsimony I will share the experiences of others. Because they are highly personal, I share the following comments unedited in an effort to share the unselfish character of the man we all respect.

I met Arch at AUT in Auckland when he was an adjunct professor (also called extraordinary professor in South African terminology) and I was immediately drawn in by his tremendous sense of humour and willingness to help everyone (young and old, new and experienced) with their research. Most impressive (even mind-boggling to me) was his willingness to help me, a late bloomer and early-career researcher. At the time, I had just joined the academic research fraternity after more than 26 years as business executive and a member of the teaching staff at AUT. Arch acted as catalyst. After many months of considering and reconsidering whether I should embark on the long, uphill road of doing a PhD, he got me motivated and excited about a PhD, studying executive decision-making. He is truly, in every sense of the word, an extra-ordinary researcher and truly a brilliant supervisor.

To demonstrate his generosity, a short story. During the first few minutes of us meeting to discuss my PhD, I boldly, naively and arrogantly stated that I have no intention of taking six years to complete my dissertation. Arch immediately confirmed that there is no need to take six years, part-time or not, and that once the data are collected, one should be able to write the dissertation in a weekend. At the time I did not know Arch well enough, but now that I do, I am quite sure that HE can write the full 80,000 word dissertation and less than that... but not other mere mortals like myself. What Arch did succeed in doing, was to support me in such a manner that I did complete my dissertation in 2 years and 2 months, largely due to his generosity. What do I mean by that? Over the very many months of my PhD studies, every request for information or guidance was met with generous amounts of genuine assistance and support. Documents flew back and forth across the oceans via e-mail and comments and reviews were returned to me literally overnight. The time difference between Auckland, New Zealand and Boston, USA worked in my favour. I would send a document or request to Arch tonight and get the detailed, valuable comment-ridden response as I awake tomorrow morning. AMAZING. Many, MANY hours were spent on SKYPE on weeknights and weekends. Never once did he complain about the time taken or the amount of effort he had to expend on my studies. To top it all, my antsiness increased in December when I took a new position at the University of Waikato. The urgency escalated. I wanted to complete the PhD in order to accept a more senior position. In the remaining three months of my employment at AUT, Arch was, once again, willing to help and wrote several documents and support letters to help me to secure the position and get funding to visit him in Boston to complete the analysis of my data. This is by no means the most impressive example of his generosity.

He put me up in his own house, over a very hectic period in his own career, and helped me day in and day out for 14 days to come to grips with the ins-and-outs of fsQCA. I left Boston on 26 January this year with the dissertation just-about ready for submission. Arch is truly a generous man and an extra-ordinary human being.

Rouxelle de Villiers, Ph.D.

I am delighted at the thought of contributing a little something to this tribute. The tribute is to an absolutely superb storyteller, great marketing academic, and a lifelong friend and mentor. Professor Arch Woodside through his professorial positions, teaching, international activities, editorial contributions and PhD supervisory work, journal publications, and book publishing has without a doubt altered the global practice of marketing for generations to come.

As my Ph.D. supervisor, I can truly say Arch helped me understand the true meaning of Robert Frost's power of standing still, to step back from the messiness of life, and walk in the shoes of others. He taught me how to find my own inner voice and self-identity through not only discovering Jungian archetypes but phenomenological research exploring the lived experiences of others. I continue this gift from Arch of research going beyond numbers and analytics to incorporate storytelling research amongst students under my supervision.

Arch has been truly a great role model providing light at the end of a tunnel when choosing to return to Ph.D. study in my fifties. When others around me believed humans are unable to build relationships with brands, Arch understood and showed me the way of the human psyche to transcend the mundane by finding excitement and happiness amongst brand destinations. I am forever grateful for having the time to have such rich, deep and meaningful discussions with Arch to help refine my lifelong thinking and will truly be grateful for the words write, write, write.... For me the US Army's loss of such a great psychologist is the gain of marketing academia and practice everywhere.

Suresh Sood, Ph.D.

Several years ago, Arch Woodside appeared on my doorstep. He arrived to teach a summer course and to conduct research at my university. Arch loves to visit Hawaii, so we were both very happy about the experience. I assumed six weeks of working with Arch might lead to a publication and a chance to observe how he works (best sung to the Gilligan's Island theme song ...a three-hour tour). Eight years later, I remain mystified how one person can accomplish so much.

Less than one week after meeting Arch, I was sucked into the Woodside Vortex. He invited me to start a book project to be completed in nine months. The book project just started my journey. Co-chairing conference tracks, guest-editing journal special editions, and even participating in a geriatric fashion show followed. Little did I realize, starting a project with Arch means the fun never stops. Communication about new projects and ideas arrive frequently. Over time, I have come to recognize dozens of new and seasoned scholars traverse the Vortex. When I do not hear from Arch for two weeks, my assumption is he must be writing another book.

My favorite story about Arch involves an exchange of e-mail messages with the publisher of about a forthcoming book. The discussion involved deciding what picture to put on the book's cover. Arch suggested a picture of William Shatner dressed as Star Trek's Captain Kirk. His feeling was William Shatner's character was the ultimate traveler, so he perfect fits the profile a best-selling tourism book. The publisher's contact wrote back asking if Arch recently had a head injury! Unfortunately, we did not get William Shatner on our book cover. I cannot afford to retire early and live off the book's royalties. Maybe we should have stuck with the Star Trek theme?

Drew Martin, Ph.D.

Thanks for the opportunity of saying a few words about Arch Woodside. Like so many others fortunate enough to be drawn into his intellectual orbit, I am forever grateful for the profoundly positive impact he had on my career.

An intellectually gifted rascal, Arch is an Old School charmer with a wonderfully inquiring mind straddling many and varied aspects of human behaviour. One of his extraordinary talents is his memory: Mm. This reminds me of the November 1974 paper by Smith and Jones in JM. That memory extends to his filing system (sic). An Arch Woodside office is literally littered with printed journal articles, on the floor, on tables, and in filling cabinets with unlabelled drawers. For all that apparent confusion, he knows exactly where each article is located.

I'll share a couple of revealing comments from Arch. The first is his admission that publishing for him is an addiction. It's like being a heroin addict. I need to publish and I need to do it often. The other is about one of his proudest publications: I conducted a survey on the Monday, did the analysis on Tuesday and wrote the paper on Wednesday. As you do.

Roger March, Ph.D.

The life story continues

As the preceding tributes express, Arch is a tireless spirit who is always looking forward in the pursuit of new knowledge. Today he remains pioneering in the application of storytelling in marketing, which in my case served as the basis of web analytics using consumer blogs. Moreover, examine his most current publications (selected from a total of 78 peer-reviewed journal articles published between 2011 and 2013) and you will find that he is impelling us into new and useful research directions and methods. It is these qualities that will keep his body of knowledge in the forefront of academic research long after we are gone.

Arch, you continue, make us better, and inspire us all. Thank you for all you do.

Selections from most recent journal publications

Chang, C-W., Tseng, T-H., & Woodside, A. G. (2013 in print). Configural algorithms of patient satisfaction, participation in diagnostics, and treatment decisions' influences on hospital loyalty. *Journal of Services Marketing*.

Eng, S., & Woodside, A. G. (2012). Configural analysis of the drinking man: Fuzzy-set qualitative comparative analyses. *Addictive Behaviors, 37*(4), 541–543.

Hsu, S., Woodside, A. G., & Marshall, R. (2013 in print). Critical tests of multiple theories of cultures' consequences comparing the usefulness of models by Hofstede, Inglehart and Baker, Schwartz, Steenkamp, as well as GDP and distance for explaining overseas tourism behavior. *Journal of Travel Research*.

Li, C-S., Lin, C-H, Liu, C-C, & Woodside, A. G. (2012). Dynamic pricing in regulated automobile insurance markets with heterogeneous insurers: Strategies nice versus nasty for customers. *Journal of Business Research, 65*(8), 968–976.

Lloyd, S., & Woodside, A. G. (2013). Animals, archetypes, and advertising (A3): The theory and the practice of customer brand yymbolism. *Journal of Marketing Management, 29*(1), 5–25.

Martin, D., & Woodside, A. G. (2012). Structure and process models of leisure travel decisions and behavior: Mapping how visitors interpret own travel plans, actions, and outcomes. *International Journal of Contemporary Hospitality Management, 24*(6), 855–872.

Megehee, C. M., Strick, S. K., & Woodside, A. G. (2013 in print). Overcoming the bystander apathy and non-intervention effect (BANE) in alcohol-poisoning emergency situations: Advancing field testing of training-for-intervention theory via thought experiments. *International Journal of Business and Economics*.

Muller, C., & Woodside, A. G. (2012). Epiphany travel and assisted-subjective personal introspection. In K. Hyde, C. Ryan, & A. G. Woodside (Eds.), *Field Guide to Case Study Research in Tourism, Hospitality and Leisure, Advances in Culture, Tourism and Hospitality Research* (*Vol. 6*, pp. 259–273). Bingley, UK: Emerald.

Rageh, A., Melewar, T. C., & Woodside, A. (2013 in print). Using netnography research method to reveal the underlying dimensions of the customer/tourist experience. *Qualitative Market Research: An International Journal*.

Woodside, A. G. (2012a). Economic psychology and fashion marketing theory appraising Veblen's theory of conspicuous consumption. *Journal of Global Fashion Marketing, 3*(1), 55–60.

Woodside, A. G. (2012b). Incompetency training: Theory, practice, remedies. *Journal of Business Research*, *65*(3), 279–293.

Woodside, A. G. (2013a). Proposing a new logic for data analysis in marketing and consumer behavior: case study research of large-N survey data for estimating algorithms that accurately profile X (extremely high-use) consumers. *Journal of Global Scholars of Marketing Science.*, *22*(4), 277–289.

Woodside, A. G. (2013b). Moving beyond multiple regression analysis to algorithms: Call for a paradigm shift from symmetrical to asymmetrical data analysis and crafting theory. *Journal of Business Research*, *66*(4), 463–472.

Woodside, A. G., & Baxter, R. (2013 in print). Achieving Accuracy, Generalization-to-Contexts, and Complexity in Theories of Business-to-Business Decision Processes. *Industrial Marketing Management*.

Woodside, A. G., Chang, M-L, & Cheng, C-F (2013 in print). Government regulations of business, corruption, reforms and the economic growth of nations. *International Journal of Business and Economics*.

Woodside, A. G., Ko, E., & Huan, T. C. (2012). The new logic in building isomorphic theory of management decision realities. *Management Decision*, *50*(6), 765–777.

Woodside, A. G., Sood, S., & Muniz, K. M. (2013). Creating and interpreting visual storytelling art in extending thematic apperception tests and Jung's method of interpreting dreams. In A. G. Woodside & E. Ko (Eds.), *Luxury Fashion and Culture* (pp. 15–45). Bingley, UK: Emerald.

Woodside, A. G., & Zhang, M. (2012). Identifying x-consumers using causal recipes: 'Whales' and 'jumbo shrimps' casino gamblers. *Journal of Gambling Studies*, *28*(1), 13–26.

Woodside, A. G., & Zhang, M. (2013). Qualitative comparative analysis of cultures' consequences on fairness and punishment in ephemeral exchanges. *Psychology & Marketing*, *30*(3), 263–276.

Arie Reichel: pioneer, mentor, and leader

Natan Uriely

Introduction

When offered to present a portrait of Prof. Arie Reichel, my first reaction was that "it is too close for comfort." Twenty-four years ago, Reichel was the person who recruited me to the university and the department, where I still work. He became a colleague and friend with whom I collaborated on many research projects, celebrated personal achievements, and on several occasions "crossed stormy waters" together in our academic lives. I thought that I might not be removed far enough to paint an objective portrait of him, that I might skip an achievement he considers to be important, or stress another accomplishment that he regards as marginal. Worse, I might write another boring paper, this time about an interesting person. Although I was aware of the risks, I could not resist the opportunity to pay a tribute to someone who deserves it. I hope the following sketch of Arie Reichel's biography and his contribution to the study of tourism in general and to Israeli academia in particular will disprove my initial concerns.

Personal background

Arie Reichel was born in Kfar Saba, Israel (1950), and spent his childhood and adolescence in Kfar Maas, a small village near Tel Aviv. After three years of military service (1968–1971), he began his academic education at Tel Aviv University, where he earned a BA degree in sociology and social anthropology (1971–1974), and continued for a graduate degree at the School of Management. His interest in tourism was sparked when he was a graduate student at Tel Aviv University, by his encounter with Prof. Abraham Pizam, who became his mentor and eventually his close colleague. As a young student with academic aspirations, Reichel wanted a campus job, and Pizam was looking for a research assistant. This random match became a life-changing event for Reichel. Without completing his graduate studies at Tel Aviv University, he followed his mentor to the University of Massachusetts, US, to pursue his doctoral studies, where he received strong foundations in management, with further specialization in tourism management (1976–1980).

After graduation, he served as Assistant Professor of management at New York University, US (1979–1984), and also taught a course in tourism planning and development at The New School for Social Research (1982–1984). Living in Manhattan in the early 1980s was exciting for the young scholar, who found himself at what he used to call "the center of the world." Yet, on one of his visits to Israel he realized how difficult it was for his ageing parents to be so far away from their son, and felt that his long sojourn abroad might soon become irreversible. He therefore accepted an offer from Ben-Gurion University of the Negev (BGU), where he ended up spending most of his academic career (1984–2019). In subsequent years, he became increasingly interested and active in the field of tourism and hospitality research, which was at that time a somewhat obscure but challenging and relatively intimate field. Tourism became the main area of research for Reichel from 1994 onward, when he founded the Department of Hotel and Tourism Management at BGU.

Style of academic work

Consistent with the mentor- follower academic models, Reichel often stressed the need for intensive teamwork when articulating a research problem, formulating a research design, collecting data, and conducting the rest of the scientific process. In Israel, this style of academic work has the additional value of ensuring that graduate students and young researchers emulate the particular style of English language used in writing research papers. Under his leadership, teamwork has been a key element in the organizational culture of our department, and an effective way to undertake research projects indented for publication in leading journals. Working together, in pairs or triads, for long hours, in our small offices, and arguing about the correct interpretation of findings or the appropriate words to use, has resulted in effective brainstorming and a personal form of association that contains elements of pleasurable sociability.

Equipped with knowledge, experience, and an open mind, Reichel was a principal actor in these teamwork sessions. His mentorship was mostly evident in his ability to synthesize and guide the ideas of research students and young scholars in the direction of publishable research papers. As founder and the first chairperson of the department, he deserves the credit for the brainstorming style of teamwork established at the BGU Hotel and Tourism Department. He was also the knowledgeable researcher to be approached when deciding which journal is appropriate for a certain paper, and the experienced scholar who taught his young colleagues the practice of revisions, including how to handle rejections.

Streams of research

Arie Reichel is a versatile researcher who writes about a range of topics, mainly in the field of tourism scholarship. He draws on concepts and theories from different areas of knowledge, including marketing, strategic management, sociology, and social psychology, and his studies apply both quantitative and qualitative methodologies. The following account of the topics he studied over the years is not complete, but it covers the core of his research agenda.

One stream of research that Reichel conducted over the course of decades is the study of residents' attitudes towards tourists and tourism, a topic that has recently took centre stage in public attention, with the emerging interest in the concept of over-tourism (Seraphin, Sheeran, & Pilato, 2018). Note that this "hot" topic recycles ideas from early tourism studies, in which the problem of carrying capacity and its effect on locals at tourist destinations have already been recognized (Butler, 1980; Pizam, 1978). The importance of residents' attitudes for the success of tourism and the wellbeing of locals was first introduced to Reichel by his mentor, Abraham Pizam, when he arrived at the University of Massachusetts at Amherst, in the late 1970s. Residents of Cape Cod, Massachusetts, had mixed feelings towards tourists (Pizam, Neumann, & Reichel, 1978). On one hand, the tourists were a main source of income and were clearly welcome, but on the other, some residents felt that they would prefer to be elsewhere during the high season. Ambivalent and diverse attitudes towards tourists and tourism have been observed in other locations as well, where Reichel and colleagues conducted research, including the city of Nazareth (Israeli, Uriely, & Reichel, 2002; Uriely, Israeli, & Reichel, 2002, 2003) and the Sinai Peninsula (Uriely, Maoz, & Reichel, 2009).

Yet, Reichel suspected that when "community" was treated as a unified entity that ostensibly stood against the development of tourism, especially in developing countries, it often reflected a paternalistic ideology rather than a rigorous empirical approach. Reichel's call for a balanced perspective and empirical research was evident in his studies of tourism development, where in addition to local residents, attention was paid to other stakeholders, including consumers, entrepreneurs from the private sector, and governmental agencies (Haber & Reichel, 2005; Reichel & Haber, 2005; Reichel & Uriely, 2003; Reichel, Uriely, & Shani, 2008).

Another stream of research conducted by Reichel concerns tourist behaviour, mainly from the perspective of marketing and consumer behaviour. His studies about tourists' risk perception (Fuchs & Reichel, 2006; Fuchs & Reichel, 2011; Reichel, Fuchs, & Uriely, 2007, 2009) received considerable attention and initiated enlightening discussions about the definition and measurement of such concepts as "perceived risk" and "worries" (Larsen, Brun, & Øgaard, 2009; Wolf, Larsen, & Ogaard, 2019). His studies in this line of research were based on the notion of tourists as risk-averse consumers, and stressed the multidimensionality of tourists' perceived risks. To gain a wider understanding of risk-related behaviour by tourists, Reichel and colleagues shifted attention away from risk-averse to voluntary risk-taking by tourists, when visiting destinations exposed to terror in Sinai (Fuchs, Uriely, Reichel, & Maoz, 2013; Uriely, Maoz, & Reichel, 2007), undertaking health tourism at volatile destinations (Fuchs & Reichel, 2010), and participating in Scuba diving (Fuchs, Reichel, & Shani, 2016). These studies shed light on behaviours and rationalizations of tourists who either seek or ignore various aspects of risk.

Reichel's inclination to examine tourist behaviour from the perspective of consumer behaviour is also evident in a series of studies about particular segments, including backpackers (Reichel et al., 2007, 2009), visitors at heritage attractions (Biran, Poria, & Reichel, 2006; Poria, Biran, & Reichel, 2009; Poria, Reichel, & Biran, 2006a, 2006b; Reichel et al., 2007), and tourists with disabilities, such as the movement-challenged, blind, and obese (Poria, Reichel, & Brandt, 2009, 2010, 2011). The studies about the handicapped tourists turned the spotlight on a population that was discriminated against, and suggested relatively simple means to alleviate existing difficulties. Sensitivity and empathy to the needs of marginalized people and peripheral regions is evident in Reichel's research as well as in his administrative activity within the academic sphere and beyond it.

Academic entrepreneurship and leadership

As noted, Reichel founded the first Department of Hotel and Tourism Management in Israel (1994). The accreditation of a previously non-existent bachelor's degree, followed by master's and Ph.D. degrees, in the area of hospitality and tourism management attests to the field coming of age as an independent academic domain in Israel. The success of the programme at BGU and its accreditation prompted a surge in similar programmes across Israel. Reichel understood the academic arena, and promoted the vision that the department at BGU should be the flagship of tourism research in Israel. Although there are highly skilled, world-renowned scholars of tourism at various academic institutions and programmes in Israel, only the BGU department was able to achieve a high ranking, among the top 20 universities worldwide, in research contribution to the field (Li & Xu, 2014).

The success of the BGU Hotel and Tourism Department was attained in a two-stage process implemented by Reichel. In the first stage, he recruited scholars, like myself, who began their academic careers in other disciplines, and had some sort of connection to tourism or hospitality research. In my case, it was a year of post-doctoral scholarship at the Sociology and Anthropology Department of the Hebrew University in Jerusalem, where I met Erik Cohen, who kindled my curiosity for the sociology of tourism. Under the guidance of Arie Reichel, I shifted the focus of my research towards tourism, mainly, but not only, from a sociological perspective. Other colleagues, such as Aviad Israeli, had a similar experience. In the second stage, Reichel invested resources in developing a generation of scholars who specialize in tourism already in their undergraduate or graduate degree – often referred to in the department as the "T generation." Promising students from the department and other related units at BGU, such as Yaniv Poria,

Yaniv Belhassen, Amir Shani, and Galia Fuchs, were sent to Ph.D. and post-doctoral programs at leading tourism and hospitality departments worldwide, and returned as highly-skilled faculty members to the Hotel and Tourism Department. I daresay that for all of us, the initially recruited faculty and members of the T-generation, meeting Reichel was a life-changing event. He was the entrepreneur who provided us with a platform for pursuing an academic career in the area of tourism and hospitality research, the influential administrator who assisted in advancing our academic promotions, and the senior faculty member who guided us in organizational citizenship at BGU.

Reichel eventually founded and became the Dean of the Eilat campus of BGU (2001–2004), an extension of the main hotel and tourism programme. Located in a popular Israeli tourist destination on the Red Sea, the Eilat extension supplies the local hospitality and tourism industry with educated young employees, and offers an excellent location for research. Equally important for Reichel, the Eilat campus serves the academic needs of local residents in a distant peripheral town, with limited access to higher education. A similar vision, in which welfare is considered to be as important as profit, guided Reichel in other entrepreneurial activities and administrative positions, such as being a member of a group that founded the Guilford Glazer Faculty of Business and Management at BGU, and serving as Dean of the Faculty for two terms (2005–2011). Reichel's period as Dean was the golden age for departments that are often located at the fringes of business schools, such as Management of Health Systems, Public Policy and Administration, and Hotel and Tourism Management.

Conclusion

The above-portrayal of Arie Reichel reveals a pioneer in Israeli academic life. Reichel founded the first and leading academic department of tourism and hospitality in Israel, created the first and only university-level campus in the peripheral tourist destination of Eilat, and initiated the School of Business and Management at BGU. Under his leadership as chairperson or dean, these academic units emphasized the importance of diversity and empathy towards marginalized people and regions. His exceptional entrepreneurship and intensive involvement in academic administration were not carried out at the expense of research activity. As a busy chairperson and later as dean, he always found the time and invested the effort to advance his research agenda, which produced many highly-quoted papers in top-tier academic journals. As noted above, he collaborated intensively with students and young colleagues for whom he served officially or informally as a mentor. Reichel's ability to empower his colleagues appears to be the most important feature of his academic leadership.

Disclosure statement

No potential conflict of interest was reported by the author.

References

Biran, A., Poria, Y., & Reichel, A. (2006). Heritage site management: The link between visitors' pre-visit perceptions, motivations and expectations. *Anatolia, 17*(2), 279–304.

Butler, R. W. (1980). The concept of a tourist area cycle of evolution: Implications for management of resources. *Canadian Geographer, xxiv*, 5–12.

Fuchs, G., & Reichel, A. (2006). Tourist destination risk perception: The case of Israel. *Journal of Hospitality and Leisure Marketing*, *42*(2), 81–106.

Fuchs, G., & Reichel, A. (2010). Health tourists visiting a highly volatile destination: A three segment exploratory study. *Anatolia*, *21*(2), 205–227.

Fuchs, G., & Reichel, A. (2011). An exploratory inquiry into destination risk perceptions and risk reduction strategies of first time vs. repeat visitors to a highly volatile destination. *Tourism Management*, *32*(2), 266–276.

Fuchs, G., Reichel, A., & Shani, A. (2016). Scuba divers: The thrill of risk or the search for tranquility. *Tourism Recreation Research*, *41*(2), 145–156.

Fuchs, G., Uriely, N., Reichel, A., & Maoz, D. (2013). Vacationing in a terror-stricken destination: Tourists' risk perceptions and rationalizations. *Journal of Travel Research*, *52*(2), 182–191.

Haber, S., & Reichel, A. (2005). Physical design correlates of small tourism ventures' profitability. *Annals of Tourism Research*, *32*(1), 269–272.

Israeli, A., Uriely, N., & Reichel, A. (2002). Attitudes of local residents vs. residents of surrounding areas toward tourism development. *Anatolia: an International Journal of Tourism and Hospitality Research*, *13*(2), 145–158.

Larsen, S., Brun, W., & Øgaard, T. (2009). What tourists worry about — Construction of a scale measuring tourist worries. *Tourism Management*, *30*, 260–265.

Li, J., & Xu, Y. (2014). Author analyses of tourism research in the past thirty year - Based on ATR, JTR and TM. *Tourism Management Perspectives*, *3*, 1–6.

Pizam, A. (1978). Tourism's Impacts: The social costs to the destination the destination community perceived by its residents. *Journal of Travel Research*, *16*(4), 8–12.

Pizam, A., Neumann, Y., & Reichel, A. (1978). Dimensions of tourist satisfaction with a destination area. *Annals of Tourism Research*, *5*(3), 314–322.

Poria, Y., Biran, A., & Reichel, A. (2009). Visitors preferences for interpretation at heritage sites. *Journal of Travel Research*, *48*(1), 92–105.

Poria, Y., Reichel, A., & Biran, A. (2006a). Heritage site management: Motivation and expectations. *Annals of Tourism Research*, *33*(1), 162–178.

Poria, Y., Reichel, A., & Biran, A. (2006b). Heritage site management: Motivations and perceptions. *Journal of Heritage Tourism*, *1*(2), 121–132.

Poria, Y., Reichel, A., & Brandt, Y. (2009). People with disabilities visit art museums: An exploratory study of obstacles and difficulties. *Journal of Heritage Tourism*, *4*(2), 117–120.

Poria, Y., Reichel, A., & Brandt, Y. (2010). The light experience of people with disabilities: An exploratory study. *Journal of Travel Research*, *49*(2), 216–222.

Poria, Y., Reichel, A., & Brandt, Y. (2011). Dimensions of hotel experience of people with disabilities: An exploratory study. *International Journal of Contemporary Hospitality Management*, *23*(5), 571–591.

Reichel, A., Fuchs, G., & Uriely, N. (2007). Perceived risk and the non-institutionalized tourist role: The case of Israeli student ex-backpackers. *Journal of Travel Research*, *46*(2), 217–226.

Reichel, A., Fuchs, G., & Uriely, N. (2009). Israeli backpackers: The role of destination choice. *Annals of Tourism Research*, *36*(2), 222–246.

Reichel, A., & Haber, S. (2005). A three-sector comparison of small enterprises performance: An exploratory study. *Tourism Management*, *26*(5), 681–690.

Reichel, A., & Uriely, N. (2003). Sustainable tourism development in the Israel Negev desert: An integrative approach. *Journal of Park and Recreation Administration*, *21*(4), 14–29.

Reichel, A., Uriely, N., & Shani, A. (2008). Ecotourism and simulated attractions: Tourists' attitudes toward integrative sites in a desert area. *Journal of Sustainable Tourism*, *16*(1), 23–41.

Seraphin, H., Sheeran, P., & Pilato, M. (2018). Over-tourism and the fall of Venice as a destination. *Journal of Destination Marketing & Management*, *9*, 374–376.

Uriely, N., Israeli, A., & Reichel, A. (2002). Heritage proximity and resident attitudes toward tourism development. *Annals of Tourism Research*, *29*(3), 859–861.

Uriely, N., Israeli, A., & Reichel, A. (2003). Religious identity and residents' attitudes toward heritage tourism development: The case of Nazareth. *Journal of Hospitality & Tourism Research*, *27*(1), 69–84.

Uriely, N., Maoz, D., & Reichel, A. (2007). Rationalizing terror-related risks: The case of Israeli tourists in Sinai. *International Journal of Tourism Research*, *9*(1), 1–8.

Uriely, N., Maoz, D., & Reichel, A. (2009). Israeli guests and Egyptian hosts in Sinai: A bubble of serenity. *Journal of Travel Research*, *47*(4), 508–522.

Wolf, K., Larsen, S., & Ogaard, T. (2019). How to define and measure risk perceptions. *Annals of Tourism Research*, *79*, 1–9.

Bihu (Tiger) Wu: the tourism scholar ironman of China

Mimi Li and Alastair M. Morrison

Introduction

It was not an easy task to craft a portrait for Professor Bihu (Tiger) Wu, although both authors have been acquainted with Tiger for nearly twenty years, as colleague (second author), former student (first author), and very close friend. Wu is a professor at College of Urban and Environment Sciences, Peking University, China. He is the founding director of the International Center for Recreation and Tourism Research (iCRTR) at Peking University. iCRTR was one of the first organizations devoted to the tourism research and education in China. As a researcher, Tiger excels both in geography and in "tourismology" (the term he created to refer to tourism studies, see Wu, 2010, p. 177). Three of his many publications (Wu, 1994, 2001; Wu et al., 1997) in geography rank in the top ten in terms of impact in the past three decades (ranked first, third, and fourth, respectively). Two articles published in *Acta Geographica Sinica* (Wu, 1994; Wu et al., 1997), the most prestigious journal in geography in China, were awarded 4th and 15th place for high citation in the 80 years since the journal was established.

In the field of tourism, Wu is recognized as one of the most innovative and productive Chinese scholars who made a "significant contribution to the development of tourism as an academic area of work in China – especially for destination planning" (email correspondence with Professor Chris Ryan, 15 September 2017). Tiger's research impact was the highest among all Chinese scholars from 1982 to 2012, publishing over 220 journal articles and authoring or co-authoring 12 books and 34 edited/ translated books and conference proceedings. He also made more than 100 conference presentations. His *magnum opus*, *Regional Tourism Planning Principles* (published in 2001 and 2010 by China Tourism Press), was commented as distinguishing "itself from other texts on tourism…include Clare Gunn's two books … and C. Michael Hall's …", demonstrating his "profound knowledge of regional tourism planning" (Morrison & Cai, 2002, p. 640), and making "a significant contribution to the research and practice of tourism planning" (Morrison & Cai, 2002, p. 641). The book ranks 8th in academic impact among all Chinese books in humanities and social sciences.

Wu is an active member of several associations and committees. Domestically, he is a member of the Advisory Committee of China Tourism Reform and Development, China National Tourism Administration (CNTA), and the Founding President of China National Conference on Historic Villages. Internationally, he is the founding member and Secretary-General of the International Tourism Studies Association, the first China-based international academic organization in tourism providing a platform for collaboration among tourism scholars within and outside of China. Due to his achievements in tourism geography and planning, Wu was elected in 2015 as a Fellow of the

International Academy for the Study of Tourism, which is the world's most elite honorary organization for tourism scholars.

Apart from these recognitions as a scholar, Tiger is known as a practitioner and knowledge diffuser, actively applying his research into the practice of tourism development and planning in China. Jafar Jafari commented that "he (Tiger) knows both the theory and practice of tourism; few tourism scholars fall in the category" (email correspondence, 17 September 2017). Tiger has served as the Principal Investigator for more than 100 tourism planning projects in Mainland China, ranging from provincial to local levels. He has made over 400 speeches to executives and government officers. Tiger is regarded as "the most significant knowledge broker that bridges academia and industry in China" (personal communication with Mr Shunli Gao, former President of China Tourism News, 11 September 2017).

This rather long resumé only partially sheds light on who Tiger is as a scholar and practitioner. To portray a broader picture of Tiger, the authors had many conversations with his colleagues and peers, collaborators, and former students. Individuals who shared their perspectives for this portrait included Professor Jafar Jafari (University of Wisconsin-Stout, U.S.A.), Professor Chris Ryan (University of Waikato, New Zealand), Professor Yanjun Xie (Dongbei University of Finance & Economics, China), Mr Shunli Gao (China Tourism News, China), Ms Xiaoyan Qiao (Overseas Chinese Town, China), Dr Honggen Xiao (The Hong Kong Polytechnic University, Hong Kong), Dr Lina Zhong (Beijing International Studies University, China), Mr Ping Su, Ms Xiaolan Yang, Dr Lan Xue (Pennsylvania State University, U.S.A.), Mr Tao Xue (BES Cultural Tourism Group), Dr Yiyi Jiang (China Tourism Academy, China), Dr Xiaobo Xu (Shanghai Normal University, China), Dr Xiaoting Huang (Shandong University), and Dr Ning Dang (East China Normal University, China).

A researcher

Tiger was born in a poor village in North Jiangsu Province in 1962 when the entire country was struggling to recover from the three-year natural disaster period when millions died of starvation. Despite the ever-present feeling of hunger, he was fortunate to be given the opportunity to receive a formal education, thanks to both, his parents and the then Party President, Deng Xiaoping. He was admitted to the Department of Geography at East China Normal University (ECNU) in 1980. Wu received his degrees of Doctor of Philosophy, Master of Science, and Bachelor of Science in geography from ECNU (1984), and spent 17 years there both as a student and as a faculty member. Being invited by Professor Lu Peiyuan, the then Department Head, he joined the Department of Urban and Environmental Sciences at Peking University as a Postdoctoral Research Fellow (1997). He worked closely with late Professor Chen Chuankang, "the founder of contemporary tourism geography and tourism planning studies in China" (Wu, 2010, p. 173), Professor Wang Enyong and Professor Guo Laixi after the passing away of Professor Chen (1997). Wu became a faculty member of Department of Urban and Environmental Sciences at Peking University (1999).

His destiny to be a tourismologist was determined by his vast interest in various disciplines and his passion to explore nature and culture. Xiao Honggen recalls:

> As a human geographer engaged in travel and tourism research, Tiger is a ceaseless and tireless learner, as much as a curious and keen explorer on the way. I remember we travelled together to the 2010 ISA World Congress of Sociology in Goteborg, where he was to assume his term of co-presidency of the International Tourism Working Group. As side trips after the Congress, we explored Oslo and Copenhagen as "serious" tourists and travel researchers. In the Chinese spirit of learning from the West for applications, Tiger performed his part as a fictional county magistrate where I served (or acted) as his secretary. With these staged-up roles, he was able to probe and learn about city planning and urban tourism development through "real" encounters and conversations. I could tell that the locals were totally amazed by the types of questions he raised and the way he asked them. (email correspondence, September 20, 2017)

Tiger's path in academia was in four stages as he has described in his autobiography: a physical geography student who was crazy about Chinese literature and history, a human geographer, a tourism geographer, and a tourismologist (Wu, 2010). This can be seen from domains of his publication over the years as shown in Figure 1. Before 1999, Tiger mainly examined tourism phenomenon from a geographical perspective, later expanded to wider aspects of tourism including knowledge development

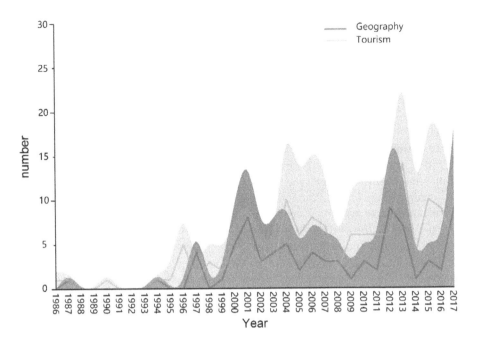

Figure 1. Domains of publication (1986–2017).

in tourism (e.g. Zhong, Wu, & Morrison, 2013), tourist behaviour (e.g. Cong, Wu, Morrison, Shu, & Wang, 2014; Zhang, Morrison, Tucker, & Wu, 2017; Zhang, Tucker, Morrison, & Wu, 2017), tourism in heritage sites (e.g. Gao & Wu, 2017; Li, Wu, & Cai, 2008), destination image (e.g. Tseng, Wu, Morrison, Zhang, & Chen, 2015; Zhang, Wu, Morrison, Tseng, & Chen, 2016), rural tourism (e.g. Sia, Wu, Park, Shu, & Morrison, 2013), and so on.

After graduating with a Bachelor of Science in physical geography from ECNU (1984), Tiger was admitted to the Master's programme in the same institution (1984). The legacy of following the then Soviet Union-styled curriculum design, in which great emphasis and resources were given to science education, left the liberal arts obsessed Tiger not much choice and he started to pursue his Master's in Human Geography under the supervision of Professor Chu Shaotang. Chu is a historical geographer and his area of study was the travel history of China. This gave Tiger his first academic exposure to tourism. Tiger's passion for tourism was stimulated by a talk on tourism geography made by Professor Chen Chuankang at ECNU in 1985, and was later enlightened by his encounter with *Recreation Geography* by Stephen Smith in the ECNU library, which was one of the very few university libraries with literature in foreign languages at that time. The Chinese version of this book was translated by Tiger and published in 1992 by the Beijing-based Higher Education Press and later by the Taiwan-based Garden City Publishers in 1996.

The 1990s was a remarkable period for the tourism industry in China as it gradually became an important sector of the national economy. Favourable policy was formulated to encourage development and enormous funds were invested on tourism resource development, infrastructure and facility construction, education, and research. To capitalize on the opportunity, many universities in Mainland China started to run tourism-related programmes, although under different names. ECNU established the Department of Tourism Education (as a Normal University, everything had to be related to education even if only nominal) in 1992. Tiger was transferred to the new department from the Department of Geography and "officially" became a researcher in tourism.

When being asked about the critical "milestones" in his career as a researcher, the first one to pop up was his first major research grant from the National Natural Science Foundation of China (NSFC) in 1992. The study investigated travel behaviour patterns of domestic tourists in China from a geographic perspective. This grant laid a solid foundation for his endeavours as a tourism geographer.

Based on its findings, he identified the geographical patterns of Chinese urban residents' domestic travel behaviour (*Wu's Curve*), and proposed the concept of the *Recreational Belt around Metropolis* (*ReBAM*) to describe the spatial patterns of recreation/tourism facilities around urban areas. Articles on *Wu's Curve* and *ReBAM* were published in top-tier journals of geography and tourism including *Acta Geographic Sinica* (Wu, 1994; Wu et al., 1997) and *Annals of Tourism Research* (Wu & Cai, 2006).

One of the byproducts of the unprecedented growth of Chinese economy since the 1990s was the remarkable increase of tourism, both in terms of numbers of trips made and total expenditures. This rapid development exemplified the *ReBAM* theory in various contexts, and provided incomparable opportunities for Tiger to further develop the theory. Informed by *ReBAM*, several graduate students completed their dissertations under Tiger's supervision and many publications were generated. Without doubt, *ReBAM* is one of the key theories in urban tourism, tourism geography, and tourism planning, which encouraged thousands of publications as shown by Google Scholar.

Planning is an important application of geography and geographers were always pioneers in tourism planning. Tiger was not an exception. After getting involved in several tourism planning projects in Shanghai (1994, 1995, and 1996), Wuxi (1995), and Lunan (1995), Tiger started to reflect on the foundation, principles and guidelines of regional tourism planning. This became the study area for his postdoctoral research. According to Tiger, the second important milestone for his career was being a Visiting Scholar at Purdue University in the summer of 2000. Being invited by Professors Alastair Morrison and Liping Cai, Tiger spent several months in the tranquil surroundings of this top research university, immersing himself in seemingly endless reading and writing about tourism planning. By the end of his Visiting Scholar stint, he finished the first draft of *Regional Tourism Planning Principles* (2000). The experience at Purdue University was very important to Tiger because it was his first international exposure and laid the foundation for his contributions to international collaboration between China and other countries. Mr Gao commented, Tiger "has made significant contributions to the international collaboration in the field of tourism".

Tourism research in China is dominated by theories and frameworks developed in Western countries. Although a theory is meant to be universally applicable, researchers in China were always eagerly calling for conceptual approaches that were applicable to China's unique situation. In this sense, Tiger is undoubtedly one of the most innovative Chinese scholars developing and applying original theories from and for China's tourism.

A knowledge broker

The beginning of the twenty-first century witnessed the rapid development of tourism in China, providing Chinese tourism academics an unprecedented platform to apply their theoretical constructs and creative thoughts. This became the focus of the second stage of Tiger's career: to blend academic knowledge into practice and to conduct practical research relevant to the development of the tourism industry. *Regional Tourism Planning Principles* provided a starting point for such a shift. Among all the original concepts proposed in the book, probably the *1231 framework*, the *Resource-Market-Product* (*RMP*) *framework*, and *ReBAM* were to become the most well-known and widely applied. The former two delineated the steps to be followed follow when preparing a tourism plan. Although proposed 17 years ago, these approaches remain relevant and are applied by many tourism planners in China. The behavioural patterns of urban residents and spatial patterns of tourism/recreation facilities around cities, as described by *ReBAM*, provide the guideline for most, if not all, urban destination planning. It is fair to say that *ReBAM* has become an indispensable component of urban tourism planning in China.

Apart from providing the theoretical groundwork for tourism planning practice, Tiger has actively participated in over 1,000 tourism planning projects to various degrees: as Principal Investigator, member of expert teams, and reviewer of planning reports. As Principal Investigator, his planning consultancy projects cover almost all major urban destinations in China including Beijing (1997), Hangzhou (2003), Xi'an, Lhasa, and Chengdu. The Hangzhou Tourism Master Plan set a new benchmark for tourism planning. While many urban destinations at that time were striving for attraction admission ticket income, the Hangzhou plan suggested a shift from sightseeing to leisure and vacations, revitalization of heritage sites and intangible cultural heritage, and development of the Grand Canal, for which Hangzhou was the southern start point.

To bridge the gap between academia and the industry, Tiger conducted destination-based research with research problems generated from practice. As shown in Figure 2, his research covered 19 provincial-level regions. He launched the journal, *Tourism Planning and Design*, with China Architecture and Building Press in 2010. This publication is patterned after the *Cornell Hospitality Quarterly* but focuses on tourism planning, landscape architecture, and tourism destination management. The journal has published 24 volumes since its foundation and has become a must-have item for practitioners and government officers. Capitalizing on his academic achievements, Tiger also provides professional advice on tourism development for state government on policy formulation, resource allocation, destination planning, and destination management. As an active member of the think tank of CNTA, Tiger led a group of experts to develop the *Best Tourist City Evaluation Criteria* (BTC) in 2001, a first of its kind across the globe. And building upon this, Tiger was appointed in 2011 by CNTA as the Principal Investigator to develop an attractiveness index for urban destinations. BTC have been widely applied as a development guideline by many urban destinations in China in the past decades.

In traditional Chinese culture, devotion to academic research is only part of the role a scholar should play in society. Importantly, a scholar should cultivate himself, regulate his family, and govern the state to achieve world peace (Zengzi, 505–437 BC). This philosophy has been the principle for many scholars in China, including Tiger. Apart from being productive in research and publishing, Tiger is eagerly sharing the most updated research, best practices around the world, and his own academic thoughts via various channels with enterprise executives and government officers from national to county levels, especially the latter since in a socialist market economy like China, government plays a vital role in every aspect of industry. It is sad to say but in many occasions, only the top leaders (normally the Party Secretary) have the final say on the strategic direction of destinations

Figure 2. Distribution of destination-based research. (Source: Authors).

and these people may have limited knowledge about tourism. Keeping the actual decision-makers well informed and educated is therefore a huge challenge for the sustainable development of tourism. Working closely with public agencies, Tiger has delivered more than 400 speeches to government officers. His talks have influenced over 10,000 attendees working at the front line of tourism development and governance, as well as the decision-makers. Ms. Qiao Xiaoyan from Overseas Chinese Town commented, "Professor Wu has made significant contributions to tourism development in the country through knowledge dissemination" (personal communication, 15 September 2017). Tiger also enthusiastically shares his thoughts about various social and environmental issues, and even criticizing public policy in different media, which demonstrates "a strong sense of social responsibility" (Mr Su Ping, personal communication, 13 September 2017), and "scholastic independence" (Mr Gao, 11 September 2017).

The second author likens Tiger Wu as the "rock star" of Chinese tourism and recalls doing a keynote speech in Kunming just after Tiger and before the start of the China International Tourism Mart:

> Tiger delivered his speech and there were parts of it when many in the audience laughed. I didn't at that time completely understand what was being said, but he was cracking some good jokes. I had worked very hard at preparing a good presentation on consumer trends, but nobody even broke a smile when I used humor. At the end of our speeches, Tiger was mobbed by people as I stood by and watched. This is tourism fandom in China, I thought, and Tiger Wu rocks.

A mentor

For many of his students, Tiger is not only a world-leading researcher but also a great teacher, mentor, and "easy-going friend with whom you can share anything" (Ms Xiaolan Yang, personal communication on 20 September 2017). The first author recalls taking Tiger's subject on Regional Tourism Planning during her junior year at Peking University:

> Tiger is a very innovative and inspiring professor. He was actually the first one in our department to introduce the "concept" of group project and encouraged undergraduate students to do research. In his class, we had to work in groups to examine a tourism-related phenomenon, collect and analyze data, and report our findings to the class. This approach intrigued our interest in tourism and tourism research. Now three (out of 23) of my classmates are tourism researchers.

Almost all his students have a common memory of going to Karaoke with him, liking each other's posts on social media, and being corrected by him via the most "in" instant messenger. As Dr Xiaoting Huang (his former Ph.D. student) recalls that "I remember vividly how Tiger panned me on MSN because of the inappropriate use of punctuation" (personal communication, 27 September 2017).

As a professor at Peking University, he has supervised 36 Doctoral students, 76 Master's students, and countless undergraduate honour theses. He has collaborated with four Postdoctoral Fellows and 38 Visiting Scholars and serves as a Visiting Professor at top-tier universities including Shaanxi Normal University, Harbin Institute of Technology, Huaqiao University, and his Alma Mater, East China Normal University.

Tiger's students are always impressed by his diligence, persistence, and passion for what he is doing. Mr Ping Su, Tiger's former Master's student, says:

> Tiger's attitude to work has had a great influence on my career development. The most important thing I learned from him is to be passionate about what you are doing, devote wholeheartedly to it, and always strive for excellence.

Dr Lina Zhong, Tiger's Doctoral student and Associate Professor at Beijing International Studies University, adds:

> We always call Tiger "iron man". It seems to us that he doesn't need to sleep. I remember once we traveled to Sinkiang for a very intensive field visit. We worked until 1 am almost every night and got up early in the morning. The whole team rested only for five or six hours per day for more than 10 days. Everybody in the team felt exhausted, except Tiger. One day we arrived in an area that is rich in fruits, our local collaborator recommended us to visit a place that produces a special type of fruit. It sounded appealing but we were scared off by the fact that we had to get up at 6am in the next morning. Then Tiger visited the place alone with our local collaborator

and came back from the visit sharing with us the potential of that place, energetically and excitedly. He even brought some fresh fruit back for us. It tasted awesome but we all felt a little shamed. On our way back to Beijing, he fell into a deep sleep on the plane. I realized that he is not tireless, he is just more persistent in working hard to achieve his goal than anyone else. We always respect him for his modesty and continuous learning. As the old Chinese saying goes, it is not difficult to teach others with excellent professional knowledge, but it is difficult to teach others how to be a man with his profound knowledge and noble personality. As a teacher, Tiger set a good example for me and he is always my role model.

Tiger is an inspiring mentor. He respects students' research interests and provides endless support even after they graduate. Mr Tao Xue, Tiger's former Master's student, explains:

> I had a difficult time to decide the topic for my Master's thesis. Since I came from a landscape architecture background, I couldn't propose any real tourism problem, and I was afraid that the committee will not let me pass. Then Tiger told me, there is no bad research, any research that contribute to the knowledge advancement is meaningful. He encouraged me to develop the research problem from my academic background and my thesis was not only praised by the committee but also published on Journal of Asian Architecture and Building Engineering.

A sign of a good mentor is when mentees become research colleagues and time and time again this has happened with Tiger's graduate students and others that he has advised. However, Tiger's influence has spread much further than China as his research publications and association work has built an international network of colleagues.

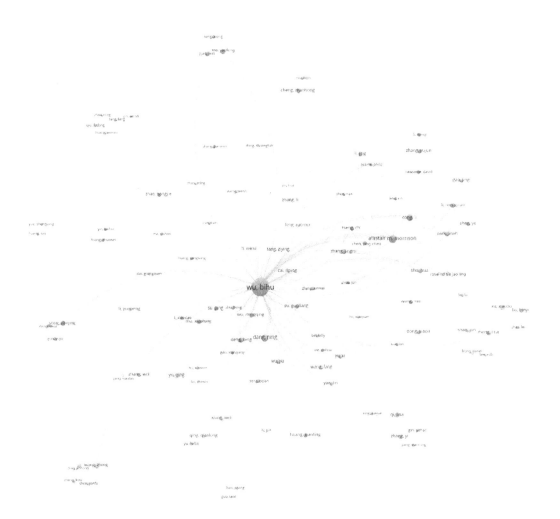

Figure 3. Co-authorship network of Bihu Wu.

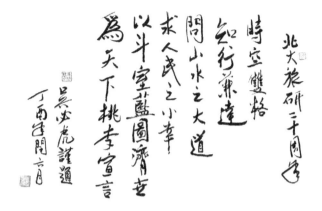

Time evolves along with space,
Knowledge in action corroborates.
Mountains and waters uphold the truth,
To which the wellbeing of people subdues.
Mapping and preaching are dual a goal,
Regardless of what's global and what local.

Figure 4. Calligraphic expression of his work by Bihu Wu.

A valued colleague

A final perspective on Wu is from the second author and based on comments contributed by several mutual colleagues. Tiger's publishing history is a testimony to his great ability to collaborate with other scholars, in China and around the globe (Figure 3). All those who know him characterize Tiger as affable, witty, energetic, and tireless. On the latter point, the second author witnessed Tiger climbing the 75-metre, Dave Evans Bicentennial Tree in Western Australia, and was amazed by his bravery. Others will remember Tiger as a shutterbug, taking thousands of photos each day. The second author has the following to say about Tiger as a colleague, and not just as a tree-climber and cameraman:

> I first met Tiger in 2000 when we invited him as a Visiting Scholar to Purdue University. He impressed me right from the start with his quick wit and knowledge of tourism. He is one of a handful of Chinese tourism scholars of his generation to have made an impact and engaged internationally. Additionally, Tiger is one of only two Chinese scholars who are Fellows in the International Academy for the Study of Tourism (IAST).

Conclusion

2017 is a remarkable year for Tiger. On 15 July 2017, the International Center for Recreation and Tourism Research at Peking University celebrated its twentieth anniversary with over 100 iCRTR alumni and nearly 200 attendees from academia and industry. For the ceremony, Tiger shared a poem in calligraphy as shown in Figure 4. This is how he positions himself and practices, as a scholar and a mentor.

And so, readers now know more about the Tourism Ironman of China, Bihu "Tiger" Wu. It is quite a story of how a boy from rural Jiangsu has become a famous professor at China's top university in Beijing. While it will be hard for anyone to emulate this success, it is surely inspirational to young Chinese scholars who wish to make a mark on the world.

Acknowledgements

The authors would like to express their gratitude to Huang Jiacheng and Li Qing, Master's student at iCRTR, for their assistance in organizing the bibliographic information, analysing the data, and developing the first three figures. The translation of Wu Bihu's calligraphy in Figure 4 was expertly crafted by Honggen Xiao of The Hong Kong Polytechnic University.

Disclosure statement

No potential conflict of interest was reported by the authors.

References

Cong, L., Wu, B., Morrison, A. M., Shu, H., & Wang, M. (2014). Analysis of wildlife tourism experiences with endangered species: An exploratory study of encounters with giant pandas in Chengdu, China. *Tourism Management, 40*, 300–310.

Gao, J., & Wu, B. (2017). Revitalizing traditional villages through rural tourism: A case study of Yuanjia Village, Shaanxi Province, China. *Tourism Management, 63*, 223–233. doi: 10.1080/09669582.2017.1329310

Li, M., Wu, B., & Cai, L. (2008). Tourism development of world heritage sites in China: A geographic perspective. *Tourism Management, 29*(2), 308–319.

Morrison, A., & Cai, L. (2002). Regional tourism planning principles: Wu, B.; China Travel and Tourism Press, Beijing, China, 2001, 711 pp., price 58 yuan, 639–641, ISBN 7(5032), 1825, 8. *Tourism Management, 23*(6), doi:10.1016/S0261-5177(02)00034-1

Sia, R., Wu, B., Park, J., Shu, H., & Morrison, A. M. (2013). Women's role in sustaining villages and rural tourism in China. *Annals of Tourism Research, 43*, 634–638.

Tseng, C., Wu, B., Morrison, A. M., Zhang, J., & Chen, Y.C. (2015). Travel blogs on China as a destination image formation agent: A qualitative analysis using Leximancer. *Tourism Management, 46*, 347–358.

Wu, B. (1994). A research on urban recreationist's traveling behaviour in Shanghai. *Acta Gegraphica Sinica, 49*(2), 117–127.

Wu, B. (2001). A study on recreational belt around metropolis (ReBAM): Shanghai case. *Scientia Geogrpahica Sinica, 21*(4), 354–359.

Wu, B. (2010). The way to and from Shanghai: A Chinese tourism geographer's story. In S. L. J. Smith (Ed.), *The Discovery of Tourism* (pp. 163–178). Bingley: Emerald.

Wu, B., & Cai, L. (2006). Spatial modeling: Suburban leisure in Shanghai. *Annals of Tourism Research, 33*(1), 179–198.

Wu, B., Tang, J., Huang, A., Zhao, R., Qiu, F., & Fang, F. (1997). A study on destination choice behavior of Chinese urban residents. *Acta Gegraphica Sinica, 52*(2), 97–103.

Zengzi. (505–437 BC). *Great learning.* (J. Legge, Trans.). Shanghai: Commercial Press.

Zhang, J., Morrison, A., Tucker, H., & Wu, B. (2017). Am I a backpacker? Factors indicating the social identity of Chinese backpackers. *Journal of Travel Research.* doi: 10.1177/0047287517702744

Zhang, J., Tucker, H., Morrison, A.M., & Wu, B. (2017). Becoming a backpacker in China: A grounded theory approach to identity construction of backpackers. *Annals of Tourism Research, 64*, 114–125.

Zhang, J., Wu, B., Morrison, A.M., Tseng, C., & Chen, Y.C. (2016). How country image affects tourists's destination evaluation: A moderated mediation approach *Journal of Hospitality & Tourism Research.* doi: 10.1177/1096348016640584

Zhong, L., Wu, B., & Morrison, A.M. (2013). Research on China's tourism: A 35-year review and authorship analysis. *International Journal of Tourism Research, 17*(1), 25–34.

Bob McKercher: serendipity, passion and a commitment to excellence

David C. W. Chin

Introduction

I stumbled into tourism and hospitality academia a few years ago while working in Hong Kong Disneyland Resort, having over 20 years cross-industry experience in a variety of marketing and market research related positions. I believed further studies would enhance my knowledge, and subsequently enrolled in the Doctor of Hotel and Tourism Management programme at the School of Hotel and Tourism Management, The Hong Kong Polytechnic University, Hong Kong, China. There, I encountered Professor Bob McKercher for the first time. I did not know him but fellow students said he was well-known in the field. My naiveté soon gave way to the realization that he is more than well-known; in fact, he is a well-respected authority in the field. If one were to be serious about studying tourism theory, it would be difficult not to come across his work at some point in time. Being a prolific author, his works have helped shape how we think about tourism. His contribution to the field has been well-recognized: elected as a Fellow of International Academy for the Study of Tourism, and selected as a Fellow of the Council for Australasian University Tourism and Hospitality Education (CAUTHE) and the Academy of Culture, Tourism and Hospitality Research, where he also received a lifetime achievement award.

I met Bob when I enrolled in my first doctoral subject: Theories and Concepts of Tourism. First impressions indicated he was somewhat serious, reserved and down to earth, but had a good sense of humour. Bob likes his students to call him Bob. Like any other new kid on the block, I asked fellow students about his teaching standards. They said he was extremely knowledgeable, tough, but fair. Recently, I interviewed him as part of my own doctoral thesis research on academic research and career development. His insightful feedback provided many "ah–ha!" moments, which led to the idea of sharing his perspectives with others. It was on this basis that this portrait article was born, using a constructivist and narrative approach (Del Corso & Rehfuss, 2011).

Serendipity – the winding road from student to professor

Bob's road to a tourism academic involved a series of what he calls "serendipitous events" that, at the time seemed disconnected, but ultimately led to where he is now. He was born in Ottawa, Canada in 1954 and has three siblings. One sister is an archaeologist. The other sister was the first female foreign correspondent for Canadian Press before embarking on her own career as a Professor of Journalism. His brother was born with Downs Syndrome and died at a relatively young age of 42. His dad was a medical doctor with close relatives being lawyers. With his family background of professionals and upbringing, there was a general expectation that he would pursue a university education, but there was no pressure on the specific field he would study.

The idea of being an academic has always been at the back of his mind. While still in high school, he thought about being a scientist with the Geological Survey of Canada. That dream seemed very far off, as he spent too much time enjoying himself as an undergraduate student majoring in Geography at York University in Toronto, Canada but did not spend enough time studying. He still wanted to do something related to research when he graduated and took his first job as an insurance claims adjuster, investigating a range of property, personal injury and automobile claims. Despite its clerical nature, his next job brought him closer to geography when he worked as the Mission Planner for the Canada Center for Remote Sensing.

It was while working there that he discovered tourism, first, by joining a new adventure tourism organization initially as a client, and then later as a trip leader and tour guide, leading hiking, cycling, canoeing and cross–country ski tours; second, by pursuing a Master's degree in tourism. His initial plan was to study something related to remote sensing, but during one (boring) class, he started to wonder about the price/value relationship in selecting different types of hotels. The spark was ignited. By the end of that class, he had drafted the outline of the thesis, written the first version of the questionnaire and decided on the research method. His remote sensing professor complimented him on taking such detailed notes, but Bob did not have the heart to tell him the notes had nothing to do with the topic. This signalled a seismic shift in his career path.

After graduation, he worked briefly as a tourism consultant and researcher, and then was hired as the Executive Director of a trade association, representing the interests of 1000 wilderness lodges and resorts. This job entailed writing policy, attempting to influence government to protect nature-based tourism values and representing the needs of the association's members. His exposure to industry had the dual effect of convincing him tourism was the right career choice, and simultaneously helping him realize that the single biggest thing holding back the sector was the lack of skills among many people working in it.

The idea of becoming a teacher was thus born. He had never really travelled much internationally, so when the time came to leave the trade association, he started to look for opportunities outside of Canada. Serendipity raised its head once more when his Master's degree supervisor received a letter from a new university in rural Australia that was recruiting academic staff. He applied for the post and was lucky enough to be offered a job at Charles Sturt University (CSU) in Albury, NSW, Australia (1990). Australia was undergoing a massive expansion in tourism programmes at the time, and universities were seeking staff that had postgraduate qualification and extensive industry experience. Neither a doctorate nor a publication track record was required. CSU proved to be a good fit for a new academic like him and it allowed him to develop his teaching and research skills, in a non-competitive environment. Having been in Australia for just three months, Bob realized that teaching as a tourism academic is his life's calling. The satisfaction from teaching as well as the freedom to express one's opinion through intellectual exchanges makes it worthwhile to pursue this as a lifelong career.

Bob, like with many other Australian academics recruited at the same time, realized they needed doctoral qualification and publication to advance in their careers. In 1991, while working full time as a teacher and Sub-Dean in tourism and marketing, Bob pursued his Ph.D. part-time at the Department of Geography at the University of Melbourne, Australia. He graduated five years later when he was 42. Having relevant work experience, Bob knew exactly from the beginning what he wanted for his doctoral thesis research. In addition, much research he subsequently embarked on in his career could be related back to pragmatic industry and enterprise-level issues with practical implications, rather than simply addressing theoretical or global policy issues from a pure academic perspective. In fact, when Bob started teaching, he introduced himself as an industry professional who teaches.

He submitted his first paper to *Annals of Tourism Research*, at about the same time. *Annals* was chosen because that was the only journal he had heard about. Of course, it was rejected. A few months later he received a letter from the editor, Jafar Jafari, asking why he had not resubmitted a revised version of the paper. He went back through his files and re-read the "rejection" letter. It was not a rejection at all, but rather a request to revise and resubmit. His first ever journal paper was subsequently published in *Annals* (McKercher, 1992). He then targeted *Tourism Management* and the *Journal of Sustainable Tourism* with his next two papers and they too, were accepted (McKercher, 1993a, 1993b). Having the first three papers accepted by top journals in the field was a great confidence booster.

Serendipity came calling again when he received a phone call from the secretary of the then Head of the Department of Hotel and Tourism Management at the Hong Kong Polytechnic University (PolyU) asking if he was available for an interview. To this day, he does not recall ever having applied for a position there. So, he asked the logical question "for what job?" and was told it was for an Associate Professor position. He joined PolyU in 1999 and was promoted to Full Professor in 2005.

Lessons learned

Serendipity plays a role in everyone's career, some more so than others. If Bob had not joined the adventure tourism business, he would not have been introduced to tourism. Had the letter from the Australian university arrived one week later, he would not have moved there. Had he not left the trade association six months earlier than planned, who knows what would have happened instead. And, had he not moved to Hong Kong, his life would have been quite different. But, luck and good fortune only go so far. They may open doors, but developing a career requires passion, a commitment to excellence and continuous skills development. He identified the following key factors that he felt made him a successful academic during his 30-year career.

Teaching and research go hand in hand

He feels teaching and research go hand in hand, for teaching informs research, just as much as research informs teaching. Teaching provides a golden opportunity to challenge some of the assumptions, as so much of what we teach is repeated as "absolute truth," which may not be the case. By questioning what we teach, new insights can be gained. Bob recalled some "ah–ah" moments that occurred in class whereby subsequent reflections resulted in studies, ranging from questioning Plog (McKercher, 2006), to developing a cultural tourism segmentation model (McKercher, 2002b), to wondering if intention to return is a valid proxy for actual repeat visitation (McKercher & Tse, 2012), to challenging the wrong method used in defining special interest tourism markets (McKercher & Chan, 2005).

As such, he takes teaching seriously. He won a teaching award early in his career at CSU. It saddens him when he encounters academics who see teaching as a "hygiene" task or a necessity to endure while they focus on research. They are missing out on so much. But one does not become an accomplished teacher overnight. Like anything else, it takes practice. He describes the journey as akin to the Japanese term 'kaizen', a process of continuous improvement over time. Part of the process involves updating one's skills, where he has undertaken a series of professional develop-ment programmes, including the Certified Hospitality Educator programme offered by the American Hotel and Lodging Educational Institute. The other part involves trying new things, even if they do not work. A third component is to stay current with both practice and theory. Students have an expectation of learning the most up-to-date materials. Of course, real-life experience always helps by providing a perspective of what the real world out there is like, as well as demonstrating through case examples. For academics who do not have many years of working experience, Bob's recommendation is to be out of their office from time to time; travel, observe and talk to people. This provides insights to practice, as opposed to just working in a vacuum.

Bob has taught undergraduate subjects in transport and tourism, tourism and society, research methods, hotel management and strategic marketing, as well as post graduate subjects in research methods, tourism theory and concepts, cultural tourism and strategic marketing. While senior academics generally prefer to teach senior level courses, Bob volunteers to teach introductory courses periodically. He believes it is important for students to hear from a senior staff to establish a good foundation for their skills. As well, teaching introductory course requires the ability to explain concepts clearly in a manner that lay people can understand. This hopefully balances out the situation where introductory subjects are only taught by more junior staff.

Students are part of the teaching and learning process and not 'clients'

Bob's teaching and learning philosophy involves two simple beliefs. First, students are as important to the teaching and learning process as the lecturer. He rejects a widely held belief that we should treat students as "clients" that the teacher needs to go out of their way to please the clients. Instead, he sees the relationship more in terms of "management" and "staff" creating an experience together. Bob is the manager while students are staff, and together they produce a quality educational outcome called "the subject." This approach places the onus on both the teacher and students to perform. The teacher has an obligation to come to class prepared, teach to the best of his or her ability, and be fair and transparent. This also means students have obligations to come to class prepared, do the work required and contribute to class. Indeed, he sees the course outline as a contract whereby each party agrees to certain terms and conditions if they remain in the subject. The other benefit of this approach is that it places the onus on students to perform. He reminds students that they earn a grade on their assignments, rather than him giving them a grade. A student who receives an "A" has earned that grade by the quality of the work produced. In a similar fashion, someone who is awarded an "F" earned that grade based on the same guidelines as the student who earned an "A."

His second belief is that teaching should be fun! Students will learn much more if they are engaged, especially millennials who tend to multi-task. Deep down, the students need to be curious about what they learn, and realize the end benefit of the learning process is to help prepare them to face future life difficulties and decisions, and the experience can be supportive as well as fun. Challenge yourself and the student. Engage students through activity-based group interactions and debates. When asked about Bob's demeanour in class, that he was described as somewhat quiet, reserved and serious, he said part of it has to do with emerging into the discussions, thinking and shaping the key message 'on the fly'. Another part is the larger responsibility that students learn by example, so the stamina and posture of how one conducts himself or herself will have a cascading effect, particularly with doctoral students who will learn from their professors on how to teach.

To date, Bob has supervised over three dozen doctoral students. Many graduates have excelled in teaching and research, in places including Hong Kong, Macau, Thailand, Malaysia, Taiwan and Korea. Others have developed strong consultancy profiles. Bob's students love him. A second year doctoral student mentioned, "Bob is very constructive and supportive on his teaching and mentoring. He has never interrupted but co-created upon his students' creativity... I felt my ideas were being swirled around and synthesized to new knowledge." Another third year doctoral student said, "Bob made a seemingly boring theory course very interesting with lots of personal examples and jokes. He has a great sense of humour which definitely made our lives easier. Talking to him is truly inspiring and I do not feel any distance talking to him!" Past students also have fond memories of being taught by Bob. One recent doctoral graduate mentioned, "As an international student of colour, my great concern is a genuine person to work with and I found that in him." Another recent graduate recalled, "Talking to Bob is like talking to a friend. He is a teacher, a mentor and a friend with great wisdom."

Research is about making a difference and not the number of papers you publish!

I asked Bob how he became a prolific researcher. His answer was that his vision when entering academia 30 years ago was to be recognized as someone who has made a significant contribution to the field. Promotion, recognition and awards would follow, but are not ends in themselves. He sees research as a two-fold process that involves both knowledge creation and knowledge dissemination. Knowledge creation is great, but if no one has ever heard about it the work really does not count for much. In practical terms, this means quality research needs to be published in top tier journals, which are read disproportionately more than those published elsewhere. So, if the work is really good, aim high so others can benefit.

But as Bob recalled, when he first started, it took him seven to nine years to learn to conduct research. It takes many years to learn one's craft. One starts as an apprentice, hopefully working under a master craftsperson to learn a whole array of skills before heading off on your own. That takes time. Today, the situation has changed significantly. Fresh doctoral graduates have to be research ready, and they need to land with their feet running in order to hit certain high performance criteria (particularly in Asia). Too much research is produced on an assembly line, where junior staff are asked to perform one task without developing their skills. Yes, they may have what appears to be a strong publication record, but at the expense of failing to learn all the tasks and becoming reliant on others.

Bob believes academic research should be about exploring ideas, and pursuing interests to understand this phenomenon we call tourism, or its components. Unfortunately, he feels the metrification and marketization of scholarly work has meant these ideals have been lost and instead research is now seen as competition that is all about churning as many publications as possible. The result is "much of a muchness," where the same methods are used to produce the same "publishable" results, even if they add little to the development of the field. Indeed, one of the ironies he noted in a recently published commentary in hospitality and tourism research is that the more we publish, the less knowledge we actually create (McKercher, 2018b).

So, what does Bob feel are the keys to good research? For Bob, good research is all about asking and answering questions. Bob researches what interests him. He questions the world around him, or something that does not fit with the existing knowledge. The idea is most important and the one question from this idea is to be answered. Sometimes, it can take months or even a number of years for the essence of the idea to percolate and the study to come to fruition. One also needs to really know about the topic before one can answer this one question.

When asked what motivates him to do what he does day in and day out, he said: "this is just how my brain was built." He referred to Jim Davis, the creator of Garfield cartoons – when asked how he came up with his ideas, he said he did not know and he just came up with the ideas. Bob is curious: seeing something and wondering, why? Maybe because he came from industry, he is naturally predisposed into looking at how industry really works and wondering why differences exist.

The experience of being a poor undergraduate student resulted in him not being completely immersed in a single discipline or way of doing things. This gave him the freedom to explore different approaches when he began his academic career. Tourism is multi-disciplinary. If there is an idea, explore the idea. Bob considers his relatively weak quantitative skills as a blessing in disguise. This makes him always put the research question as key, allowing him to look into different disciplines including geography, sociology, marketing and anthropology; rather than simply plugging numbers into software to churn out results. Therefore, he is not bound by a particular school of thought and methodology employed.

Yet, Bob typically changes his research focus about every five to seven years, partly because his interests change, and partly when he feels he has explored current issues to the extent of his skills. He started out in ecotourism, then shifted to cultural tourism and tourism movements, then time, space and distance, before moving to some climate change and broader theory topics; with an ongoing interest in professional development. He believes it is important for aspiring academics to develop a couple of areas that one wants to be known for, instead of publishing anything anywhere.

If one were to look at influence based on citations, Bob is probably best known for his work in cultural tourism, whereby his book is now in its second edition (McKercher & Du Cros, 2008; McKercher & Du Cros, 2002). It takes a different approach to cultural tourism in that it focuses largely upon the product development and sustainable use sides of the issue, with each author contributing as a tourism expert and a cultural heritage manager respectively. Another piece of related work includes the development of a cultural tourism typology based on examining the centrality of cultural heritage in the trip purpose and the depth of experience; yielding five segments which include purposeful, sightseeing, casual, incidental and serendipitous cultural tourists. This work is significant in that the framework was adopted by the UNWTO, as well as many European and North American tourism marketing and cultural tourism agencies, and spawned a number of follow-up studies (McKercher, 2002b; McKercher & Du Cros, 2003). Other seminal work includes a number of studies researching distance decay, location and travel movements. Distance, in addition to influencing volume of tourists, also influences who can travel, how their motives differ as well as how their subsequent behaviour differ. While distance has been treated as a seemingly less important factor, it functions as a valuable proxy for a wide range of factors including time, cost, willingness to visit strange places and party size, and has a profound effect on tourism (Lau & McKercher, 2006; McKercher & Du Cros, 2008; McKercher, 2018a, 2008b; McKercher, Chan, & Lam, 2008; McKercher & Lew, 2003; Shoval, McKercher, Ng, & Birenboim, 2011).

If good tourism research is about interesting ideas and borrowing theories, Bob has an uncanny ability in doing just that. He applied the principles of chaos and complexity theories to explain why seemingly stable systems can all of a sudden be propelled into chaos. This challenges the belief that tourism functions in a mechanistic manner (McKercher, 1999). In a similar vein, building on the Boston Consulting Group (BCG) Growth Share matrix on portfolio analyses, and the strengths of Butler's Life Cycle and Plog's behavioristic models, a Destination-Market (DMM) matrix was conceptualized to visually explain the inter-relationship between a destination and the markets it serves. Through the use of NEST analysis, which classifies the relative position of markets into New, Expanding, Stable and Tired, insights can be drawn to reflect the health and marketing needs of a destination area (McKercher, 1995). Another note-worthy conceptual paper, stemming from the need for a holistic classification of tourism products and drawing from Linnean Taxonomy and Philip Kotler and others on product family, product class and product lines, Bob proposed a seven-tier taxonomy of tourism products, based on five need families including pleasure, personal quest, human endeavour, nature and business; together, they encapsulate 27 product families and 90 product classes (McKercher, 2016).

A recurrent line of thinking in Bob's research and classroom teaching is that he tends to go back to basics, and asks the question of what is truth and what is non-truth, challenging certain accepted beliefs or assumptions, be it noting the fundamental truths about tourism development in relation to social, cultural and environmental impacts to the host communities (McKercher, 1993a), re-examining whether intention to return is a valid proxy for actual repeat visitation using longitudinal and cross-sectional data (McKercher & Tse, 2012), or identifying the methodological flaw in analyzing activities to infer trip purpose in defining special interest (SI) tourism market segments to differentiate them from other tourists (which assumes activities are valid proxies for underlying motives) and tested the assumptions empirically through participation and motivation rates using omnibus survey (McKercher & Chan, 2005). Aside from this, his professional development research work yielded insights in academic performance (McKercher, 2005; McKercher, Law & Lam, 2006), publishing and referee process (McKercher, 2002a; McKercher, Law, Weber, Song, & Hsu, 2007; McKercher, 2015; McKercher & Tung, 2016; McKercher & Tung, 2015) and academic career management (Tung & McKercher, 2017). Accounting for the state of hospitality and tourism research and noting some of the systemic issues, based on his 30 plus year experience as an academic, Bob offered some practical advice to those who want to excel in academic research (McKercher, 2018b).

On mentorship

For Bob, a mentor has many roles. Sometimes, it is like a father figure to students, and he has joked with some that he felt like being their Hong Kong father during school. Other times, it is as a guide, helping students see the light and gain insights into their work. A mentor is an expert advising students on how to strive for excellence, or simply a friend. When asked about Bob's own mentor, he mentioned many people who helped him along the way, but there was no single mentor. His master's supervisors taught him how to do good research. The executive members of the trade association taught him about tourism and small business. The colleagues and peers he met in Australia allowed him to do research in a very welcoming environment. His colleagues and peers at the School of Hotel and Tourism at the Hong Kong Polytechnic University were instrumental too.

Conclusion

As mentioned, the aim of this article is to share Bob's insightful experience about his career journey. Bob was not my thesis supervisor; nor have I coauthored a paper with him. I ran into Bob purely by chance and stayed in touch with him. Yet, with my 20 plus years of industry experience, many of which in senior management positions, there are a few things about Bob that I feel are noteworthy. First, he is very passionate and serious about his teaching. His teaching is impactful. The concepts are articulated clearly and the content is updated regularly, and tied to current research. He once told me he takes the time to prepare a course by writing out the entire series of lectures long hand to see the themes that flow through and develop the lecture outcomes. Second, while Bob talked about serendipity, it is perseverance that counts – whereby he aims to make a significant contribution through research and teaching. Bob does give time to his students. He is a good listener and coach, takes the patience to hear what a student has to say. This is not something to be taken lightly, particularly for professors in research-oriented institutions where time is a scarcity. Third, Bob's research is significant. I know he does not measure research success by the number of publications, but for those who do, he is an influential scholar with over 300 publications and reports, which include over 150 refereed articles, many of which were in high tier journals. At the time of writing, his citations were over 13,000 as recorded by Google Scholar. Yet, when asked about what he considers to be his best top three articles, he noted it would be his works on special interest tourism, destination-market matrix and defining cultural tourists; the common thread being these studies question accepted dogmas through rigorous analyses, and change people's thinking about how tourism works (McKercher, 1995, 2002b; McKercher & Chan, 2005).

Summarizing his 30 years' career, Bob's closing advice is to make a research career through "vocation and avocation." Treat the career both as a job and a hobby, then everything in tourism will be interesting. If it were just a job, one would not be able to excel. If it were only a hobby, then it would not be productive. As research productivity means words on paper, it is critical to focus on the outcome as opposed to only the process of doing research. Focus on fire and not smoke. Fire is aiming for a research with outcome being published in a top tier journal or an interesting idea that answers a "so what" question.

Acknowledgments

The author would like to thank Ms. Margaret Chin and Professor Stephen Pratt, University of The South Pacific, for providing feedback to earlier versions of this paper.

Disclosure statement

No potential conflict of interest was reported by the author.

ORCID

David C. W. Chin http://orcid.org/0000-0002-7868-038X

References

Del Corso, J., & Rehfuss, M. (2011). The role of narrative in career construction theory. *Journal of Vocational Behavior, 79*(2), 334–339.doi: https://doi.org/10.1016/j.jvb.2011.04.003]

Lau, G., & McKercher, B. (2006). Understanding tourist movement patterns in a destination: a gis approach. *Tourism and Hospitality Research, 7*(1), 39–49.

McKercher, B. (1992). Tourism as a conflicting land use. *Annals of Tourism Research, 19*(3), 467–481.

McKercher, B. (1993a). Some fundamental truths about tourism: Understanding tourism's social and environmental impacts. *Journal of Sustainable Tourism, 1*(1), 6–16.

McKercher, B. (1993b). The unrecognized threat to tourism: Can tourism survive 'sustainability'? *Tourism Management, 14*(2), 131–136.

McKercher, B. (1995). The destination-market matrix: A tourism market portfolio analysis model. *Journal of Travel & Tourism Marketing, 4*(2), 23–40.

McKercher, B. (1999). A chaos approach to tourism. *Tourism Management, 20*(4), 425–434.

McKercher, B. (2002a). The privileges and responsibilities of being a referee. *Annals of Tourism Research, 29*(3), 856–859.

McKercher, B. (2002b). Towards a classification of cultural tourists. *International Journal of Tourism Research, 4*(1), 29–38.

McKercher, B. (2005). A case for ranking tourism journals. *Tourism Management, 26*(5), 649–651.

McKercher, B. (2006). Are psychographics predictors of destination life cycles? *Journal of Travel & Tourism Marketing, 19*(1), 49–55.

McKercher, B. (2008b). The implicit effect of distance on tourist behavior: a comparison of short and long haul pleasure tourists to hong kong. *Journal of Travel & Tourism Marketing, 25*(3–4), 367–381.

McKercher, B. (2015). Why and where to publish. *Tourism Management, 30*(3), 97–102.

McKercher, B. (2016). Towards a taxonomy of tourism products. *Tourism Management, 54*, 196–208.

McKercher, B. (2018a). The impact of distance on tourism: A tourism geography law. In *Tourism geographies,* 1–5.

McKercher, B. (2018b). What is the state of hospitality and tourism research – 2018? *International Journal of Contemporary Hospitality Management, 30*(3), 1234–1244.

McKercher, B., & Chan, A. (2005). How special is special interest tourism? *Journal of Travel Research, 44*(1), 21–31.

McKercher, B., Chan, A., & Lam, C. (2008). The impact of distance on international tourist movements. *Journal of Travel Research, 47*(2), 208–224.

McKercher, B., & Du Cros, H. (2002). *Cultural tourism: the partnership between tourism and cultural heritage management.* New York, NY: Haworth Hospitality Press.

McKercher, B., & Du Cros, H. (2003). Testing a cultural tourism typology. *International Journal of Tourism Research, 5*(1), 45–58.

McKercher, B., & Du Cros, H. (2008). *Cultural tourism: The partnership between tourism and cultural heritage management.* New York, NY: Routledge.

McKercher, B., Law, R., Weber, K., Song, H., & Hsu, C. (2007). Why referees reject manuscripts. *Journal of Hospitality & Tourism Research, 31*(4), 455–470.

McKercher, B., & Lew, A. (2003). Distance decay and the impact of effective tourism exclusion zones on international travel flows. *Journal of Travel Research, 42*(2), 159–165.

McKercher, B., & Tse, T. (2012). Is intention to return a valid proxy for actual repeat visitation? *Journal of Travel Research, 51*(6), 671–686.

McKercher, B., & Tung, V. (2015). Publishing in tourism and hospitality journals: Is the past a prelude to the future? *Tourism Management, 50*(C), 306–315.

McKercher, B., & Tung, V. (2016). The rise of fractional authors. *Annals of Tourism Research, 61*, 213–215.

McKercher, B., Law, R., & Lam, T. (2006). Rating tourism and hospitality journals. *Tourism Management, 27*(6), 1235–1252.

Shoval, N., McKercher, B., Ng, E., & Birenboim, A. (2011). Hotel location and tourist activity in cities. *Annals of Tourism Research, 38*(4), 1594–1612.

Tung, V., & McKercher, B. (2017). Negotiating the rapidly changing research, publishing, and career landscape. *Tourism Management, 60*(C), 322–331.

Boris Vukonić: symbiosis of symmetry and balance

Nevenka Čavlek

Introduction

To write a portrait of Professor Boris Vukonić is an honour and privilege for me, but at the same time it is a task which I perceive as one of my most difficult to achieve. As his undergraduate, graduate, and doctoral student I have always felt great respect and admiration for his academic achievements – so much so that he inspired me to embark on an academic career. I was his assistant at the Faculty of Economics & Business, University of Zagreb from 1993 to 2001 and continued working with him until his retirement from the University of Zagreb in 2004 when he founded a private business school for tourism and hotel management – Utilus. Still, I have always called him "Professor Vukonić" or "My Professor" and this is why I am loathe to refer to him in any other way. Thus, although this portrait of Vukonić might be considered overly subjective, I know that whatever I write about him will be too modest.

To prepare portraits of persons who have contributed immensely to tourism theory is not only a great idea but also a sine qua non, since not only a younger generation of tourism scholars is sometimes unaware of the leading names who pioneered and paved the way towards building the world tourism theory, especially if their research publications appeared in other languages than English.

Fortunately, Professor Vukonić has not only been writing in Croatian, but also has published some of his best scientific works in English. On the other hand, too many of his great works still remain a source of inspiration just to those who can read Croatian. Therefore, this portrait is a great opportunity to publicly acknowledge some of his most valuable publications in Croatian to a wider international audience. In his academic career, Vukonić has published over 150 scientific and professional papers in national and international journals, presented over 80 papers in conferences and congresses in Croatia and in all continents, and authored some 30 books and university course books and co-authored four additional books. His thirst for identifying new research fields has led him to write some publications that were well ahead of his time. This has made him not only the most productive and most cited scholar in the field of tourism in Croatia and previously in Yugoslavia, but has earned him a wider international recognition as well. Only these few "hard" facts may best illustrate why Professor Vukonić has merited his portrait to be published with the other internationally recognized scholars in the journal – *Anatolia*.

His life, education, and encounter with tourism

Boris Vukonić was born in Zagreb, Croatia (1938). Although he has never changed his city of residence, he has pointed out many times as a matter of interest that he has actually lived in four states – the Kingdom of Yugoslavia, the Independent State of Croatia, the Socialist Federal Republic of Yugoslavia, and the Republic of Croatia. As he himself stated in his personal history published in a book on some leading world tourism economists entitled *The Discovery of Tourism Economics* (Vukonic, 2011, p. 218) and edited by Larry Dwyer he spent most of his life in the Socialist Federal Republic of Yugoslavia, which led to his professional life and work being marked by the state doctrine and "also by the answers to the numerous questions raised by the political, economic, and other circumstances of the time". He was fortunate enough to live in the city of Zagreb where he could obtain the best possible education.

A very important foundation for his future studies he received already during his secondary school education at the Classical Gymnasium in Zagreb which focused mainly on social disciplines that later facilitated his better understanding of tourism and broadened his horizons. Although he initially wanted to study architecture, he graduated from the Faculty of Economics of the University of Zagreb (1962). As he himself described in the aforementioned book, the studies gave him a "controlled" understanding of economics based on Marxist thought and the teaching curriculum was replete with macroeconomics and industrial economics. Tourism was not even mentioned during his entire repertoire of the field. However just as he graduated, the Faculty of Economics of the University of Zagreb launched the first postgraduate study programme in Tourism Economics in this part of Europe and he was invited to enrol in the programme. He completed his master's degree in the field of tourism economics (1965). What began as a hasty decision ended up influencing his entire professional life.

Prior to subsequently obtaining a doctoral degree, Vukonić gathered ample experience connected to tourism in different fields ranging from spatial planning, marketing, and consultancy in tourism to travel agency business operations. At first he worked in the Croatian Urban Planning Institute where he was engaged in a large spatial planning project for the South Adriatic, conducted by the World Bank. Experts from the most prestigious European research institutes of that period were involved in the project introducing tourism marketing research into professional circles for the first time in Yugoslavia. This experience turned out to be a trigger for his more specific research efforts in tourism and the topic of his doctoral thesis therefore came as a logical choice. Vukonić defended his doctoral thesis entitled *Primjena marketinga u prostornom planiranju u turizmu* [Implementation of marketing in the spatial planning of tourism] at the Faculty of Economics, University of Zagreb (1979). His dissertation was the first scientific research in the field that combined tourism with a marketing concept on the one hand and spatial planning on the other. This was definitely a revolutionary approach towards the economics of space in relation to tourism since it introduced a new planning method that was predicated on market conditions.

While still working as a director of the tourism department in a large company in Zagreb he devoted some of his time to pedagogical activities and was duly elected lecturer at the Zagreb Department of the Pula College of Economics. In this part time job he discovered his passion for teaching. It thus came as no surprise that in 1973 he decided to dedicate himself to a scholarly career by becoming a full time employee with Senior Lecturer status at the College of Foreign Trade which later became the Faculty of Foreign Trade of the University of Zagreb. When this faculty merged with the Faculty of Economics (1982), he continued his career there. Owing to his productive research and publication record his academic career progressed rapidly. In 1983, he was promoted to the rank of Associate Professor and just one year later to that of Full Professor. He created and lectured in courses on the *Management of Travel and Tourism Intermediaries* and *Tourism Policy and Development* at the undergraduate and graduate levels. He also served as the Head of the postgraduate study programme in *Tourism Economics* from 1984 to 1986 and later on in *International Tourism in the National Economy* where he developed a course on *Economic Theory and Tourism*.

I was fortunate to attend his most interesting and engaging lectures during my study of *Tourism* at the Faculty of Foreign Trade. All the students of that time were fascinated by his vivid lectures (without modern technical support!) because he would always take us on a new exciting intellectual journey that facilitated our better understanding of tourism as a system by broadening our horizons in many aspects and reinforcing our love for future work in tourism. The journey would always start with a thorough overview of tourism theory from different author's perspectives and continued with ample examples on how to apply tourism theory to practice. He illustrated the best and worst practices of tourism development, policy and planning from different parts of the world with anecdotal evidence derived from working in the field and travelling to many countries in and outside of Europe. He also served as an UNDP and UNWTO tourism development consultant and advisor to governments on tourism development in Bangladesh, India, Egypt, Guyana, Afghanistan, Zanzibar, and Tanzania (1974–1984). Unlike many of my then professors, he was able to take the circumstances in which we lived and which were different from those that prevailed in the West, and turn them into intriguing challenges seen through the eyes of a globetrotter (as we the students perceived him to be).

His own private library featured a considerable amount of scientific tourism literature published in English, French, German, Spanish, and Italian. His knowledge of languages and cultures allowed him to make his students aware of the different approaches to tourism studies, and to critically assess alternative points of view – always daring us to express our own opinions, which was a challenge in itself considering the regime in which we all lived then. Owing to the widely read Professor Vukonić generations of students heard from him about the early contributions to tourism theory by the likes of Walter Hunziker, Kurt Krapf, Pierre Defert, Paul Bernecker, Robert Glucksman, to name just a few. He was the first to encourage us to read the publications of doyens of scientific tourism theory like Erik Cohen, Graham Dann, Jafar Jafari and many others in such leading journals as *Annals of Tourism Research*.

When I once asked him about who had the greatest effect on his academic career he proudly mentioned the following names: Srđan Marković, Walter Hunziker, Piere Defert, Geoffrey Wall and J. R. Brent Ritchie. Srđan Marković was the founder and the first director of the Institute for Tourism in Zagreb. It was the influence of his lectures at the postgraduate level that Boris Vukonić found the most inspiring and thus they particularly shaped his understanding of tourism. In the international tourism arena he was recruited by Hunziker who enrolled him into the AIEST at its congress in Villach, Austria, where he came into contact with numerous leading scholars of the time (1973).

Research spectrum

Professor Vukonić's scientific publications reflect a broad spectrum of his interest in the field of tourism. This necessarily brief portrait cannot allow for even a summary listing let alone a thorough analysis of his books and scientific articles. Therefore and as a compromise, let me call your attention to the publications that to my mind best illustrate his scientific interest and research achievements. His work can be divided into seven major areas of specialization: tourism marketing, travel agency operations, policies of tourism development, history of tourism and tourism theory, tourism and religion, and tourism and political relations.

Although during Professor Vukonić's working career, scholarly achievement in Croatia was evaluated more by the numbers of published books than the quantum of articles, he was proliferate in both outlets of academic communication. He was also very much aware of the importance of supplying students with references to the appropriate literature as it was before the age of information technology. His first textbook dealing with the operation and economics of travel agencies appeared in 1972 under the title *Organizacija i tehnika poslovanja turističkih agencija* [Organisation and Business Techniques of Travel Agencies]. At that time he was working in a travel agency and was asked, as a practising expert in the field and the person with a Master of Science degree in tourism economics, to write a book for tourism secondary vocational schools. According to him:

> This was an excursion into microeconomic issues, but an excursion that lasted quite a long time due to the lack of other authors or their interest in the operations of travel agencies. Later, this publication, in an amended and revised format, now as a university textbook, went through nine editions. (Vukonic, 2011, p. 222)

Indeed, his name was for a very long time associated with this emerging field of tourism and gained him a reputation of specialist expert. His choice to appoint me as his assistant and possible successor at the Faculty of Economics was also partially a result of my working experience in the field of tour operating business and my Master of Science degree in the field of economics. As my mentor on the doctoral thesis *Utjecaj turoperatora na svjetska turistička kretanja* [The Impact of Tour Operators on International Tourism Flows] he encouraged me to use economic theories in the field which had been overlooked by tourism theory and encouraged me to always take *the road less travelled*. It is interesting to mention that we co-authored only one paper because he always encouraged me to write independently explaining that his job was primarily to read my papers and give me feedback. The same applied also to his other doctoral students whom he successfully mentored and who now hold important positions at institutions in Croatia or abroad, like Neven Ivandić (Institute for Tourism, Zagreb, Croatia), Dora Smolčić Jurdana (Faculty of Tourism and Hospitality Management, University of Rijeka, Croatia), Lidija Petrić (Faculty of Economics, University of Split, Croatia), Mitre Avramovski (University of Ohrid, The Former Yugoslav Republic of Macedonia), and Nexhat Muhadjeri (Republic of Kosovo).

In 1982a, Professor Vukonić published the first book on tourism marketing in Croatia *Marketing u turizmu* [Marketing in tourism]. Later on the book was published twice in co-authorship in an extended version (Vukonić & Senečić, 1993, 1997) becoming the first university course book in this field. For years the book was the major text for undergraduate and postgraduate tourism study programmes at the universities of Zagreb, Rijeka, and Split.

Boris Vukonić published his key contribution to the economic research of tourism in 1987 in the book *Turizam i razvoj* [Tourism and Development]. By using an econometric model he revealed the three major factors of special significance for the development of tourism: the political circumstances and potential turbulences in the environment, the dominant religion, and the extent of state indebtedness. A year earlier he co-authored a paper with Šemso Tanković on the same topic (1986) in which they explained the use of stepwise regression in their statistical analysis.

As he stated in his chapter in the book *The Discovery of Tourism Economics* (Vukonic, 2011, p. 223), the book Tourism and Development was extremely well received by the Croatian professional public, which encouraged him to continue his research. His most productive years followed. In 1990a, he published the book *Turizam i religija* [Tourism and Religion] and during the Croatian Homeland War another book entitled *Turizam u vihoru rata* [Tourism in the Whirlwind of War, 1993]. Croatian versions of both books were translated into English and published in 1996 and 1997, respectively. Although by then he had published many articles in Croatia and abroad (1982b, 1983a, 1983b, 1985, 1985, 1986a, 1989, 1990b, 1990c, 1990d, 1991, 1992a) including three articles in *Annals of Tourism Research* (1984, 1986b and 1992b), the book *Tourism and Religion* granted him a special place in the international scientific community since it was the first such extensive study on the topic published in the world. It analysed the mutual relationship between the two phenomena – tourism and religion – that had marked the history of modern civilization, each in its own way. Special attention was given to the relationship of Christianity and Islam towards the phenomenon of tourism. He published four more texts dealing with tourism and religion in 1998, 2002a, 2006, 2010a.

The book *Tourism in the Whirlwind of War* represented another instance of Professor Vukonić's pioneering research work for which he also received a special "Mijo Mirković" award (1996). It was written as his reaction to the war of aggression on Croatia (1991) and prepared a solid ground for further research on the relationship between tourism and political circumstances in any discipline that focused on both phenomena.

Another book published during the war period in Croatia had an intriguing title *Turizam u susret budućnosti* [Tourism Approaching the Future, 1994a]. It represented a continuation of Professor Vukonić's research that dated back to the 1980s. He first provided a theoretical research background and then discussed the connections between the theory of development, economic theory, and tourism development in different parts of the world. Although he thought that this book meant for him the end of his theoretical discussions about tourism development, the dramatic events at the end of twentieth and the beginning of twenty-first century, which significantly influenced tourism development in the world, prompted him to write another book entitled **Turizam** *Budućnost mnogih iluzija* [**Tourism** Future of Many Illusions, 2010b]. It explored the barriers or threats to tourism development like global warming, new "economic players" in the global economy, war and terrorism, religious prejudices and religious fundamentalism, hunger, health, and risks to health.

A special part of Professor Vukonić's scientific contribution belonging to a series of monographs on the history of tourism. His devotion to the topic and his inclination for assembling historical documents and producing an intriguing and easily readable text from "dry" material showed how well balanced his analytical research skills and his literary writing skills had been. All these books on the history of tourism in Croatia could be read as well-documented and scientifically classified historical facts in the form of a bestseller. The first such book entitled *Tempus fugit: Povijest turizma Zagreba* [Tempus Fugit: The History of Zagreb's Tourism] was published in 1994b.

Deciding to write and edit a book entitled *Povijest hrvatskog turizma* [The History of Croatian Tourism, 2005] was a much more demanding research task. Here, he assembled an impressive number of associates from all over Croatia who voluntarily worked on the project. I was proud to be part of it. The book represented the first ever published monograph about the history of tourism in Croatia from 1863 until the beginning of the twenty-first century. He dedicated the book to recognizing the values of Croatian tourism in the European Union and in the world. Why has he been so interested in the history of tourism? He answered this question of identity in this very book by stating that history obliges us to be responsible. After all, *Historia est magistra vitae* [History is the teacher of life].

His inclination towards history was not only related to the history of tourism in Croatia but also, and more importantly for the international scientific community, towards the history of scientific thought on tourism worldwide. Professor Vukonić's impressive knowledge of published tourism research in many disciplines, tourism economics and beyond, was fortunately recognized by several members of the International Academy for the Study of Tourism (IAST) who persuaded him to write a text on the history of scientific thought on tourism in the world. The paper was originally presented to the IAST members in Beijing in 2005 under the title *An Outline of the History of Tourism Theory: Source Material*, and was later published as a chapter in *The Routledge Handbook of Tourism Research* (2012). There he covered the period from the initial stages of scientific research on tourism until the end of the twentieth century – thus paving the way for future research in the field.

To write about the development of tourism theory in the world and not to devote a special paper on the development of tourism theory in the Former Yugoslavia would represent unfinished business for Professor Vukonić. In the paper *Tourism Theory in the Former Yugoslavia* published as a chapter in the book edited by Dann and Liebman Parrinello (2009) he showed how political ideology shaped tourism theory and how the consequences of different kinds of tourism development in each republic of a single state affected the theoretical approaches of scientists.

Another area of interest to him, not only from an historical perspective, was education in tourism. Thus, to mark 40 years of education for tourism at our Faculty he initiated an international conference entitled *Rethinking of Education and Training for Tourism* (2002b) which gathered a respectable number of scientists from all over the world who presented 42 papers. His presentation focused on *Tourism at the Graduate School of Economics and Business, University of Zagreb: 1962–2002*. All the contributions were published in the ensuing conference proceedings that we jointly edited.

Professor Vukonić's inexhaustible source of ideas also directed him to the field of lexicography. In 2001 the first *Rječnik turizma* [Tourism Dictionary] appeared in Croatia. A total of 13 scholars from the Department of Tourism at the Faculty of Economics and Business prepared 2300 entries from all tourism fields complementing them with English–Croatian or German–Croatian tourism equivalents. It was an extraordinary experience for me to work with him on the project as co-editor and author as he shared the experience gained from working in the editorial team of the first *Encyclopedia of Tourism* (2000) edited by Jafar Jafari.

The credit for establishing the oldest scientific journal at the Faculty of Economics & Business in Zagreb *Acta Turistica*, also goes to Professor Vukonić who was the journal's Editor-in-Chief from its beginnings in 1989 to 2004 when he passed the job on to me.

Wide recognitions of his academic achievements

Professor Vukonić's devotion to science, research, and pedagogical work has been widely acknowledged in Croatia, but even more so internationally. This only proves the old biblical saying that it is more difficult to be a prophet in one's own country. I will mention here only his most distinguished awards.

In 1995, he was elected into the IAST. In 1997, he was given an award of *International Recherche de la Qualité* (International Quality Research) by *the Order de Saint Fortunat* for life achievement in tourism. In 1998, the President of the Republic of Croatia bestowed on him the Order of the Croatian Braid.

In addition to his prolific authorship in scientific publishing, he was also very active in commenting on daily topics dealing with Croatian tourism and was known for his columns in the journal *Ugostiteljstvo i turizam* [Catering and Tourism] where he published 99 columns, which earned him a membership in FIJET (International Federation of Tourism Journalists and Writers). In 2001, he received FIJET's special award for his contribution to research and education in tourism. From 1992 to 2005 he was a member of the Education Council of the World Tourism Organisation and his dedicated work was acknowledged with UNWTO recognition for his *Contribution to the Global Development, Research, Education and Training in Tourism* (2002).

With greater academic recognition, Professor Vukonić was also entrusted with higher managerial tasks at his institution. Thus, he first served two mandates as Vice Dean of the Faculty of Economics and later as its Dean. In 2003, as the first European he was awarded the *International Dean of the Year* by the International Management and Development Association. The Croatian National Tourist Board recognized his life achievements in tourism (2014).

Conclusion

Looking back on Professor Vukonić's multifaceted career one can easily see that he has devoted his entire life to tourism. Indeed, he was successful in every position and every task connected to his professional standing. However, something seems to be missing. He has never been appointed as the Minister of Tourism of the Republic of Croatia. Although many experts in the tourism field would have wanted to see him in this post and whereas there have been some discussions on the topic, and in spite of the realization that he had outstanding qualifications for the job, he did not fulfil the major political condition: he has never been a member of any political party. He never agreed to trade his academic independence and freedom of thinking, saying, writing, and acting the way he thought was right for any benefits that any political function would bring him. He has always kept his integrity and this is why I respect him totally.

Professor Vukonić stands out with his scientific achievements and with his pedagogical work; he has been an exceptional educator and an outstanding researcher. He has contributed immensely in putting Croatia on the international scientific tourism map. One of our former Deans, Professor Emeritus Soumitra Sharma once said about him: "Such symmetry and balance in a professional profile can be achieved only by the best and the most successful scholars". I could not agree more!

References

Jafari, J. (2000). *Encyclopedia of tourism*. London: Routledge.

Vukonić, B. (1982a). *Marketing u turizmu* [Marketing in tourism]. Zagreb: Vjesnik – Agencija za marketing.

Vukonić, B. (1982b). The problem of finding a market for an agency's travel tour and the distribution channels of an agency's operation. *The Tourist Review, 1,* 10–14.

Vukonić, B. (1983a). Touristic marketing or marketing in tourism. *The Tourist Review, 38,* 2–4.

Vukonić, B. (1983b). Strategija diferenciranog proizvoda kao strategija nastupa Jugoslavije na međunarodnom turističkom tržištu [Strategy of differentiated product as appearance strategy of Yugoslavia in international tourism market]. *Marketing, 3–4,* 5–8.

Vukonić, B. (1986a). Temeljni teorijski aspekti pojma i problema motiva i motivacija u turizmu [Fundamental theoretical aspects of the notion and issue of motive and motivation in tourism]. *Turizam, 9,* 235–238.

Vukonić, B. (1986b). Foreign tourist expenditures in Yugoslavia. *Annals of Tourism Research, 1,* 59–78.

Vukonić, B. (1987). *Turizam i razvoj* [Tourism and development]. Zagreb: Školska knjiga.

Vukonić, B. (1989). The analysis of the existent development level and the problem of saturation in tourism. *Acta Turistica, 1,* 41–47.

Vukonić, B. (1990a). *Turizam i religija* [Tourism and religion]. Zagreb: Školska knjiga.

Vukonić, B. (1990b). Alternative tourism or an alternative to tourism. *Acta Turistica, 1,* 50–59.

Vukonić, B. (1990c). Some hypotheses for tourism development in developing countries. *Acta Turistica, 2*, 194–208.

Vukonić, B. (1990d). Od dogovorne do tržišne ekonomije – novi marketing u turizmu [From command to market economy – New marketing in tourism]. *Turizam, 9–10*, 127–131.

Vukonić, B. (1991). Il tourismo in Yugoslavia [Tourism in Yugoslavia]. *Politica Del Turismo, 2*, 51–55.

Vukonić, B. (1992a). Turizam u vrijeme rata [Tourism in war time]. *Turizam, 9–10*, 131–136.

Vukonić, B. (1992b). Medjugorje's religion and tourism connection. *Annals of Tourism Research, 1*, 79–91.

Vukonić, B. (1993). *Turizam u vihoru rata* [Tourism in the whirlwind of war]. Zagreb: Mate & EP '64.

Vukonić, B. (1994a). *Turizam ususret budućnosti* [Tourism approaching future]. Zagreb: Ekonomski fakultet Zagreb & Mikrorad.

Vukonić, B. (1994b). *Tempus fugit: Povijest turizma Zagreba* [Tempus fugit: The history of Zagreb's tourism]. Zagreb: HAZU & AGM.

Vukonić, B. (1996). *Tourism and religion*. London: Pergamon.

Vukonić, B. (1997). *Tourism in the whirlwind of war*. Zagreb: Golden marketing.

Vukonić, B. (1998). Religious tourism: Economic value or an empty box. *Zagreb International Review of Economics & Business, 1*, 83–94.

Vukonić, B. (2002a). Religion, tourism and economics: A convenient symbiosis. *Tourism Recreation Research, 2*, 61–67.

Vukonić, B. (2002b). Tourism at the Graduate School of Economics and Business, University of Zagreb: 1962–2002. In B. Vukonić & N. Čavlek (Eds.), *Rethinking of education and training for tourism* (pp. 1–12). Zagreb: Graduate School of Economics and Business & Mikrorad.

Vukonić, B. (2005). *Povijest hrvatskog turizma* [The history of Croatian tourism]. Zagreb: HAZU & Prometej.

Vukonić, B. (2006). Sacred places and tourism in the Roman Catholic tradition. In D. Timothy & D. Olson (Eds.), *Tourism, religion and spiritual journeys* (pp. 217–229). London: Routledge.

Vukonić, B. (2009). Tourism theory in the former Yugoslavia. In G. Dann & G. Liebman Parrinello (Eds.), *The sociology of tourism: European origins and developments* (pp. 195–219). Bingley: Emerald.

Vukonić, B. (2010a). Do we always understand each other? In N. Scott & J. Jafari (Eds.), *Tourism in the Muslim world* (pp. 31–45). Bingley: Emerald.

Vukonić, B. (2010b). *Turizam Budućnost mnogih iluzija* [Tourism future of many illusions]. Zagreb: Plejada & Utilus.

Vukonić, B. (2011). On the road to tourism economics. In L. Dwyer (Ed.), *The discovery of tourism economics* (pp. 217–229). Bingley: Emerald.

Vukonić, B. (2012). An outline of the history of tourism theory: Source material (for future research). In C. H. C. Hsu & W. C. Gartner (Eds.), *The Routledge handbook of tourism research* (pp. 3–27). London: Routledge.

Vukonić, B., & Bujas, V. (1972). *Organizacija i tehnika poslovanja putničkih agencija* [Organisation and business techniques of travel agencies]. Zagreb: Školska knjiga.

Vukonić, B., & Čavlek, N. (2001). *Rječnik turizma* [Tourism dictionary]. Zagreb: Masmedia.

Vukonić, B., & Dujović, S. (1985). Potrošnja agencijskih inozemnih turista [The expenditure of international travel agency tourists]. *Turizam, 7–8*, 201–209.

Vukonić, B., & Senečić, J. (1993). *Marketing u turizmu* [Marketing in tourism]. Zagreb: Školska knjiga.

Vukonić, B., & Senečić, J. (1997). *Marketing u turizmu* [Marketing in tourism]. Zagreb: Ekonomski fakultet & Mikrorad.

Vukonić, B., & Tanković, Š. (1985). Primjena matrice rasta u planiranju razvoja turizma [Application of growth matrix in tourism development planning]. *Ekonomist, 38*, 37–48.

Vukonić, B., & Tanković, Š. (1986). Snaga utjecaja pojedinih faktora na razvoj turizma [The effect of specific factors on the development of tourism]. *Turizam, 35*, 70–72.

Vukonić, B., & Tkalac, D. (1984). Tourism and urban revitalization: A case study of Poreč, Yugoslavia. *Annals of Tourism Research, 11*, 591–605.

Brent Ritchie: one of the truly great pioneering researchers in tourism

Simon Hudson

Introduction

I can remember reading *The Five People You Meet in Heaven* by author Mitch Album a few years ago, in which the main character in the book meets five people that have changed his life. At the time I started to think about people who have had the most influence on my life-path, and the first name that came to mind was Brent Ritchie. So to be asked to write this "portrait" of Brent is real honour, and is a small way of saying thank you to the best mentor a tourism academic could ever have. Although the majority of this portrait is in my own words, I decided to seek the views of others who have worked with Brent over the years, and I would like to thank each one of them for their contribution.

I first met Brent at a conference in Cleveland, Ohio in 1998. At the time I was based in England, and at the conference, I was presenting the results of my Ph.D. research on constraints to skiing participation. Brent approached me after my talk and said he was looking for someone like me to come and work alongside him at the University of Calgary. Although I had a young family, and had spent the better part of 30 years on the south coast of England, it did not take much to persuade me to move the 5000 miles across the pond. The opportunity to learn from arguably tourism's most esteemed academic was too good to pass up. Sixteen years later, I can categorically say that Brent has had a tremendous impact on my life as a tourism professor, and I know I am not the only one who would say this. With Brent's retirement in 2014, tourism's academic community has lost a hugely influential scholar.

Recognition

Just the list of his national and international awards is a testament to his stature in tourism research. He has been handed the Tourism Industry Association Award, the Commemorative Medal for the 125th Anniversary of the Confederation of Canada, the Achievement Award of the International Travel and Tourism Research Association, the Calgary Convention & Visitors Bureau's Certificate of Appreciation, the Macleod Dixon International Achievement Award, the International Society of Travel & Tourism Educators (ISTTE) Martin Oppermann Memorial Award, the World Tourism Organization Ulysses Prize, the John Wiley & Sons Research Award, the Tourism Industry of Alberta ALTO Award, and the United Nations World Tourism Organization (UNWTO) Science Fellowship Award amongst many others.

Academic appointments

But let's step back a little and look at Brent's roots. Brent obtained his Bachelor and Master's degrees from Queen's University in Canada, and his Ph.D. (1966–1971) from the University of Western Ontario. He taught at l'Institut pour les Etudes des Methodes de Direction de l'Enterprise, Lausanne, Switzerland, and at Université Laval, Québec before he moved to the University of Calgary as Assistant Dean (Graduate Programs) in 1978. At Calgary, he was instrumental in the designation of the University as a World Tourism Education and Research Centre (WTERC) in 1989, and served as Chair of the Centre until retirement. He also served as Associate Dean (both Academic and Research & Development) in the School of Business, and as Director of the Division of International Business for the University's International Centre. In 1995, he became the inaugural holder of the University of Calgary's Professorship in Tourism Management.

Research accomplishments

Brent has published extensively in all the top tourism journals in addition to several leading business journals. His work appears in *Annals of Tourism Research, Journal of Travel Research, Journal of Tourism Studies, Journal of Leisure Research, Tourism Review, Event Management, Journal of Teaching in Travel and Tourism, Journal of Business Research, Journal of Marketing Research, Journal of Marketing, Journal of Consumer Research, Journal of Public Policy in Marketing, Journal of Travel and Tourism Marketing, Journal of Convention & Exhibition Management, Visions in Leisure & Business, Tourism Economics, Tourism Management, Tourism Analysis*, and the *Journal of Sustainable Tourism*. He is also co-author and co-editor of five books. He was the associate editor of the *Journal of Travel Research* for over 20 years and served on the Editorial Review Boards of numerous other leading journals in the field.

He has served as president of the Administrative Sciences Association of Canada, as Vice-President of the Social Sciences Federation of Canada and was a member of the Industry Council of the Pacific Asia Travel Association. He was instrumental in establishing the Calgary Consortium for Tourism & Hospitality Studies, and was a founding Director of the Canadian Tourism Research Institute and the Alberta Tourism Education Council. In 2001, Brent was elected as the inaugural Chair of the UNWTO Education Council. As a result of his international reputation, he has acted as consultant to many private and public sector organizations.

When one looks at Brent's research areas over the years, there are a few key areas where he has really excelled. One of those is *destination competitiveness*. I arrived in Calgary at about the same time Dr Geoff Crouch was heading back to Australia, so I had some big shoes to fill. Geoff had been with the University of Calgary for five years, and worked closely with Brent on competitiveness and tourism. Their book, *The Competitive Destination: A Sustainable Tourism Perspective*, published by CABI in 2003, has become one of the seminal works in tourism research and engendered a number of major research papers on the subject (Ritchie & Crouch, 2003). Their work culminated in an excellent edited book called *Competitiveness and Tourism*, published by Edward Elgar in 2012 (Crouch & Ritchie, 2012). The book is a two-volume set that brings together key scholarly articles that discuss the challenges of managing, maintaining and enhancing competitive tourism destinations.

Geoff is now Professor of Tourism Policy & Marketing at La Trobe University, Melbourne, and had this to say about his work with Brent.

> I enjoyed very much the experience of working with Brent on our collaborative research into the topic of destination competitiveness. When we began our work in the early 1990s, research into destination competitiveness was just being pioneered. Our styles of working were very compatible. Our views and ideas were usually very similar while we each

contributed important perspectives and suggestions. Our writing styles also fitted together very nicely and so our book on the subject came together very successfully. I particularly admired Brent's ability to always focus on the big, important issues in tourism research and our work together on destination competitiveness certainly represents an excellent example of this. While I was located at the University of Calgary in the mid 1990s working with Brent on this research area was a joy. Unfortunately my return to Australia in 1997 made it a little more difficult to so freely collaborate after that but we have always continued to enjoy a wonderful professional and personal relationship. Brent has been one of the truly great pioneering researchers in tourism.

Brent is also really well known for his work on *destination image*. His publications with Charlotte Echtner (Echtner & Ritchie, 1991, 1993, 2003) in particular are well known and widely cited – especially the 1993 paper that proposed a scale for measuring destination image. In the paper, the authors presented a framework which suggests that to completely measure destination image, several components must be captured. These include attribute-based images; holistic impressions; and functional, psychological, unique, and common characteristics. They proposed that a combination of structured and unstructured methodologies is necessary to measure destination image as envisaged in the conceptual framework. A series of open-ended questions and scale items were developed and were shown to successfully capture all of the components of destination image. Brent continued to work with other scholars on this subject, publishing a paper in 2009 for example, with Sergio Moreno Gil from the University of Las Palmas, Gran Canaria (Moreno Gil & Ritchie, 2009). Their work provides a deeper understanding of the image formation process as it relates to museums finding that residents and tourists have differences in their image formation process following visitation to a museum.

Sergio Moreno Gil had this to say about Brent.

Brent is, no doubt, one of the most outstanding researchers in tourism and the person that caused a major influence in my career. When he started his career he was a marketing man, but he told me 'I didn't want to promote cigarettes', so he decided to pick a much social and sensitive topic: tourism. That's Brent. When he takes a topic, he just takes 'the topic'. I remember when I first arrived to Calgary from Spain for my post doc. He told me one of the most important pieces of advice in my academic career that I do not always get to follow. 'Sergio, you have to keep focused on the topic'. Brent visited us in the Canary Islands a few times, and from every visit, I learned so much. But of course behind every great man there's a great woman; his wife Rosemary is not only a lovely woman but a great and invaluable support.

Another strand of Brent's research explores the relationship between *destination management* organizations and their stakeholders. Beginning in 1985 when he studied consensus policy formulation in tourism (Ritchie, 1985), he moved on to work with Lorn Sheehan on several papers related to stakeholder theory (Bornhorst, Ritchie, & Sheehan, 2010; Presenza, Sheehan, & Ritchie, 2005; Sheehan & Ritchie, 2005; Sheehan, Ritchie, & Hudson, 2007). In their well-cited 2005 paper published in *Annals of Tourism Research*, they applied a stakeholder theory analysis to the empirical study of chief executive officers of tourism destination management organizations. Lorn Sheehan is now Professor and Associate Director for the Rowe School of Business at Dalhousie University, and had this to say about Brent.

Brent was initially skeptical about applying the stakeholder lens to tourism destination management. This critical perspective forced justification of the theoretical grounding and practical relevance of our work. In the end, our work was well received. Brent has an unfailing belief in the academy and has been so generous with his time to guide and mentor graduate students and early career academics. I want to congratulate Brent on his outstanding career.

More recently, Brent has once again put his name on a relatively new area for tourism researchers, looking at the creation of *memorable experiences*. Building on his earlier interest in service experiences (Otto & Ritchie, 1995, 1996), he first worked with Jong-Hyeong Kim and Vincent Tung (Kim, Ritchie, & Tung, 2010; Tung & Ritchie, 2011) developing and testing a model that investigated the effects of memorable tourism experiences on future behavioural intentions. A structural equation modelling analysis revealed that the memorable experiential components of involvement, hedonism, and local culture positively affect behavioural intention to revisit the same destination, engage in the same tourist activities, and generate positive word-of-mouth. Following this, he developed a 24-item memorable tourism experience scale that could be applicable to most destination areas. The scale comprises seven domains: hedonism, refreshment, local culture, meaningfulness, knowledge, involvement, and novelty (Kim, Ritchie, & McCormick, 2012). Brent has further publications on this topic including a paper with his son Robin (Ritchie, Tung, & Ritchie, 2011) and an edited book called *The Tourism and Leisure Experience: Consumer and Management Perspectives* (Morgan, Lugosi, & Ritchie, 2010).

Vincent Tung worked under Brent as a Ph.D. student for five years, and is now Assistant Professor for the School of Hotel and Tourism Management at The Hong Kong Polytechnic University. Commenting on his relationship with Brent, Dr Tung said:

> Brent is truly a visionary researcher and teacher. From his knowledge and experiences, he is able to identify upcoming trends with stellar insight on how they will impact the field. More importantly, perhaps, is his enthusiasm and energy that opens your eyes to new perspectives and research possibilities. As a teacher, he is genuine and sincere; he shares his passion and wisdom with his students, and provides them with the guidance they need to succeed. Nevertheless, Brent certainly has high standards! He is frank and straightforward with his comments, and pushes his students to publish work of the highest quality. His goal is to refine our skills to produce the next generation of independent researchers that can make positive contributions to the field. He stresses the importance of collaborations and publications: as he always says, 'publications are diamonds and diamonds are forever!' To conclude, Brent is undoubtedly the single most influential person in my career as an academic.

There are other areas where Brent has carved out a name for himself, and I was fortunate enough to work with him on some of these topics, or build on the research foundations he had already established. One of these was managing the *tourism impact of mega-events*. He was one of the first researchers to study the impacts of mega-events on host destinations, focusing particularly on the Calgary Olympics of 1988 (Ritchie, 1984, 2000; Ritchie & Aiken, 1985). I have since had a keen interest in the tourism impacts of events and how destinations can leverage events. Our mutual interests in this area (as well as his expertise in destination image) led to some joint research on *destination marketing* (Hudson & Ritchie, 2002) and then *destination branding* specifically (Hudson & Ritchie, 2009).

We also collaborated on research related to sustainability (Hudson & Ritchie, 2001; Ritchie, Hudson, & Timur, 2002), and his work in the Banff Bow Valley (Ritchie, 1999) inspired me to develop my own stream of research about the delicate balance between tourism development and environmental protection in sensitive areas (Hudson, 2002). Likewise, Brent's interest in *tourism poverty alleviation* (Zhao & Ritchie, 2007) influenced my research in the area of tourism ethics (Hudson, 2007). Brent was never afraid to dive into new and exciting areas of tourism research, and partnered with me a decade or so ago to study the *film tourism* phenomenon. At the time, there were very few academics looking at this, whereas now it has become a popular topic of study. We published two influential papers together – one that focused on the marketing initiatives that destinations can use to leverage film tourism (Hudson & Ritchie, 2006a);

the other that illustrated the influence that the movie Captain Corelli's Mandolin had on the island of Kefalonia (Hudson & Ritchie, 2006b).

Finally, we collaborated on research related to *tourism education*, a subject very dear to Brent's heart (see Jafari & Ritchie, 1981; Ritchie & Sheehan, 2001). At Calgary, Brent was instrumental in helping develop a hybrid Bachelor of Hotel and Restaurant Management (BHRM) degree that represented a learning track especially adapted for students seeking long-term careers rather than simply a job in the tourism and hospitality sector. In a joint paper with Lorn Sheehan in 2012 (Ritchie, Hudson, & Sheehan, 2002), we described the rationale and the details of this hybrid programme, outlining how the programme had expanded from coast to coast across Canada through the development of affiliation arrangements with some 19 institutions. It also described the academic and practical difficulties that were encountered in the establishment, delivery, and marketing of the programme and outlined the potential of similar hybrid models for other sectors.

Finally, most undergraduate students (and the tourism professors that teach them) will know Brent Ritchie for his book *Tourism: Principles, Practices and Philosophies*, now in its 12th edition (Goeldner & Ritchie, 2012). Once a year in Calgary, I witnessed Brent and co-author Chuck Goeldner, lock themselves in a room for days on end to work tirelessly on the next edition. The current edition explores major concepts in tourism, providing an overview of the principles, practices, and philosophies that affect the cultural, social, economic, psychological, and marketing aspects of human travel and the tourism industry. The two have also worked together on an edited handbook for managers and researchers focused on the latest research methodologies, statistics and techniques relevant to tourism and hospitality (Ritchie & Goeldner, 1994).

Hi co-author on these books, Dr Goeldner, who is Emeritus Professor of Marketing and Tourism at the University of Colorado, Boulder, said:

> I have had the good fortune to have known and worked with J. R. Brent Ritchie for over 40 years. First, we worked together on Travel and Tourism Research Association (TTRA) projects as Brent went through the officer ranks. After he finished serving as TTRA president our work led to the publication of Travel, Tourism and Hospitality Research: A Handbook for Managers & Researchers in 1987 by John Wiley and Sons with the help of TTRA. Wiley asked us to do a second edition which we did and it was published in 1994. I still admire Brent's work and skill in organizing the contributions of the 57 contributors to the 2nd edition. As indicated above Brent and I are best known as co-authors of book Tourism: Principles, Practices and Philosophies. Brent joined me as a co-author for the 7th edition published in 1995 and the book has enjoyed great success. Because Brent had resources available at the University of Calgary, he invited me to come up each time a new edition needed to be prepared. His hospitality, the help of his wife Rosemary, and his assistant Deb Angus, greatly contributed to the success of the book. It was always a pleasure to travel to Calgary and work with Brent.

Personal qualities

Not only was Brent a prolific researcher, the comments by Vince Tung above alluded to the fact that he also had the qualities of a truly inspiring leader: someone who motivates everyone to give their best all the time; someone who challenges their employees by setting high but attainable standards and expectations; and someone who gives them the support, tools, training, and latitude to pursue those goals. When I arrived in Calgary, Brent said "Give me five good years" (he did not think he could keep me in Canada for longer). I stayed for ten years mainly because of him. What I particularly appreciated about Brent was his trust in me – there was no micro-management as far as Brent was concerned. He did not seem to mind where I was in the world, as long as I was publishing and contributing to the credibility of our small but renowned tourism department. As Theodore Roosevelt said, the best leader "is the one who has sense enough to pick good men to do what he wants done, and self-restraint enough to keep from meddling with them while they do it". Brent was such a leader.

Finally, Brent has another characteristic of a great leader – he is also a very humble man. Humility doesn't mean that you're weak or unsure of yourself. It means that you have the self-confidence and self-awareness to recognize the value of others without feeling threatened. It means that you are willing to admit you could be wrong, that you recognize you may not have all the answers. Moreover, it means that you give credit where credit is due. That was Brent. He was not the type to jump up and down in celebration after hitting a top journal or winning a major award – but if one of his staff was successful in any way, he was always the first to offer congratulations.

Conclusion

Even in his retirement, Brent continues to give back to the tourism field. The Canada Chapter of Travel and Tourism Research Association (TTRA) has just launched the TTRA Lifetime Contribution Award to recognize an individual whose outstanding scientific contributions to travel and tourism research have substantially enhanced the stature of the Canada Chapter and its members. Brent is the sponsor of this prestigious award and instigated the whole process. His vision for the award is to recognize someone whose dedication and service to the Chapter have been uniquely invaluable and lasting in nature. "I would like the Award to recognize individuals whose contributions to tourism research, over his or her lifetime, have been so significant and substantial, that they bring international recognition to the Canada Chapter and its members," he said, when setting up the award. "I believe we should recognize these individuals." If Brent were eligible for this award, he would receive my nomination as its first winner.

References

Bornhorst, T., Ritchie, J. R. B., & Sheehan, L. (2010). Determinants of tourism success for DMOs and destinations: An empirical examination of stakeholders' perspectives. *Tourism Management, 51*, 572–589.

Crouch, G. I., & Ritchie, J. R. B. (Eds.). (2012). *Competitiveness and tourism*. Cheltenham: Edward Elgar.

Echtner, C. M., & Ritchie, J. R. B. (1991). The meaning and measurement of destination image. *Journal of Tourism Studies, 2*, 2–12.

Echtner, C. M., & Ritchie, J. R. B. (1993). The measurement of destination image: An empirical assessment. *Journal of Travel Research, 31*, 3–13.

Echtner, C. M., & Ritchie, J. R. B. (2003). The meaning and measurement of destination image. *Journal of Tourism Studies, 14*, 37–48.

Goeldner, C. R., & Ritchie, J. R. B. (2012). *Tourism: Principles, practices and philosophies* (12 ed.). New York, NY: John Wiley.

Hudson, S. (2002). Environmental management in the Rockies: The dilemma of balancing National Park values while making provision for their enjoyment. *Journal of Case Research, 22*(2), 1–14.

Hudson, S. (2007). To go or not to go? Ethical perspectives on tourism in an "outpost of tyranny". *Journal of Business Ethics, 76*, 385–396.

Hudson, S., & Ritchie, J. R. B. (2001). Cross-cultural tourist behavior: An analysis of tourist attitudes towards the environment. *Journal of Travel and Tourism Marketing, 10*(2/3), 1–22.

Hudson, S., & Ritchie, J. R. B. (2002). Understanding the domestic market using cluster analysis: A case study of the marketing efforts of Travel Alberta. *Journal of Vacation Marketing, 8*, 263–276.

Hudson, S., & Ritchie, J. R. B. (2006a). Promoting destinations via film tourism: An empirical identification of supporting marketing initiatives. *Journal of Travel Research, 44*(4), 1–10.

Hudson, S., & Ritchie, J. R. B. (2006b). Film tourism and destination marketing: The case of Captain Corelli's Mandolin. *Journal of Vacation Marketing, 12*, 209–221.

Hudson, S., & Ritchie, J. R. B. (2009). Branding a memorable destination experience. The case of "Brand Canada". *International Journal of Tourism Research, 11*, 217–228.

Hudson, S., Ritchie, J. R. B., & Timur, S. (2004). Measuring destination competitiveness: An empirical study of Canadian ski resorts. *Journal of Tourism and Hospitality Planning and Development, 1*, 79–94.

Jafari, J., & Ritchie, J. R. B. (1981). Toward a framework for tourism education: Problems and prospects. *Annals of Tourism Research, 8*, 13–34.

Kim, J.-H., Ritchie, J. R. B., & McCormick, B. (2012). Development of a scale to measure memorable tourism experiences. *Journal of Travel Research, 51*, 12–25.

Kim, J.-H., Ritchie, J. R. B., & Tung, V. (2010). The effect of memorable experience on behavioral intentions in tourism: A structural equation modeling approach. *Tourism Analysis, 15*, 637–648.

Moreno Gil, S., & Ritchie, J. R. B. (2009). Understanding the museum image formation process: A comparison of residents and tourists. *Journal of Travel Research, 47*, 480–493.

Morgan, M., Lugosi, P., & Ritchie, J. R. B. (Eds.). (2010). *The tourism and leisure experience: Consumer and management perspectives*. Bristol: Channel View Publications.

Otto, J. E., & Ritchie, J. R. B. (1995). Exploring the quality of the service experience: A theoretical and empirical analysis. *Advances in Services Marketing and Management, 4*, 37–61.

Otto, J. E., & Ritchie, J. R. B. (1996). The service experience in tourism. *Tourism Management, 17*, 165–174.

Presenza, A., Sheehan, L. R., & Ritchie, J. R. B. (2005). Towards a model of the roles and activities of destination management organization. *Journal of Hospitality, Tourism and Leisure Science, 3*(1), 1–16.

Ritchie, J. R. B. (1984). Assessing the impact of hallmark events: Conceptual and research issues. *Journal of Travel Research, 23*, 2–11.

Ritchie, J. R. B. (1985). The nominal group technique: An approach to consensus policy formulation in tourism. *Tourism Management, 6*, 82–95.

Ritchie, J. R. B. (1999). Policy formulation at the tourism/environment interface: Insights and recommendations from the Banff Bow Valley study. *Journal of Travel Research, 38*, 100–110.

Ritchie, J. R. B. (2000). Turning 16 days into 16 years through Olympic legacies. *Event Management, 6*, 155–165.

Ritchie, J. R. B., & Aiken, C. E. (1985). Olympulse II – Evolving resident attitudes toward the Olympic winter games. *Journal of Travel Research, 23*, 28–33.

Ritchie, J. R. B., & Crouch, G. I. (2003). *The competitive destination: A sustainable tourism perspective*. Oxon: CABI.

Ritchie, J. R. B., & Goeldner, C. R. (1994). *Tourism and hospitality research: A handbook for managers & researchers* (2nd ed.). New York, NY: John Wiley.

Ritchie, J. R. B., & Hudson, S. (2009). Understanding and meeting the challenges of consumer/ tourist experience research. *International Journal of Tourism Research, 11*, 111–126.

Ritchie, J. R. B., Hudson, S., & Sheehan, L. R. (2002). Hybrid programs in tourism and hospitality: A review of strengths, weaknesses and implementation issues. *Acta Turistica, 14*, 29–45.

Ritchie, J. R. B., Hudson, S., & Timur, S. (2002). Public reactions to policy recommendations from the Banff-Bow Valley study: A longitudinal assessment. *Journal of Sustainable Tourism, 10*, 295–308.

Ritchie, J. R. B., & Sheehan, L. R. (2001). Practicing what we preach in tourism education and research the use of strategic research methods for program design, implementation and evaluation (part II-focus groups). *Journal of Teaching in Travel & Tourism, 1*, 49–57.

Ritchie, J. R. B., Tung, V. W. S., & Ritchie, R. J. B. (2011). Tourism experience management research: Emergence, evolution and future directions. *International Journal of Contemporary Hospitality Management, 23*, 419–438.

Sheehan, L. R., & Ritchie, J. R. B. (2005). Destination stakeholders exploring identity and salience. *Annals of Tourism Research, 32*, 711–734.

Sheehan, L. R., Ritchie, J. R. B., & Hudson, S. (2007). The destination promotion triad: The city, the hotels and the DMO. *Journal of Travel Research, 46*, 64–74.

Tung, V. W. S., & Ritchie, J. R. B. (2011). Exploring the essence of memorable tourism experiences. *Annals of Tourism Research, 38*, 1367–1386.

Zhao, W., & Ritchie, J. R. B. (2007). Tourism and poverty alleviation: An integrative research framework. *Current Issues in Tourism, 10*, 119–143.

Brian Archer: the multiplier man

David Airey

Introduction

For Brian Archer's own account of his career as a tourism economist published in Larry Dwyer's edited collection, *The Discovery of Tourism Economics* (2011) he takes the title "Musings of a Multiplier Man". At one level, this title captures exactly the important aspect of Brian's academic work and indeed, as he acknowledged in a keynote speech to the IATE conference in 2011, at least for anyone over 35 it is what he is best known for – multipliers. But, at a rather more profound level, it obscures the great contribution that early scholars of economics, like Brian, made to the development of tourism as a serious field of study. He is one of those early scholars who, in common with a very small band of others, partly by design and partly accident, found himself involved in the serious study of an activity that was taking on global significance. Brian was among the first scholars and as such he set some of the first directions for tourism studies, he helped to bring economic thinking into the field, and he enhanced the understanding of tourism in a way that is still felt today.

In the mid-1960s, when Brian first began to research its economic contribution, tourism hardly existed as a subject of serious study or research. Medlik (1965) identifies some early tourism programmes at the Universities of Rome (1925), Vienna (1936), and at St Gallen and Berne in Switzerland, and of course there were some early vocational hotel schools both in Europe and North America. But for the most part, tourism did not figure as a subject either for study or for research. For that to occur, three ingredients needed to come together. First, tourism as an activity needed to be recognized as important, whether for its contributions or for its problems. This happened during the 1960s with the accelerating growth in tourist numbers and expenditure and with, for example, the recognition by the United Nations Organization of 1967 as International Tourist Year. Second, there was a need for pioneers to start developing programmes of study and research. That was happening at a few places around the world where universities began to spot new opportunities. Third, scholars, by definition from other subject areas, needed to turn their scholarly ambitions to tourism. Economists were in the vanguard of such scholars and among the first of these was Brian Archer. In other words, he was entering a new field and in entering it he helped to create it, and in helping to create it he provided a basis for subsequent scholars to develop and challenge. From this, tourism as an area of scholarly study as we know it today has emerged. This portrait of Brian Archer is, therefore, a portrait of one of the founders of the study of tourism.

Brian is currently Emeritus Professor at the University of Surrey. He retired from his full-time post there in 1994 and retired completely in 2000. Since then, tourism has remained an important part of his life, partly through occasional consultancy studies and assistance with journal editing and Ph.D. vivas, and recently through conference contributions, but much more importantly and more extensively through personal travel. For the past 20 years, he has certainly become a highly experienced practitioner of tourism.

As for me, I have now known Brian for more than 35 years. I was aware of his "multiplier" work when I was a student in the early 1970s, and we first met when he came to give a presentation (on tourism multipliers of course) at the University of Surrey which I had joined as member of academic staff in 1975. Subsequently, he became the Head of the Department at Surrey, and we worked together there for some years until I moved away in 1985. During that time, his work played an influential and important role in my development, as a lecturer in tourism and economics. Subsequently, we have kept in contact, partly through meetings at our local supermarket, and, over a pub lunch, he was kind enough to assist in providing information for the preparation of this portrait, by providing documentation, by answering questions, and by sharing anecdotes. Within these, his chapter in Dwyer's collection has provided important source material (Archer, 2011).

Background

Brian Archer was born in the suburbs of Liverpool into a long-standing dairy farming family. His father subsequently managed a milk-processing company. He was educated at a private school in Liverpool, and, as was common at the time in the UK, as a high-performing pupil at the age of 13 he was encouraged to take classical studies (Latin, Greek, and Ancient History). It was only later in his school career that he took the first of three turns in his academic direction by studying English, History, and Geography. The second turn came a few years later towards the end of his studies at the University of Cambridge when he moved away from Geography towards Economics, subsequently taking a second undergraduate degree in that subject. The third came much later when he moved also into Tourism.

When he left school, he was conscripted into the British Army for two years national service rising to Corporal within a year and then commissioned as an officer. Having finished his national service, he continued his links with the part-time Territorial Army, rising to the rank of Major. During this time, he returned to his studies gaining a place at the University of Cambridge (Fitzwilliam College) to study Geography. Interestingly, while there, he was taught by Terry Coppock, who subsequently, as Professor at the University of Edinburgh, started the Tourism Recreation Research Unit at that University. Terry was another one of those early pioneer scholars, this time a geographer, who took their academic skills into tourism, but according to Brian, at the time at Cambridge, tourism did not figure in their studies.

It is in some ways paradoxical that his turn towards Economics at the end of his time at Cambridge led him to a career as a school teacher of Geography, at Monmouth School. His explanation is that this provided him with the space to study for an external degree from the University of London in Economics and Politics. It also provided him with an opportunity to develop Economics as a subject across the School, which in itself was unusual at the time.

The appearance of tourism

Apart from cricket and rugby, and also developing his skills as an accomplished conjuror, Brian's other great passion during this time, and indeed subsequently, was travel. By the time he was at Monmouth School, he had already visited most of the countries of Western Europe and some in the east, as well as the USA, Canada, and parts of Africa. In the early 1960s, this was exceptional. His interest in tourism had an early start. As he explains it, his professional interest in economics and his personal interest in tourism came together almost by accident from a chance meeting, during a return visit to Cambridge, with a former Economics Tutor at his college who had moved to the University College of North Wales, Bangor as Professor and Head of Department. The outcome of this encounter was that he took a post as Senior Research Officer in the newly formed Economic Research Unit at Bangor. The first major project for Brian was an economic study of the Isle of Anglesey. Although not ostensibly about tourism, the nature of the region and Brian's own interests were in his words "crucial in helping to bring together the two strands of tourism and economics into a meaningful relationship" (Archer, 2011, p. 5). An outcome was one of the first so-called "multiplier studies" bearing the name of Brian Archer as a co-author (Sadler, Archer, & Owen, 1973). This then led to his studies for a doctorate examining the state of the art in tourism economics. Further regional tourism impact studies, initially in the UK and later in many other parts of the world, followed as well as a permanent lectureship at the University and eventually the Directorship of the Institute of Economic Research. This period also brought him into teaching in Macroeconomics, Regional Economics as well as a new course that he introduced in the Economics of Tourism and Recreation. It was during this time that Brian's pre-eminent role as the "Multiplier Man" was consolidated with the publication of *"Tourism Multipliers: The State of the Art"* (Archer, 1977d) which for the first time brought together the thinking to date of the position and proper use of the multiplier to understand tourism.

The final major step in Brian's career was to a Professorship at the University of Surrey, following the retirement of the Rik Medlik, who was the first professor in this field in the UK. His involvement at Surrey was to last for more than 20 years during which time he served as Head of Department and Pro-Vice Chancellor. At Surrey, Brian joined one of the few "mainstream" tourism centres at that time that offered tourism-related degree programmes and research. He continued the development of the department and continued his research work in tourism impacts and in other economic issues concerned with tourism. The subsequent appointment to Surrey of Steve Wanhill and John Fletcher, both economists and both trained at Bangor provided Surrey with a powerful economics team that brought worldwide attention to the University.

Academic and other contributions

The twin themes of economics and tourism that were brought together in the "Anglesey Study" have provided the *leitmotif* for Brian's career. The first step in this was bringing the theory of economics, particularly macroeconomics into tourism, to understand the role that tourism plays in generating incomes and employment. The fact that this was done in the context of specific studies of tourist regions also served to bring together both theory and practical implications for destinations. At the heart of this work was both the challenge of measuring the demand for tourism but conceptually more importantly of identifying tourism in models based on traditional industrial classifications, an issue that was originally solved in the Anglesey study by adding rows and columns for tourism to the input–output tables – an early precursor of satellite accounting. This work had two important effects. First, it added both the understanding and rigour to the growing field of tourism as an area of study. Brian brought this together in the publication cited earlier (Archer, 1977d), and it is not surprising that he received regular invitations to present his work at academic conferences notably, originally in the USA at, for example, Colonial Williamsburg, Virginia; Sun Valley, Idaho (Archer, 1973); and Scottdale, Arizona (Archer, 1977b). In his CV, he identifies 50 such conferences, seminars, and colloquia. Second, it took Brian into a range of other studies both in the UK and overseas on projects funded by local and national governments as well as by international agencies such as the World Bank, UN World Tourism Organization, and the United Nations Development Programme. His CV lists over 30 such studies in destinations from the Lake District in the UK, to the Bahamas, Bermuda, Fiji, Hong Kong, Mauritius, the Seychelles, and Vanuatu to name just a few. With a passion for travel, this certainly met at least one of Brian's goals. At the same time, as an economist, he increasingly looked beyond the impacts of tourism to consider also issues such as project appraisal, cost–benefit analysis, manpower and training needs, data needs, statistical needs, and more general tourism development studies, and he spent some time as Special Advisor on Tourism to a House of Commons Select Committee. Brian's skills as an economist were clearly recognized in many of the countries and regions where he worked, such that he was regularly invited to return, not only to carry out economic impact work but also to provide more general economic advice. In the case of the Bahamas his relationship lasted for 8 years and for Bermuda 28 years.

Many of these studies subsequently appeared as publications, both free standing and as journal articles. Apart from his 1977 study of tourism multipliers, he published a number journal articles on this topic (Archer, 1971c, 1972, 1976, 1984a; Archer & Fletcher, 1988, 1991; Archer & Owen, 1972). He also developed his work specifically in relation to the economic impact of domestic tourism which represented some of the earliest considerations of this element of tourism (Archer, 1977a, 1978) and on the impact of tourism on regional and island economies (Archer, 1971a, 1989a, 1998). Furthermore, he produced a series of UK and internationally based tourism impact studies for specific destinations (Archer, 1977c, 1984b; Archer, de Vane, & Moore, 1977; Archer, Shea, & de Vane, 1974). And he also began to explore in his research and publications other economic dimensions of tourism. As his career developed, he covered a wide range of such issues including, for example, manpower (Archer & Shea, 1977); evaluating publicly funded projects (Archer & Shea, 1980); gravity models (Archer, 1975a); and measuring and forecasting tourist demand and expenditure (Archer, 1975b, 1980, 1986, 1989b). Outside tourist demand and impact issues, he also considered other aspects of tourism relating, for example, to the economic dimensions of sustainability and the broader consequences of tourism (Archer, 1996; Archer & Cooper, 1994), tourist legislation (Archer, 1971b), tourism and amenity values (Archer, 1970), and broad trends in tourism (Archer & Lawson, 1982). In 1979, he brought some of his international experiences together at his inaugural professorial lecture at the University of Surrey to relate his work to the Third World, entitled *Tourism in the Third World: Some Economic Considerations* (Archer, 1979).

Together, this body of work transformed the literature about tourism. It represented work that was both theoretically based and rigorous and in the process it helped on the one hand to counter the idea that tourism was somehow of little economic worth, a "candy floss" industry, and on the other to dispel some of the exaggerated claims about the economic importance of tourism. It also added to what, at that point, was a fairly sparse, research-based literature about tourism. For the newly emerging undergraduate and postgraduate programmes in tourism, this represented a vital new resource and in many ways it is not surprising that economists at the time, including Brian, were in the forefront of the development of tourism as a field of academic endeavour. I doubt whether there was a degree programme in the Western world in the 1970s and 1980s that did not spend at least some time considering Archer's work on tourism multipliers. From the standpoint of the twenty-first century when the field of tourism research is just as likely to take an interpretivist or critical stance as it is to take a positivist stance and is just as likely to be qualitative as quantitative in methods, it is hard to remember or even imagine a time when research hardly existed. The importance of the early researchers, like Brian, in the field of economics is that they brought their academic disciplines to tourism and in doing so laid the groundwork that has been being built upon by subsequent generations of tourism scholars.

In the context of subsequent scholars, of course, Brian has been directly involved in their preparation and development and many of his former students have gone on to be world leaders in their academic field. Prominent among these are Professor John Fletcher and Professor Steve Wanhill who have been close collaborators with Brian throughout their careers, from their student and early career days at Bangor, to the time they spent with him at Surrey and in their subsequent positions. They have continued to work closely with him. As a legacy of their time with Brian, they are both recognized as leading economists in their field with Steve, for example, as the founding editor of the *Journal of Tourism Economics*. Similarly, Brian was involved in the early research work of two of the first women in this field, examining the Ph.D.s of Christine Hope and the late Thea Sinclair, both of whom went on to professorships at the Universities of Bradford and Nottingham, respectively.

Influences and legacies

In turning his attention towards tourism, Brian Archer, with a few others, was something of a new phenomenon in our field. Like other scholars at about the same time, such as Professors Terry Coppock, mentioned earlier, and Richard Butler, both geographers and Professor Erik Cohen, a sociologist, to mention just a few, he used his discipline to help explain and provide insights into a complex and increasingly important human phenomenon. In doing so, he always remained an economist, drawing on the heritage of economics and in Brian's case influenced by a few early mentors such as Professor Jack Revell, Head of Economics at Bangor and Professor Peter Sadler, subsequently Professor of the Economics of Sparsely Populated Areas at the University of Aberdeen. But at the same time he also became associated with the new field of tourism and through his association he helped to establish some of the content and boundaries of the new field. His move to the University of Surrey in 1978 was an important part of this. Over a 10-year period under the leadership of Professor Rik Medlik, another economist who had brought his skills to the hotel and tourism sector, Surrey had become established as a major centre for tourism studies. In joining Surrey, Brian was placed at a key centre of this new field.

From this position, supported and influenced by his colleagues John Fletcher and Steve Wanhill, Brian continued his research, publication, and teaching, and he began a programme of course development. This obviously placed economic issues at the centre of much of the work, but more importantly it helped to strengthen the importance of research-based scholarship. Tourism scholarship has moved on dramatically since Brian's early time at Surrey. Economics has been joined by all the other disciplines that help to explain tourism, and as noted earlier, tourism research is no longer dominated by positivist and quantitative approaches. Yet, the influences of the early scholars remain. They created the original domain of study and they began to create its content and its approaches. It is this that the subsequent generations have been able to work on. For economics, Brian Archer was one of the key early scholars and his multipliers still appear in many tourism programmes.

Brian has now been in retirement for more than a decade. During this time, as already noted, his forays into the practice of tourism have been regular and far ranging, taking him all over the world. By contrast, his involvement with the profession of tourism research and teaching has been more infrequent. However, as subsequent scholars have in their turn begun to reflect on the development of their subject, which has now become an established part of the academy, they have turned to the early scholars like Brian Archer for their reflections. It is in this context that he came out of retirement to give a keynote address at the 2011 Conference of the International Association for Tourism Economics, titled "The Trials and Tribulations of a Tourism Economist". Appearances by early scholars like Brian are important in ensuring that those who followed in their footsteps do not forget the origins of their field of study and in Brian's case will not forget the role of the early economists and of the multiplier.

References

Archer, B. H. (1970). Tourism and the preservation of amenity values. *Revue de Tourisme, 25,* 158–159.

Archer, B. H. (1971a). The impact of tourism on regional economies. *Local Government Finance, 75,* 183–185.

Archer, B. H. (1971b). Tourist organization and legislation in United Kingdom. *Travel Research Bulletin, 10*(1), 1–3.

Archer, B. H. (1971c). Towards a tourist regional multiplier. *Regional Studies, 5,* 289–294.

Archer, B. H. (1972). A regional employment multiplier. *Tourist Review, 27,* 105–107.

Archer, B. H. (1973). *The uses and abuses of multipliers.* Paper presented at the annual Travel Research Conference, Sun Valley, Idaho.

Archer, B. H. (1975a). The gravity model: A case study of Llandudno. *Revue de Tourisme, 30,* 86–91.

Archer, B. H. (1975b). Length of stay problems in tourist research. *Journal of Travel Research, 13,* 8–10.

Archer, B. H. (1976). The anatomy of a multiplier. *Regional Studies, 10,* 71–77.

Archer, B. H. (1977a). *The impact of domestic tourism.* Bangor: University of Wales Press.

Archer, B. H. (1977b). *Input–output analysis: Its strengths, limitations and weaknesses.* Paper presented at the annual conference of the Travel Research Association, Scottsdale, Arizona.

Archer, B. H. (1977c). *Tourism in the Bahamas and Bermuda: Two case studies.* Bangor: University of Wales Press.

Archer, B. H. (1977d). *Tourism multipliers: The state of the art.* Cardiff: University of Wales Press.

Archer, B. H. (1978). Domestic tourism as a development factor. *Annals of Tourism Research, 5,* 126–141.

Archer, B. H. (1979). *Tourism in the third world: Some economic considerations – Inaugural lecture.* Guildford: University of Surrey.

Archer, B. H. (1980). Forecasting demand: Quantitative and intuitive techniques. *International Journal of Tourism Management, 1,* 5–12.

Archer, B. H. (1984a). Economic impact: Misleading multipliers. *Annals of Tourism Research, 11,* 517–518.

Archer, B. H. (1984b). Tourism and the British economy. *Rivista Internazionale di Scienze Economiche e Commerciale, 31,* 596–613.

Archer, B. H. (1986). Demand forecasting and estimation. In B. Ritchie & C. R. Goeldner (Eds.), *Tourism and hospitality research* (pp. 75–85). Chichester: Wiley.

Archer, B. H. (1989a). Tourism and island economies. *Progress in Tourism, Recreation and Hospitality Management, 1,* 125–134.

Archer, B. H. (1989b). Trends in international tourism. In S. F. Witt & L. Moutinho (Eds.), *Tourism marketing and management handbook* (pp. 593–597). Hemel Hempstead: Prentice Hall.

Archer, B. H. (1996). Sustainable tourism: An economist's viewpoint. In L. Briguglio (Ed.), *Sustainable tourism in islands and small states: Issues and policies* (pp. 6–17). London: Pinter.

Archer, B. H. (1998). The impact of international companies on the economies of small islands: A case study of Bermuda. In M. Bowe, L. Briguglio, & J. W. Dean (Eds.), *Banking and tourism in islands and small states* (pp. 192–208). London: Cassell.

Archer, B. H. (2011). Musings of a multiplier man. In L. Dwyer (Ed.), *The discovery of tourism economics* (pp. 1–13). Emerald: Bingley.

Archer, B. H., & Cooper, C. P. (1994). The positive and negative impacts of tourism. In W. F. Theobald (Ed.), *Global tourism* (pp. 63–81). Oxford: Butterworth Heinemann.

Archer, B. H., de Vane, R., & Moore, J. H. (1977). *Tourism in the coastal strip of East Anglia.* London: Department of the Environment.

Archer, B. H., & Fletcher, J. R. (1988). The tourism multiplier. *Teoros, 7,* 6–9.

Archer, B. H., & Fletcher, J. R. (1991). The development and application of multiplier analysis. *Progress in Tourism, Recreation and Hospitality Management, 3,* 28–47.

Archer, B. H., & Lawson, F. R. (1982). Trends in tourism planning and development tourism management. *Tourism Management, 3,* 206–207.

Archer, B. H., & Owen, C. (1972). Towards a tourist regional multiplier. *Journal of Travel Research, 11,* 9–13.

Archer, B. H., & Shea, S. (1977). *Manpower in tourism: The situation in Wales.* Cardiff: Wales Tourist Board.

Archer, B. H., & Shea, S. (1980). *Grant-assisted tourism projects in Wales: An evaluation.* Cardiff: Wales Tourist Board.

Archer, B. H., Shea, S., & de Vane, R. (1974). *Tourism in Gwynedd: An economic study.* Cardiff: Wales Tourist Board.

Medlik, S. (1965). *Higher education and research in tourism in Western Europe.* London: University of Surrey.

Sadler, P. G., Archer, B. H., & Owen, C. B. (1973). *Regional income multipliers: The Anglesey study.* Bangor: University of Wales Press.

Carminda Cavaco: pioneer of tourism studies in Portugal

João Sarmento ⓘ and Ana Inácio ⓘ

Introduction

On a cold and misty winter morning we were warmly greeted by Carminda Cavaco on her Lisbon apartment. Serenely on her couch, lighting a cigarette at regular intervals, Carminda happily answered our endless questions and calmly (re)counted various episodes of her life. We chatted for about three hours, scribbling some notes hastily, and travelled to her youth, to her voyages and initial papers, to the development of her early career, attempting to understand the paths that brought her to become the pioneer and the most influential Portuguese academic in the field of tourism. Some weeks earlier, from the other end of the Mediterranean, Metin Kozak approached us to write her portrait, an idea to which we were immediately attracted.

Both authors are part of the same research group as Carminda – TERRITUR, Centre for Geographical Studies, University of Lisbon – and while one of us (João) is a geographer with interests in tourism like herself, the other (Ana) has a background in tourism management, communication and geography, has worked with her since 1998 in various research projects and publications (Inácio & Cavaco, 2010; Inácio & Joaquim, 2008), and is one of her few former PhD students (Inácio, 2008). Despite all our enthusiasm, we quickly realised that condensing almost 50 years of intense scholarship and publications in the field of tourism into a short paper like this would not be an easy task. Yet, it is critical to write a profile for an international audience. Firstly because Carminda's CV and academic path eludes most google endeavours. Secondly, since most of her published works are not in English (remarkable exceptions are Cavaco, 1993a, 1995b, 1995c). Thirdly, because the only publication that comprehensively reviews and analyses her life and work in detail, and perhaps the single printed document with some biographic information on Carminda Cavaco, was published in Portuguese by Luís Moreno, one of her former PhD students, on the occasion of her jubilation, ten years ago (Moreno, 2006).

Short life

Carminda Maria Mariana Cavaco was born in the rural town of Boliqueime, in the Algarve, south Portugal (1938). Daughter of two (she has a sister) she grew up in a changing Mediterranean landscape of almond and carob trees, of olive groves, oranges and figs, of small landowners, landless peasants, and fishing ports. Her family owned and run some properties and the meticulous self-sufficient local familiar economy and agricultural production were central to her early years. Post-war globalization and trade competition from California and South Spain were strongly felt in this profoundly embedded agricultural landscape and economy. In the private boarding school in Faro she remembers not only an extraordinary geography teacher (José Neves), but also the mathematics and physics teachers, who were quite influential to her love for numbers, science and the precise. When the latter two were placed in Lisbon, it was easier for her family to consent her move to study in the capital, as she was lodged at their home. Carminda was supposed to study economics, but since she felt her English was poor she chose geography, in the Arts Faculty of the University of Lisbon. Her final year dissertation from 1960 was an anthropological and ethnographical work of traditional rural life in her home region (Moreno, 2006). Yet this study already made an allusion to Vilamoura, a 1600 hectares estate of agricultural land, which was later sold and transformed to become the tourist resort touchstone of the Algarve.

From 1960 to 1964 Carminda taught at secondary level, but with a scholarship from the Institute for Higher Culture, she became a researcher in the Centre for Geographical Studies (CEG) of the University of Lisbon (1961), a research institution founded in 1949 by Orlando Ribeiro (1911–1997), and heavily influenced by the French Regional School tradition. Not long after, a scholarship from the Gulbenkian Foundation allowed her to go to Strasbourg for two years (1966–1968), with brief stays in Paris and Caen. While Strasbourg was chosen because it was a place where she could develop certain cartographic skills (pursuing the CEG's idea to make an Atlas of Portugal), she ended up being enchanted by French culture and landscapes. Going to Normandy with the purpose of learning from an Atlas of that region, she was captivated by Mont St. Michel and besotted with the lure of Deauville, attracting the high society and celebrities. Listening to and learning from various French *maîtres* on numerous subjects was part of this defining moment of her career and life, which had symptomatically began with the border crossing to France on the Sud-Espress train: "I could breathe an air of freedom". In France she met Etienne Julliard, who was involved in the production of a Tourism Atlas, and encountered his work on Saint Tropez. She was also highly impressed with Louis Burnet's 1957 PhD thesis on tourism and leisure on the French Coast. These works were used in her 1970 paper on tourism published in *Finisterra*. Still in her 20s, Paris, Deauville, Cabourg, and many other places in France captivated her forever.

Back in Portugal, and without any sort of planning or predefined goal, she became an assistant lecturer in the Geography Department of the University of Lisbon (1969), and started to collaborate with the Directorate-General for Tourism, bringing from France some of the ideas of the Tourist Atlas. Two years later, with the support of Gaetano Ferro (1920–2000), an Italian who had completed his PhD on the Algarve and whom she had met in Portugal in the late 1950s, Carminda made another study period abroad, this time in Genoa, Italy. There, travelling through Liguria, she again looked at how tourism was transforming the coast – "an almost uninterrupted series of tourism settlements", and published her findings in a publication of the University of Genoa and in Italian (Cavaco, 1974a, p. 5). It is therefore rather surprising to find that her PhD thesis, completed in 1976, is a purely regional geography work about the Eastern part of the Algarve. The thesis was jointly supervised by Gaetano Ferro, a firm supporter of her "audacious interest by the Geography of Idleness, Leisure and Tourism" (Cavaco, 1997, p. 100), and Orlando Ribeiro, a highly renowned cultural, historical and regional geographer (Daveau, 2012), who was nevertheless convinced that tourism was a minor subject (C. Cavaco [Personal Interview, December 2015, Lisbon]). Carminda's numerous efforts and even joint travels with Orlando to the Algarve were never enough to change the maître's views.

Her research was somehow decentred in the Centre for Geographical Studies of the Arts Faculty (Moreno, 2006), and unlike the other researchers, Carminda did not publish her PhD in the Research Centre collection. Instead it was published by the Planning Cabinet of the Algarve Region (Cavaco, 1976a), a clear indication that in the next years she would have several partnerships outside the Faculty. In fact she collaborated with the Catholic University and with the Gulbenkian Science Institute in Oeiras, mostly with economists and agronomists. Throughout her career, Carminda's most influential colleagues were not geographers: Licínio Cunha (tourism economics); António Covas (European economics and rural policy), Carlos Laranjo Medeiros (economics and political sciences), Fernando Oliveira Baptista (agronomy), among others. As early as 1974, she was involved in teaching tourism geography, in collaboration with Fernando Moser, in the Higher Institute of Languages and Administration (ISLA), and in the late 1970s, she started an optional Tourism Geography course in the Arts Faculty. Carminda became an Associate Professor in 1980, completing her Habilitation in Geography in 1989, also at Lisbon University. She became a Full Professor (1991) and at 68 she retired from university.

Selected publications

When asked about her favourite publications, Carminda gave us a big smile and confessed "I like beautiful things" (C. Cavaco [Personal Interview, December 2015, Lisbon]). It is the glossy publications with fine photographs for wide audiences that she is most found of: *Rural Portugal: from tradition to modernity*, commissioned by the Planning and Agriculture Directorate-General (Cavaco, 1992); *Water, a Sentimental Journey* (Simões & Cavaco, 2008); and more recently, *The land and people of Cante* (Cavaco, Medeiros, & Lima, 2012), a book implicated in the submission of Cante (a genre of traditional polyphonic a capela singing by amateur choral groups for Alentejo, southern Portugal), to the UNESCO Intangible Cultural Heritage (awarded in 2014).

Looking at all her other eclectic research outputs, we distinguish four broad temporal divisions of roughly 10–12 years each, three of which are marked by a prolific publication record in tourism. The first period encompasses the years from 1969 to 1981, and it is a time when Carminda brings tourism to the attention of Portuguese academics (Cavaco, 1970), starts to look at the changes tourism was making in the Algarve (Cavaco, 1969, 1974b, 1976b, 1979a), in the country at large (Cavaco, 1979b) and to the Estoril coast (Cavaco, 1981), the "Portuguese Riviera" from the 1920s. This latter work emerged from the "Geography of Tourism" seminar she taught at the Arts Faculty in the year 1979/1980, and involved the participation of several young students, some of whom became interested in tourism later in their academic life.

During the second period, from 1982 to 1992, Carminda's distanced herself from tourism, and focused on rural development, on agriculture, on demographic issues, on border regions, intermixing publications on these themes with others related to education. Portugal joined the EU in 1986, and this new European focus, and an emphasis on planning and on the possibilities of structural funds, strongly influenced Portuguese geographers (Sarmento, 2008). Funding was available to conduct planning studies and consultancy, and Carminda embraced the opportunities, collaborating regularly with various departments of the Ministry for Agriculture (Moreno, 2006). From the mid-1980s onwards she was also very active in the creation and running of the *Portuguese Society of Rural Studies*.

In the third period, from 1993 to 2006, Carminda "returned" to tourism research, focusing then mostly on Rural Tourism. Her views from economics and local and regional development combined with spatial planning resulted in several important publications (Cavaco, 1993b, 1995a, 1996, 1999a, 1999b, 2003a, 2003b). This was a period when she interacted with Alberto Montanari, Allan Williams and Russell King – regular visitors to the Centre for Geographical Studies in Lisbon – and published some texts in English (Cavaco, 1993, 1995b, 1995c). It was also during this time that Carminda had an unforeseen opportunity to establish stronger connections with Brazil. It all started with an invitation to deliver some talks and participate in seminars, which then evolved into a research project within the context of a protocol between the universities of Lisbon and São Paulo (Moreno, 2006). As a result of these networks some publications emerged (see Cavaco & Fonseca, 2001), which are widely used particularly in Brazil. This period "ended" with an important contribution to a 4 volume publication edited by Carlos Alberto Medeiros: *The Geography of Portugal* (Medeiros, 2006). Among other chapters, Carminda wrote a 60 pages *portrait* of Tourism in Portugal (Cavaco, 2006), where she provided an outlook of tourism in the country, focusing on resources and products, rural tourism, second homes, local and regional development, and sustainability.

The fourth period, from 2006 to the present, coincides roughly with her retirement. As she happily told us, "now I could finally start doing what I liked", and in fact, in the last ten years Carminda refocused and directed her publishing energies on tourism. Although she has an interest on and keeps publishing in rural development and agriculture themes – one of her key subjects in the last 4 decades – she kindly told us: "I leave that to Luís Moreno now" (C. Cavaco [Personal Interview,

December 2015, Lisbon]), referring to one of her closest rural geography disciples (Moreno, 2002). In the past decade Carminda has worked on Health and Wellness Tourism (Cavaco, 2008, 2010a 2010b; Medeiros & Cavaco, 2008), Senior Tourism (Cavaco, 2009), an older interest that grew in the early 2000s with the supervision of Carlos Ferreira's PhD (2004), Wine Tourism (Cavaco, 2008; Inácio & Cavaco, 2010; Medeiros & Cavaco, 2008); and the urbanization and resilience of cold water resorts (Cavaco, 2013, in press).

Conclusion

It is not an easy task to establish Carminda's influence in tourism in Portugal, but also in Brazil and elsewhere. Unquestionably one of her greatest academic achievements was to initiate tourism studies in Portugal in the 1960s, when tourism was still regarded by many academics as a subject not worth looking at. It is remarkable how in 1969, in full dictatorship, Carminda highlighted so clearly issues such as land speculation, unplanned growth and environmental damages in the context of tourism in the Algarve: "at times imprudent, maybe even forged in offices and without the basic knowledge of the unity and diversity of the province" (Cavaco, 1969, p. 217). Her ground-breaking spirit was also felt in tourism education with her timely courses on Tourism Geography in the 1970s. Her strong commitment to teaching and to undergraduate and postgraduate students inspired many to embrace tourism studies within Geography certainly, but also within the disciplines of Tourism, Sociology, Economics and Rural Studies. In the 1980s and 1990s she also played a vital role in introducing tourism to rural studies, exploring the diversity and multifunctionality of rural spaces in a changing Europe and Portugal.

For many decades now Carminda's pioneering work has accustomed us to read her long and dense texts and look for trends, insights and inspiration. Before we left her home on that winter day, Carminda showed us the contents of her latest project, a book (almost concluded) on "Tourism and the New Elites in Europe". In times when mobility and doing fieldwork is harsher for her, Carminda enthusiastically explained how this new book is built upon a meticulous analysis of local newspapers and real estate minutiae conducted online, with a special focus on France: the Côte D' Azur, Saint Tropez and Deauville. In a sense Carminda went full circle and returned to her "dear places" (C. Cavaco [Personal Interview, December 2015, Lisbon]), the old resorts in France and also Italy, that many considered in decline. As she recently wrote, 'the unsustainability of a destination has nothing to do with its natural conditions or the life-cycle ending, but with the rigidity and inadequacy of the project itself, an exclusively human and political error' (Cavaco, 2013, p. 191). Carminda confided to us that her present project is as daring as more than 40 years ago Gaetano Ferro considered her tourism work brave. Carminda Cavaco is an independent thinker, who freed from her academic duties can now think about tourism with pleasure and creativity.

ORCID

João Sarmento http://orcid.org/0000-0002-4770-2427
Ana Inácio http://orcid.org/0000-0002-5004-2634

References

Cavaco, C. (1969). Geografia e turismo no Algarve. Aspectos contemporâneos [Geography and tourism in the Algarve: Contemporary aspects]. *Finisterra, 4*, 216–272.

Cavaco, C. (1970). Geografia e turismo: exemplos, problemas e reflexões [Geography and tourism: Examples, problems and thoughts]. *Finisterra, 5*, 247–282.

Cavaco, C. (1974a). *Aspetti geografici del Turismo nella Riviera di Ponente (Da Finale a Laigueglia)* [Geographical aspects of tourism in the Ponente Riviera (from Finale to Laigueglia)], Publicazioni Dell' Instituto di Scienze Géographiche, 24(March). Genoa: Universitá di Genova.

Cavaco, C. (1974b). Monte Gordo: aglomerado piscatório e de veraneio (Primeira Parte) [Monte Gordo: Fishing and summer settlement (first part)]. *Finisterra, 9*, 75–99.

Cavaco, C. (1976a). *O Algarve Oriental: as vilas, o campo e o mar* [Eastern Algarve: Towns, countryside and the sea]. Faro: Gabinete de Planeamento da Região do Algarve.

Cavaco, C. (1976b). Monte Gordo: aglomerado piscatório e de veraneio (Segunda Parte) [Monte Gordo: Fishing and summer settlement (second part)]. *Finisterra, 9*, 245–300.

Cavaco, C. (1979a). *Turismo e demografia no Algarve* [Tourism and demography in the Algarve]. Lisbon: Center for Geographical Studies.

Cavaco, C. (1979b). *O turismo em Portugal: aspectos evolutivos e espaciais* [Tourism in Portugal: Dynamic and spatial aspects]. Lisbon: Center for Geographical Studies.

Cavaco, C. (1981). *A costa do Estoril: esboço geográfico* [Estoril Coast: A geographic outline]. Lisbon: Center for Geographical Studies.

Cavaco, C. (1992). *Portugal Rural: da tradição ao moderno* [Rural Portugal: From tradition to modernity]. Lisbon: Ministry for Agriculture.

Cavaco, C. (1993a). A place in the sun: Return migration and rural change in Portugal. In R. King (Ed.), *Mass migrations in Europe. The legacy and the future* (pp.174–191). London: Belhaven Press.

Cavaco, C. (1993b). Da Integração na PAC ao Turismo Cinegético [From the integration in CAP to hunting tourism]. *Inforgeo, 6*, 37–53.

Cavaco, C. (1995a). Turismo rural e desenvolvimento local [Rural tourism and local development]. In C. Cavaco (Ed.), *As regiões de fronteira – inovação e desenvolvimento na perspectiva do mercado único europeu* [Border regions – Innovation and development from a single European market perspective] (pp. 351–401). Lisbon: Center for Geographical Studies.

Cavaco, C. (1995b). Rural tourism: The creation of new touristic spaces. In A. Montanari & A. Williams (Eds.), *European tourism regions, spaces and restructuring. Restructuring in Europe* (pp. 127–149). Chichester: Wiley.

Cavaco, C. (1995c). Tourism in Portugal: Diversity, diffusion, and regional and local development. *Tijdschrift voor economische en sociale geografie, 86*, 64–71.

Cavaco, C. (1996). Turismo rural e desenvolvimento local [Rural tourism and local development]. In A. B. Rodrigues (Ed.), *Turismo e Geografia. Reflexões teóricas e enfoques regionais* (pp. 94–121). São Paulo: Hucitec.

Cavaco, C. (1997). Gaetano Ferro. *Finisterra, XXXII*, 99–102.

Cavaco, C. (1999a). Turismo rural e turismo de habitação em Portugal [Rural tourism and residential tourism in Portugal]. In C. Cavaco (Ed.), *Desenvolvimento Rural, Desafio e Utopia* [Rural development, challenges and utopias] (pp. 293–304). Lisbon: Center for Geographical Studies.

Cavaco, C. (1999b). Turismo rural nas políticas de desenvolvimento do turismo em Portugal [Rural tourism in the politics of tourism development in Portugal]. In C. Cavaco (Ed.), *Desenvolvimento Rural, Desafio e Utopia* (pp. 281–293). Lisbon: Center for Geographical Studies.

Cavaco, C. (2003a). Ambiente e usos do Território: reflexões incómodas [Environment and spatial uses: Troubled reflections]. In J. Portela & J. C. Caldas (Eds.), *Portugal Chão* (pp. 189–198). Oeiras: Celta Editora.

Cavaco, C. (2003b). Permanências e mudanças nas práticas e nos espaços turísticos [Permanencies and changes in practices and in tourism spaces]. In O. Simões & A. Cristóvão (Eds.), *TERN – Turismo em Espaços Rurais e Naturais* (pp. 25–38). Coimbra: Instituto Politécnico de Coimbra.

Cavaco, C. (2006). O turismo e as novas dinâmicas territoriais [Tourism and the new spatial dynamics]. In C. A. Medeiros (Ed.), *Geografia de Portugal* [Geography of Portugal] (Vol. III, pp. 367–427). Lisbon: Círculo de Leitores.

Cavaco, C. (2008). Turismo de saúde e bem-estar. Inovação das práticas, renovação dos lugares [Health and wellness tourism: Innovation in practices, renovation of places]. *Proceedings of the 1st Seminar Tourism and Spatial Planning* (pp. 19–64). Lisbon: Centre for Geographical Studies.

Cavaco, C. (2009). Turismo sénior: perfis e práticas [Senior tourism: Profiles and practices]. *Cogitur, Journal of Tourism Studies, 2*, 33–64.

Cavaco, C. (2010a). Tourisme, santé, wellness: une ressource importante pour les territoires [Tourism, health and wellness: An important resource for territories]. In S. Richoz, L.-M. Boulianne, & J. Ruegg (Eds.), *Santé et développement territorial. Enjeux et opportunités* [Helth and spatial development. Challenges and opportunities] (pp. 77–92). Lausane: Presses Polytechniques et Universitaires Romandes.

Cavaco, C. (2010b). Água doce: agricultura versus Lazeres e Turismo [Fresh water: Agriculture versus leisure and tourism]. In E. B. Henriques, J. Sarmento, & M. A. Lousada (Eds.), *Water and tourism: Resources management, planning and sustainability* (pp. 223–259). Lisbon: Centre for Geographical Studies.

Cavaco, C. (2013). Resiliências dos destinos turísticos das praias frias: do Canal da Mancha ao Golfo da Finlândia. In F. Cravidão & N. Santos (Eds.), *Turismo e Cultura. Destinos e Competitividade* [Tourism and culture: Destinations and competitiveness] (pp. 137–192). Coimbra: Universidade de Coimbra.

Cavaco, C. (in press). *Tourism and the new elites in Europe.*

Cavaco, C., & Fonseca, M. L. (2001). *Território e turismo no Brasil: uma introdução* [Territory and tourism in Brazil: An introduction]. Lisbon: Center for Geographical Studies.

Cavaco, C. Medeiros, C. L., & Lima, P. (2012). *As Terras e as Gentes do Cante* [The land and people of Cante]. Lisbon: IPI.

Daveau, S. (2012). Orlando Ribeiro (1991–1997). In H. Lorimer & C. W. J. Withers (Eds.), *Geographers – Biobibliographical studies* (Vol. 31, pp. 30–55). London: Bloomsbury.

Ferreira, C. (2004). *Portugal, Destino Turístico da População Idosa Europeia. Abordagem Geográfica do Turismo Sénior Internacional* [Portugal, tourism destination of elderly people in Europe: A geographical approach to international senior tourism]. PhD in Human Geography. Lisbon: University of Lisbon [Published in 2006 by Turismo de Portugal].

Inácio, A. (2008). *O enoturismo em Portugal: da "cultura" do vinho ao vinho como cultura: a oferta enoturística nacional e as suas implicações no desenvolvimento local e regional* [Wine tourism in Portugal: From the "culture" of wine to wine as culture: The national wine tourism offer and its implications in local and regional development] (Unpublished PhD thesis). Lisbon: University of Lisbon.

Inácio, A., & Cavaco, C. (2010). Enoturismo em Portugal: forma de desenvolvimento regional e afirmação cultural local [Winetourism in Portugal: Ways of regional development and assertion of local culture]. *Turismo & Desenvolvimento, 2,* 761–769.

Inácio, A., & Joaquim, G. (2008). A Sofisticação da Oferta Termal na Europa, and A Sofisticação da Oferta de Thalassoterapia na Europa [The sophistication of the thermal offer in Europe and the sophistication of the talassoteraphy offer in Europe]. In C. L. Medeiros & C. Cavaco (Eds.), *Turismo de Saúde e Bem-estar. Termas, Spas Termais e Thalassoterapia* (pp. 59–66; 66–70). Lisbon: UCP – Centro dos Estudos dos Povos e Culturas de Expressão Portuguesa.

Medeiros, C. A. (Ed.). (2006). *Geografia de Portugal* [Geography of Portugal] (Vol. 3). Lisbon: Círculo de Leitores.

Medeiros, C. L., & Cavaco, C. (Eds.). (2008). *Turismo de Saúde e Bem-Estar, Termas, SPAS Termais e Talassoterapia* [Health and wellness tourism, spas and thaassotherapies]. Lisbon: Universidade Católica Portuguesa.

Moreno, L. (2002). *Desenvolvimento local em meio rural – caminhos e caminhantes* [Local development in rural areas – Ways and 'way-makers'] (Unpublished PhD thesis). Lisbon: University of Lisbon.

Moreno, L. (2006). Carminda Cavaco – sentidos e contextos de uma singular vida académica e científica [Carminda Cavaco – Senses and contexts of a singular academic and scientific life]. In M. L. Fonseca (Eds.), *Desenvolvimento e Território. Espaços Rurais Pós-agrícolas e Novos Lugares de Turismo e Lazer* [Development and territory: Post-agricultural rural spaces and new places of tourism and leisure] (pp. 19–57). Lisbon: Centre for Geographical Studies.

Sarmento, J. (2008). Searching for cultural geography in portugal. *Social & Cultural Geography, 9,* 573–600.

Simões, J. M., & Cavaco, C. (2008). *A Água: Uma Geografia Sentimental* [Water: An emotional geography] (bilingual edition). Mirandela: Ed. João Azevedo Editor.

A portrait of Carson L. Jenkins

Roy C. Wood

Introduction

Metin Kozak's invitation to contribute to this series of profiles on eminent tourism scholars struck me as an intriguing proposition. Mulling the nature of the task, it quickly dawned on me how little we really know about people who we think we know well. As I write this, it has been my privilege to be acquainted with Carson L. Jenkins, Emeritus Professor of International Tourism at the University of Strathclyde, Glasgow, for exactly 30 years. For 17 of these years, until I left Strathclyde in 2001, he and I were colleagues and we have remained on good terms and in regular contact since. I know (a very limited) something of his immediate family but beyond this our relationship has not been one of especial intimacy. Professor Jenkins has kindly co-operated with the preparation of this article by answering a lot of (possibly impertinent) questions not covered by the information already known to me or supplied in his résumé/curriculum vitae. The final article is, however, "all my own work" and the responsibility for any error of fact, judgement or good taste is, accordingly, mine.

Early life, academic appointments, and career

Carson L. Jenkins – known to most of his intimates as Kit Jenkins – was the eldest of four children, two sons and two daughters, born into a South Wales coal mining family in 1940. The diminutive "Kit", normally the English contraction for the male name Christopher, was conferred in adulthood and references the nineteenth century American frontiersman Kit Carson.

The families of the coal mining industry which once dominated South Wales always faced very particular pressures and dangers. Although coal reserves were nationalized for reasons of war in 1942, the mining industry itself remained in (often rapacious) private hands until being taken into public ownership by the post-war Labour government led by Prime Minister Atlee. Throughout the 1940s and 1950s (even during war and the subsequent peacetime Conservative government of Churchill that followed Atlee), great social changes were wrought not least in the fields of public provision of health and education services. Kit Jenkins did not sit the selective examination that would have seen him, from ages 11 to 18, attend a "grammar school" and pursue a possibly easy route to the university entrance matriculation examinations that these schools specialized in. Instead he attended a so-called secondary modern school leaving at the age of 15 to work in a local factory and subsequently winning a scholarship to Bridgend Technical College and then Tonyrefail Grammar School. Unusually, he sat the necessary "A" (advanced) level examinations (required for entrance to university in England and Wales) as an external student while in employment.

By the late 1950s and early 1960s, Jenkins was able, like many British people of his – and subsequent – generations, to take advantage of a national higher education system that, though still essentially élitist, had opened up considerably to those from less privileged backgrounds. Being the first in his family to so benefit, he studied economics at the University of Hull in the English county of Yorkshire (still only the 14th university to be established – in 1954 – in England see http://www2.hull.ac.uk/theuniversity/his tory.aspx) graduating BSc (Econ) in 1964. He then moved to the recently created University of Strathclyde in Glasgow for his doctoral studies which focused on the economics and industrial relations systems of the shipbuilding industry, hitherto a mainstay of the local economy which (as we now know with the benefit of hindsight) was then well along the path of its long and painful decline. The beneficiary of a UK Social Science Research Council grant in 1966, Jenkins remained in the Economics Department at Strathclyde as a Research Fellow for two years, completing his doctorate and continuing this strand of work which eventuated in his first book co-authored with the distinguished Scottish economist and Strathclyde professor Sir Kenneth Alexander (Alexander & Jenkins, 1970).

Kit Jenkins' interest in tourism began with his next appointment as a Research Fellow in the Institute of Social and Economic Research (eastern Caribbean) at the University of the West Indies, Barbados, where he remained for three years from 1968 until 1971. His research here ranged over three main areas: (a) opportunities for, and obstacles to, the development of manufacturing industries in Barbados and the eastern Caribbean; (b) the socio-economic impacts of tourism on Barbados (inspired by the work of Professor G. V. Doxey, himself another noted early contributor to tourism studies, see Doxey, 1971); and (c) studies in labour supply with a particular focus on the hotel sector. It was in Barbados that Jenkins' particular focus on tourism in developing countries began to crystallize, a focus which rapidly became a passion.

In 1971, Jenkins returned to Glasgow's Strathclyde University but this time as a lecturer in tourism in the Scottish Hotel School (SHS), the only faculty member then with a doctorate. Established in 1944 as an independent institute on the model of the then world leaders in hotel management education, Cornell University (USA) and Lausanne Hotel School (Switzerland), the SHS was one of the several institutions that came together in 1964 to form the new university, and was a department of the Strathclyde Business School. The new institution began development of its campus centred on one of its antecedent institutions (the Royal College of Science and Technology), a few steps to the east of the city centre, but the SHS remained in its original premises – an old mansion, Ross Hall – in the south of the city until the early 1980s when it occupied the top floor of a refurbished publisher's building acquired by the university in Cathedral Street (Gee, 1994).

Strathclyde University's internal promotion system was competitive and applications for advancement were carefully scrutinized. Jenkins won promotion to senior lecturer in 1977 and the rest of his conventional academic career was to be spent in the SHS, 31 years in all, the last 13 of these, from 1989, holding a personal chair as Professor of International Tourism, (Emeritus Professor after his early retirement in 2002). He also holds or has held a number of visiting professorial appointments at the Shanghai Institute for Tourism, the University of Stirling (Scotland) Chengdu University, China, and Chiang Mai University, Thailand, and is a Fellow of the International Academy for the Study of Tourism.

Service at the University of Strathclyde

No account of Kit Jenkins' career would be complete without reference to the service he rendered The Scottish Hotel School at the University of Strathclyde being, from 1986–1995 Acting Head and then Head of Department (being succeeded by the present author). The years of his stewardship of the SHS (1986–1995) were among the most difficult in the School's history. Within Strathclyde, there were those who felt the provision of hospitality education inconsistent with the status aspirations of a university, and the future of the department was more or less constantly questioned during the period. Despite this institutional uncertainty, the School went from strength to strength during Jenkins' stewardship (it had to wait until 2009 before being finally closed by the University in what many viewed as an act of – unprotested – vandalism).

Jenkins' success as head of department was attributable to something akin to "big stick" ideology – the notion derived from President Theodore Roosevelt's comments on his own foreign policy style – "speak softly and carry a big stick". To this day quietly spoken (though with a good baritone singing voice) and always judicious in choosing how and when (and with what observations) to intervene in any debate, Jenkins networked effectively within the university and particularly the Business School to build confidence in the work of the department. His long association with the University from its early days helped with this as did the fact that he was a tourism specialist (tourism being viewed as a more "respectable" subject than hotel management – how little things change). His personal achievements also became the SHS's. With colleagues he was instrumental in establishing the taught MSc in Tourism programme, one of the first of its kind anywhere in the world, and he proved adept at attracting doctoral students – especially from developing countries – to the School. Upon his retirement in 2002, he had supervised around 45 doctoral students to successful completion and acted as external examiner to countless others at universities around the globe. Many of Jenkins' postgraduate students at master and doctoral levels have built distinguished careers of their own, including David Airey, Peter Dieke, Zainab Khalifa, Brian King, Richard Sharpley, Cevat Tosun, and Hanqin Zhang.

A further factor in Jenkins' success as head of department was the standing he enjoyed because of his reputation as a consultant with many international organizations and governments. One of Strathclyde's Principals (Principal is the preferred title for Vice-Chancellor in Scotland) embarked on a promotional tour of the Far East with a small entourage. Visiting a university in one of the region's more obscure areas, he was greeted by his opposite number, a former government tourism functionary, with the salutation "How very nice to meet you – now please tell me, how is my good friend Professor Jenkins?" Although this vignette has all the properties of a joke articulated by a stand-up comedian, it is all too believable because this writer has experienced a similar situation on at least two occasions!

Post-Strathclyde

After taking early retirement from Strathclyde, Jenkins accepted the position of Adviser on Economic Development and Tourism Promotion to the city of Al Ain (United Arab Emirates) a position he occupied for 15 months until March 2004. Throughout this period and subsequently, he remained active in various consultancy projects. In a curious instance of symmetry (or perhaps asymmetry) in June 2006, Jenkins succeeded this writer as Principal and Managing Director of IMI School of Hotel and Tourism Management in Luzern, Switzerland, a private educational institution on whose advisory board he had been a long-serving member. He stayed for two years in Switzerland and since then has once again returned to the role of a freelance consultant, most recently working on projects in Thailand and Vietnam.

Approach to tourism research and scholarship

Kit Jenkins is among that small group of academics (many, like him, still active) and more imaginative industry leaders who loosely coalesced into a global network of pioneers in tourism research and education. This network delivered, as it were, the tourism baby and saw it through its infancy. Tourism as an academic subject has matured and, as is the case with most instances of disciplinary development, has become increasingly fissiparous, or more kindly, diverse, in the range of its academic practitioners' interests. The early focus on tourism policy and management remains a key area but, increasingly, sociological approaches to tourism have arguably come to dominate the field, generating an increasing number of (sometimes quite obscure) specialisms and a retreat from the realist approaches of early research.

In terms of international tourism development, Jenkins was and remains a notable enthusiast for the "big picture", for holism and for a realist perspective on tourism. Furthermore, he sees tourism as a force for good, not least in the developing world. This is not to say that recognition of the less attractive and negative impacts of tourism is absent from his consciousness or his published work, but rather to assert that his perspective lacks any of the empty sentimentality that has infused much subsequent commentary on the downside(s) of tourism. Jenkins has never been aligned with any particular "school" or "tradition" in tourism. Indeed, he has maintained a healthy but respectful scepticism of the more obscurantist sociological schools of, and contributions to, tourism. The discipline of economics has remained the main driver of his academic work. By and large a Keynesian, Jenkins' approach to the study of tourism is predicated on how academic knowledge can be employed in the improvement of people's lives. A key element in this approach is commitment to the involvement of the public sector in tourism development in the interests of accountability. Jenkins is no Marxist, but his approach to tourism studies very much reflects the views of Marx expressed in the *Theses on Feuerbach* in which he writes both that "The dispute over the reality or non-reality of thinking that is isolated from practice is a purely scholastic question" and "The philosophers have only interpreted the world, in various ways; the point is to change it". This pragmatic realism is at the heart of Jenkins' work and is further reflected in his firm and oft expressed belief that the gap between tourism academics and tourism practitioners is too wide, and probably getting wider (Jenkins, 1999).

Public output

Kit Jenkins' total published oeuvre is not, by contemporary standards, quantitatively large (although sadly, there are all too many "full" professors appointed today with much less to their credit), numbering some 60 items including books, contributions to books, journal articles and conference papers, and invited addresses. One reason for this is Jenkins' long-standing aversion to excessive "piggybacking" on the work of his doctoral students. Another is his disinclination to publish for the sake of publishing. He has been, by his own admission, fortunate to operate for most of his career in a milieu that valued academic publishing for its content rather than its quantity, a culture that in the UK at least has been infected by the "publish or perish" culture that has spread, virus like, from the USA. I well remember as a young academic his frequent imprecations on a system that insisted (and continues to insist) on quantity of output irrespective of whether authors had anything new, valuable, or interesting to say. Notwithstanding these views, Jenkins has nevertheless acted for most of his career as an exceptionally sensitive and thorough referee for countless journal article submissions and has freely lent his experience as a resource editor for *Annals of Tourism Research*; a member of the editorial advisory board of *Tourism Economics* and *Anatolia*; and a member of the editorial board of *Tourism Recreation Research*.

Most of Jenkins' initial tourism publications are, in terms of their subject matter, among the earliest of their kind, dealing with tourism policies in developing countries; the effects of the scale on tourism development projects in developing countries; the role of incentives in tourism projects in developing countries; and government intervention in tourism development in developing countries (Jenkins, 1980a, 1980b, 1982a, 1982b; Jenkins & Henry, 1982). He has consistently returned to these and related themes in tourism planning, policy, and human resources on numerous later public and private occasions (Jenkins, 1994, 2000a, 2000b; 2006, 2007; Jenkins & Singh, 2009; Liu & Jenkins, 1996; Tosun & Jenkins, 1996, 1998, Zhang, King, & Jenkins, 2002).

Among the highlights of Jenkins' publications are his two texts co-authored with Leonard J. Lickorish with whom he enjoyed a profitable collaborative relationship (Lickorish, Jefferson, Bodlender, & Jenkins, 1991; Lickorish & Jenkins, 1997). Leonard Lickorish (1921–2002) remains a little known and unsung hero of British and European tourism. After a flying career in the RAF during the Second World War, he served with what became the British Tourist Authority for most of the rest of his life, latterly as that organization's Director-General. With a particular interest in tourism statistics, he was heavily involved in European-wide tourism institutions for most of his career, co-authoring of one of the earliest "serious" UK books on tourism (Lickorish & Kershaw, 1958; see also https://groups.google.com/forum/#!topic/alt.obituaries/qUkvGsI2KFs and http://www.travel weekly.co.uk/articles/2000/04/18/6786/hall-of-fame-leonard-lickorish. html). Lickorish, like Jenkins, was softly spoken and considered in his views but was very much an establishment insider having been awarded one of the UK's arcane honours – albeit a relatively senior one – towards the end of his career (he was created CBE, Commander of the Order of the British Empire). Their 1997 *Introduction to Tourism* became a best seller twice over, first in English then in Spanish (as *Una Introduccion al Turismo*, Lickorish & Jenkins, 2000).

Private output

Kit Jenkins was one of the earliest contributors to the literature on tourism education with an article in the first volume of the journal *Tourism Management* in which he addressed the educational needs of tourism policy-makers in developing countries (Jenkins, 1980b). A commitment to education as an enabling (in more contemporary language, "empowering") force is a characteristic of Jenkins' "private" output, generated as an adviser, trainer, and consultant, which to date numbers some 70 reports and training course manuals pertaining to 80 developing countries. Among the (arguably) more recherché locations in which he has worked is the gross national happiness measuring Bhutan, landlocked Lesotho in southern Africa, and Palau (Micronesia). Sadly, much of this output, for reasons of confidentiality, is not in the public domain. Many of Jenkins' projects have been facilitated by transnational bodies such as the United Nations Development Programme; the United Nations World Tourism Organization; the United Nations Educational, Scientific and Cultural Organization; the European Union; and the World Bank. In addition, he has participated in projects promoted by the British Council and China

National Tourism Administration. His work for these and other organizations and governments have, in addition to educational issues, covered tourism policy formulation; tourism planning; institutional reform; human resources development: and, perhaps more curiously, legal frameworks for tourism. In the case of this last, Jenkins has developed expertise in the writing of tourism legislation, and his efforts in this area remain on the statute books of such countries as Zambia, Uganda, the Gambia, Namibia, Romania, Suriname, and Vietnam (C. L. Jenkins, personal communication, 3 September 2013).

Conclusion

In speaking with those who have known Kit Jenkins for some time, two descriptors of the man recur with great frequency – "discreet" and "modest". Both seem highly appropriate: in terms of discretion, it requires many years of working with Kit Jenkins to realize just how extensive has become his network of international connections, particularly at the higher levels of government and quasi-government and private organizations involved with tourism. His modesty manifests itself in a complete lack of boastfulness and an absence of the empty competitiveness that characterizes much academic life. Even his private interests are unexceptional – a love of rugby football, cats, and – in perhaps the only nod to mild academic eccentricity – submarines. Those who have worked particularly closely with him will also know that he is a considerable raconteur.

The overall impact a person has on their field of study is difficult to assess, save in the cases of those few individuals who for whatever reasons are able to transcend their discipline and become more widely known. Kit Jenkins and his contemporaries have seen a subject develop from a very minor intellectual curiosity to a full-blown field of study. When he was appointed to Strathclyde in 1971, there were no more than one or two handfuls of similar appointees in the field in the UK, and not many more worldwide. As non-economic social science perspectives – and in particular sociological approaches – have come to dominate in influence within tourism studies, then there has been a (sadly characteristic) withdrawal from the pragmatic realism that drove the management and development-oriented research agenda of the field's early days in favour of a large measure of self-indulgent and obtuse output of little apparent intrinsic or extrinsic value. There are still new generations of tourism scholars interested in the role and applications of tourism in the "real world", including the systematic and sustained analysis of tourism in developing countries, but they are, numerically, in the minority. On the one hand, this may seem like one aspect of the normal and healthy evolution of a field of study, but it can also be interpreted as being overly self-indulgent and first world centric.

Kit Jenkins remains active as an advisor, consultant, and educator, and it is, perhaps, through his professional networks in the field of development studies that his influence has been, and continues to be, at its greatest. If one requires an entrée into the world of tourism (and indeed hospitality) anywhere in the world, chances are that Jenkins will be able to arrange an introduction to some suitably influential figure. All this said, there is little doubt that in his academic output – and particularly his early output – he also succeeded in distilling with simple clarity the central issues facing tourism in developing countries, and very few of these have changed in importance over the years, it is almost literally a case of *nihil sub sole novum*. The material impacts of tourism – both positive and negative – on global society represent a tangible challenge for stewardship of the planet. Any retreat into forms of analysis that favour comfortable conceptual abstraction over a central concern with the impact of tourism on people and the environment is unlikely to have much long-term utility. With discretion, modesty, and enthusiasm, Kit Jenkins has, for nearly five decades, bridged the gap between theory and practice in the field of tourism in developing countries. That he continues to be held in high regard, with his skills and services still in demand, is testimony to the virtues of a model of academic engagement with the wider world that is fast disappearing.

References

Alexander, K. J. W., & Jenkins, C. L. (1970). *Fairfields: A study of industrial change*. London: Allen Lane, The Penguin Press.

Doxey, G. V. (Ed.). (1971). *The tourist industry in Barbados: A socio-economic assessment*. Toronto: Dukane Press.

Gee, D. A. C. (1994). The Scottish hotel school – The first fifty years. In A. V. Seaton, C. L. Jenkins, R. C. Wood, P. U. C. Dieke, M. M. Bennett, L. R. MacLellan, & R. Smith (Eds.), *Tourism: The state of the art* (pp. xvi–xxiii). Chichester: Wiley.

Jenkins, C. L. (1980a). Tourism policies in developing countries: A critique. *Tourism Management, 1*, 22–29.

Jenkins, C. L. (1980b). Education for tourism policy-makers in developing countries. *Tourism Management, 1*, 238–242.

Jenkins, C. L. (1982a). The effect of scale on tourism projects in developing countries. *Annals of Tourism Research, 9*, 229–249.

Jenkins, C. L. (1982b). The use of investment incentives for tourism projects in developing countries. *Tourism Management, 3*, 91–97.

Jenkins, C. L. (1994). Tourism in developing countries: The privatisation issue. In A. V. Seaton, C. L. Jenkins, R. C. Wood, P. U. C. Dieke, M. M. Bennett, L. R. MacLellan, & R. Smith (Eds.), *Tourism: The state of the art* (pp. 3–9). Chichester: Wiley.

Jenkins, C. L. (1999). Tourism academics and tourism practitioners – Bridging the great divide. In D. G. Pearce & R. W. Butler (Eds.), *Contemporary issues in tourism development* (pp. 52–64). London: Routledge.

Jenkins, C. L. (2000a). Tourism policy formulation in the southern African region. In P. U. C. Dieke (Ed.), *The political economy of tourism development in Africa* (pp. 62–74). New York, NY: Cognizant Communications Corporation.

Jenkins, C. L. (2000b). The development of tourism in Namibia. In P. U. C. Dieke (Ed.), *The political economy of tourism development in Africa* (pp. 113–128). New York, NY: Cognizant Communications Corporation.

Jenkins, C. L. (2006). An area of darkness? Tourism in the third world revisited. *Tourism Recreation Research, 31*, 87–91.

Jenkins, C. L. (2007, August). *How to recruit and retain talent*. New Delhi: Keynote address to the Indian Hotel Association Annual Conclave.

Jenkins, C. L., & Henry, B. (1982). Government intervention in tourism in developing countries. *Annals of Tourism Research, 9*, 499–521.

Jenkins, C. L., & Singh, S. (Eds.). (2009). Project planning and development in tourism. *Tourism Recreation Research, 34*, 3 (Special issue).

Lickorish, L. J., & Kershaw, A. G. (1958). *The travel trade*. London: Practical Press.

Lickorish, L. J., & Jenkins, C. L. (1997). *Introduction to tourism*. Oxford: Butterworth Heinemann.

Lickorish, L. J., & Jenkins, C. L. (2000). *Una introduccion al turismo*. Madrid: Editorial Sintesis.

Lickorish, L. J., Jefferson, A., Bodlender, J., & Jenkins, C. L. (1991). *Developing tourism destinations: Policies and perspectives*. London: Longman.

Liu, Z. H., & Jenkins, C. L. (1996). Country size and tourism development: A cross-nation analysis. In B. Briguglio, B. H. Archer, J. Archer, & G. Wall (Eds.), *Sustainable tourism in islands and small states: Issues and policies* (pp. 90–117). London: Frances Pinter.

Tosun, C., & Jenkins, C. L. (1996). Regional planning approaches to tourism development: The case of Turkey. *Tourism Management, 17*, 519–531.

Tosun, C., & Jenkins, C. L. (1998). The evolution of tourism planning in third world countries: A critique. *Progress in Tourism and Hospitality Research, 4*, 101–114.

Zhang, Q. H., King, C., & Jenkins, C. L. (2002). Tourism policy implementation in Mainland China: An enterprise perspective. *International Journal of Contemporary Hospitality Management, 14*, 38–42.

Cathy H.C. Hsu: a role model

Xiang (Robert) Li

Introduction

For me, to craft a portrait of Dr. Cathy H. C. Hsu, a leader in our field, is no small task. Cathy is a Chair Professor at The Hong Kong Polytechnic University's (PolyU) School of Hotel and Tourism Management and has been the editor-in-chief of the *Journal of Teaching in Travel & Tourism* for the past 16 years. Included in her extensive list of accolades are the following: she is a Fellow of the International Academy for the Study of Tourism (the youngest academic ever to be elected to the organization); a recipient of John Wiley & Sons Lifetime Research Achievement Award and Michael D. Olsen Research Achievement Award; and has served as the editor, co-editor, and/or editorial board member of over 10 academic journals. Cathy is unfailingly elegant, composed, and possesses a refreshing tenacity that sets her apart as a role model and inspiration for many.

I have had the pleasure of knowing Cathy for over a decade, having first met her as a fledgling doctoral student. We began working together in 2010 when Cathy, Dr. Laura Lawton of Griffith University, and I established a cross-continental collaboration examining the perceived impacts of the 2010 Shanghai World Expo (Li, Hsu, & Lawton, 2015). My subsequent sabbatical visit to PolyU offered me the chance to learn more from her in person.

Career take off: a destined path

English author Horace Walpole, who coined the term *serendipity*, noted that heroes in fairytales have a way of "always making discoveries, by accidents and sagacity, of things which they were not in quest of." Many leading scholars both in and outside our field have paved their career paths with healthy doses of serendipity and coincidence; Cathy is no exception. Tourism and hospitality were clearly not part of her initial career plan: upon graduating from junior high school, she intended to enter a normal college (i.e. teachers' college) in Taiwan to study to become a teacher. Thanks to a low physical education score, however, she was denied admission into the programme. While Taiwan undoubtedly missed out on a gifted teacher, our field would gain an accomplished leader. Decades later, Cathy's career came full circle as she became a chair professor, supervising students at all levels of higher education, and started editing a journal specializing in tourism and hospitality education. Nevertheless, one must connect the dots to discover how Cathy grew into her professional reputation despite life's myriad temptations, distractions, and setbacks.

In 1962, Cathy was born into a large military family in Taiwan. She was the youngest of the clan, with her closest sister eight years her senior. Cathy's home was loving, secure, and religious, although her parents were not well off. Yet even with their financial challenges, Cathy's parents prioritized experiences for their children. Her mother and father would each ride a bicycle and carry their six kids to the beach, trails, campsites, and elsewhere. Cathy soon came to love the adventure that accompanied "[going] somewhere because that's where the fond memories came from" (personal communication, 18 September, 2015).

Because Cathy did not do well on her high school entrance exams and was denied acceptance into top public senior high schools, her parents borrowed money to send her to an all-girls Catholic boarding school. Their decision would change her life. Cathy's classmates came from fairly affluent families and had cultivated a taste for the finer things. Cathy likely hailed from the most modest background of all but felt blessed to be part of this community. She strove to excel academically in order to justify her parents' investment. Sure enough, she graduated at the top of her class and became the first member of her family to attend university (Fu-Jen University, a Catholic institution) and earn a degree. Unfortunately, Cathy's performance on the college entrance exam was compromised by an unexpected health situation. Because she was in the natural science track, she was admitted to the Home Economics department, which required the lowest minimum score of all science-related majors at the time.

Fu-Jen's Home Economics programme offered three different concentrations: quantity food preparation, child development, and family studies. Cathy entered the quantity food management track and received basic training in food preparation and food service management. The university began offering minors around the same time, so Cathy decided to minor in business administration. Coursework in marketing, finance, and accounting complemented her undergraduate training in food service and ultimately came to define her academic career. Looking back, Cathy believes she was destined to attend a Catholic university and study something related to food and hospitality.

Throughout college, Cathy worked part-time during the academic year and full-time over school breaks. Her primary responsibilities were related to food and beverage (F&B). For example, she was the head cook for a kids' summer camp during her freshman and sophomore summers. She oversaw every operational aspect from menu planning, ordering, purchasing, cooking, and serving to cleaning. She also learned to appreciate the varied nature of F&B work. During her junior year, Cathy joined the banquet and catering teams at Taipei's Hilton Hotel before working in her senior year with the opening team of the first McDonald's restaurant in Taiwan. While there, she completed McDonald's diverse training programmes.

Upon completion of her Bachelor's degree (1984), McDonald's offered Cathy the chance to become a management trainee. During her brief tenure in the programme, she informed her manager that she would like to study for her Master's in the U.S. Knowing the manager himself earned an MBA in America, Cathy assumed he would support her plan. To her surprise, he simply dismissed her ambitions and assured her, "Oh, no, you don't need a Master's degree, and you don't need to go overseas. You can be a store manager in six months." Not one to be deterred, her manager's apathy only further motivated Cathy to move to the U.S. in pursuit of her dreams.

In 1984, Cathy entered Iowa State University's Master's programme in hotel, restaurant, and institution management. She intended to finish her studies in one year and then return to McDonald's. She even addressed consumer behaviour-related issues in the fast-food industry for her final research project. Once her programme of study and project were complete, however, Cathy's major professor encouraged her to take a few doctoral-level classes while working part-time in food service in case she chose to continue on for her Ph.D. If not, her professor reasoned, Cathy could always return to Taiwan and work for McDonald's as she had originally planned. Cathy knew from past experience never to turn down a new opportunity. She enrolled in a few select doctoral courses at her major professor's behest, and the rest is history.

Iowa State did not offer a doctoral program focusing exclusively on hospitality management at the time, which meant Cathy would need to pursue a dual concentration. After much consideration, she settled on Home Economics Education, given her undergraduate background in the field. Her hospitality studies were enriched by classwork related to pedagogy, higher education, administration, programme evaluation, and curriculum design. Serendipitously, this coursework effectively prepared her for an editorial position with the *Journal of Teaching in Travel & Tourism*. Looking back, Cathy conceded that,

> Everything happened like somebody was planning it for me, but I wasn't the one planning it so again, I feel lucky. It just happened that I had the opportunity to do different things at the right time and then opportunities opened up for me. (personal communication, 18 September, 2015)

Generation T: a pioneer

In 1989, Cathy graduated from Iowa State with her Ph.D. in Home Economics Education and Hotel, Restaurant, and Institution Management. Cathy was one of the first so-called "Generation T" scholars to specialize in hospitality. A few earlier tourism scholars might also belong to Generation T, namely those who studied hotel, restaurant, or tourism management as their doctoral concentration without receiving their doctorate in a specific foundational discipline. As part of the seminal cohort of Generation T scholars, Cathy demonstrated precisely how her generation could make value-added contributions to the field by acquiring multidisciplinary training and appreciating the holistic context of tourism and hospitality.

Cathy's exemplary academic record and position as one of the first hospitality-focused Ph.D. graduates garnered her a wide array of job offers. In the end, she chose to remain at her alma mater, due in part to familial matters. In an effort to satisfy a relatively vague job description to conduct "non-F&B research" and to avoid overlap with former professors and current colleagues, Cathy took the initiative to explore topics that were rarely researched. Her findings gradually took her away from F&B in favour of hotel, gaming, and tourism studies. Such diversity has become a trademark of Cathy's research career: rather than limiting herself to a handful of narrowly defined specialties, she embraces the new directions that follow from applied research. Indeed, many of her projects have been inspired by practical problems.

During her tenure at Iowa, Cathy worked with the university's extension services, which received periodic research inquiries from the field. For instance, Iowa was the first state in the U.S. to legalize riverboat gambling. One day, Cathy received a call from a local tavern in a small town on the Mississippi River, asking if she could come to assess the extent to which riverboat casinos impacted residential life and businesses. This question inspired her to examine the legitimacy of casinos as a tourism development tool and gaming's impact on residents' quality of life, local businesses, and community at large (Chen & Hsu, 2001; Hsu, 1998, 1999, 2000; Hsu & Gu, 2010). Later on, she took a more liberal approach to the effects of tourism (Huang & Hsu, 2005; Li et al., 2015) and started to look beyond residents' attitudes specifically (Hsu, Li, & Chen, 2016).

In 2001, Cathy moved to Hong Kong after a short appointment at Kansas State University. Of immediate interest to her was the emerging market for Chinese outbound tourism. In the West, China's market is largely shrouded in myth and mystery. Understanding Chinese tourists' preferences, perceptions, and behaviour can provide important insight into the market as a whole in order to better serve Chinese consumers. Hong Kong's geographic and cultural proximity to Mainland China facilitated her research focused on Chinese tourists (Fan & Hsu, 2014; Hsu, Kang, & Lam, 2006; Hsu & Song, 2012), which has recently expanded to include cross-cultural and acculturation studies as a means of bridging Eastern and Western perspectives on tourism services and similar topics (Hsu & Huang, 2016; Weber, Hsu, & Sparks, 2014).

In most cases, Cathy has chosen to examine such phenomena from a marketing perspective, as she has always been interested in the role of marketing in the hospitality field. Hence, most of her work addresses branding, service quality, and consumer behaviour. But as noted earlier, Cathy does not wish to be constrained by artificial disciplinary boundaries; instead, she takes a multidisciplinary and/or interdisciplinary approach in an effort to elevate practical problems to meaningful, intellectual inquiry (see Figure 1 for a visual depiction of Cathy's research trajectory). In doing so, she remains a strong advocate of providing solid theoretical foundation to empirical research. For instance, she and her colleagues are among the first introducing the Theory of Planned Behavior to the field of tourism (Lam & Hsu, 2004, 2006; Oh & Hsu, 2001), which paved the way for a line of tourist behaviour research.

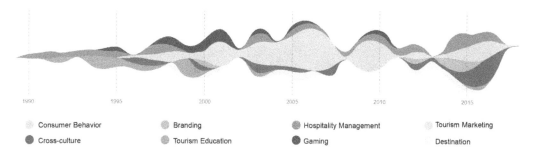

⬤ Consumer Behavior	⬤ Branding	⬤ Hospitality Management	⬤ Tourism Marketing
⬤ Cross-culture	⬤ Tourism Education	⬤ Gaming	Destination

Figure 1. Research trajectory.
Notes: This figure was modelled after charts found at https://cn.aminer.org/. It is a rough illustration of Cathy's research trajectory based on 108 refereed journal articles published between 1990 and 2016. The eight subject domains were extracted from Cathy's ResearchGate homepage, and each article was then assessed arbitrarily to fit within said domains (one article may fall into several domains). The height represents the frequency of a subject domain in a certain year; different colours represent different key words.

A role model

As one of the first female chair professors in our field, Cathy's accomplishments and personal story have been truly inspiring to today's generation of tourism and hospitality scholars. Cathy has established a global collaborative network over the years (see Figure 2) and influenced many collaborators, mentees, and colleagues through her passion, integrity, and uncompromising pursuit of excellence. Moreover, in her various roles as editor, organization president, academic administrator, and others, she pioneered this field of study and set a precedent for subsequent scholars thanks to her leadership, vision, and charisma.

Cathy's innovative spirit is not lost on those who have had the honour of working with her. Dr. Karin Weber, a frequent collaborator and colleague at PolyU, shared the following:

> I first met Cathy in the mid-1990s at various conferences in the US, before we both joined SHTM in 2001. At that time I was only aware of her excellent reputation as a scholar. Over the past 15 years working in the same school, I had ample opportunity to witness and appreciate her wide-ranging talents in and dedication to research, teaching, and providing service to our School and the academic community. Thus, it is not surprising that she has earned the admiration and respect of colleagues in the School and the academic world at large.
>
> In terms of research, I've worked with Cathy on several major research projects on the effect of acculturation in the service context where her insightful suggestions and constructive feedback were invaluable and where, despite her many commitments that often leave her with little personal time, she did not once fail to come back with very thorough and timely advice. Over the years, numerous postgraduate students have also benefited from her ready willingness to generously give her time and to impart sound research approaches and strong research ethics. I've also had the privilege to work with her for several years on the Board of ISTTE when she was the society's president, witnessing how she envisioned and then implemented numerous initiatives to elevate the society's international standing, and in the process bring diverse opinions and personalities of board members together. Despite her impressive accomplishments, Cathy is always very humble and modest. She is also easily approachable and actually has a good sense of humor.

In addition to her laudable research, teaching – Cathy's first career-related love – has remained close to her heart. In the classroom, Cathy emphasizes for her students the importance of rigorous research methodology. To her, taking the time to do the right thing throughout the research process is of paramount importance. She holds her students to the highest standards and expects quality output. As such, some of her former graduates have gone on to become world-renowned scholars. Dr. Songshan (Sam) Huang, a former doctoral student, is now a research professor at Edith Cowan University and offered the following praise:

> … I learnt a lot from Cathy when I was her student. Even after my graduation, we keep our collaboration until now. To me, Cathy is a supervisor, friend, and life mentor. On the academic research side, she is meticulous, thoughtful, and sticks to research integrity. She is hardworking, of course. She never delays things and is always

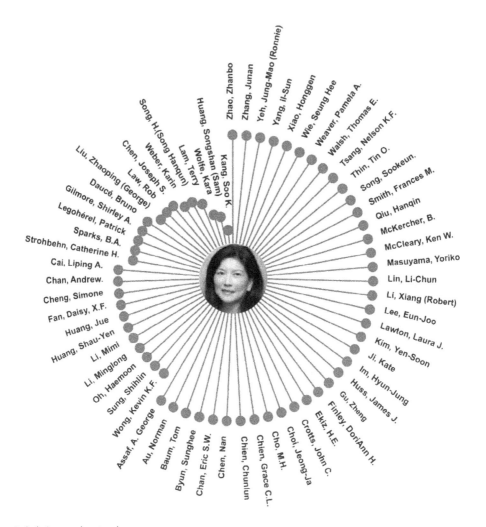

Figure 2. Cathy's research network.
Notes: This figure is modelled after charts found at https://cn.aminer.org/. It is based on the frequency of co-authorship. Each radius represents the "closeness" of academic collaboration between Cathy and her colleagues (Radius=ln(1/SumFrequency, and evenly divide the circles).

very organized. She definitely is among a small number of female academic leaders in our field. I think she is an educator as well. She contributes a lot to the teaching practices and quality curriculum systems in the field.

In personality, Cathy is a bit quiet. But she is a great listener and a silent thinker. She is not talkative as you may also see, but she expresses things precisely and is always liked and respected by people around her. I am thankful that I had her as my PhD supervisor and I can still have her as my key research collaborator …

Dr. Minglong Li, a recent graduate, added:

… Whenever I do a study, [Cathy] asks questions to guide me to think about the theoretical foundations and contributions and requires me to provide [a] detailed research process and report the research findings in a professional way. When the results of a study were not satisfactory, she suggested collect[ing] more data and [doing] cross validation … Because of this, I have confidence in her research, even though sometimes surprising conclusions may be reached.

Across the world, many co-workers and students have echoed these sentiments. Like many other successful mentors who have inspired colleagues to be their best, Cathy possesses genuine respect and deep empathy for others and enjoys leaving a positive impact on people's lives.

Conclusion

As a Gemini, Cathy is humble yet ambitious, amiable yet decisive, reserved yet witty. Having lived in both the East and West and developed a deep appreciation for each culture, she personifies the highly sought-after academic leaders and role models in today's increasingly globalized, complex world. I would be remiss to try to encapsulate Cathy's contributions to our field in a few words. Instead, I would like to close this short tribute with an eloquent quote from Cathy's former colleague Dr. Haemoon Oh, who is now Dean of the University of South Carolina's College of Hospitality, Retail, and Sport Management:

> Cathy has made a sustained contribution to and impact on the hospitality and tourism discipline. A countless number of students and educators like us have benefited from her lectures, books, and many other valuable materials she has shared. Her lifetime-devoted research, which has won every major research award in the field, has inspired us all, yet it has not lost its vibrant run. Through her vivid engagement in professional as well as administrative services in addition to research and education, Cathy remains one of the most influential educators, researchers, mentors, colleagues, and friends. We are privileged to have her in our discipline and celebrate her accomplishments that are irreplaceable.

Acknowledgement

The author gratefully acknowledges Ms. Zeya He for her assistance in preparing the two figures.

Disclosure statement

No potential conflict of interest was reported by the author.

References

Chen, J. S., & Hsu, C. H. C. (2001). Developing and validating a riverboat gaming impact scale. *Annals of Tourism Research, 28*, 459–476.

Fan, D. X. F., & Hsu, C. H. C. (2014). Potential Mainland Chinese cruise travelers' expectations, motivations, and intentions. *Journal of Travel and Tourism Marketing, 31*, 522–535.

Hsu, C. H. C. (1998). Impacts of riverboat gaming on community quality. *Journal of Hospitality and Tourism Research, 22*, 323–337.

Hsu, C. H. C. (Ed.). (1999). *Legalized casino gaming in the United States: The economic and social impact.* New York, NY: The Haworth Hospitality Press.

Hsu, C. H. C. (2000). Residents' support for legalized gaming and perceived impacts of riverboat casinos: Changes in five years. *Journal of Travel Research, 38*, 390–395.

Hsu, C. H. C., & Gu, Z. (2010). Ride on the gaming boom: How can Hong Kong, Macau and Zhuhai join hands to develop tourism in the region? *Asia Pacific Journal of Tourism Research, 15*, 57–77.

Hsu, C. H. C., & Huang, S. S. (2016). Reconfiguring Chinese cultural values and their tourism implications. *Tourism Management, 54*, 230–242.

Hsu, C. H. C., Kang, S. K., & Lam, T. (2006). Reference group influences among Chinese travelers. *Journal of Travel Research, 44*, 474–484.

Hsu, C. H. C., Li, X., & Chen, N. (2016). *From resident attitude to resident sentiment analysis: Exploring new conceptual directions.* Paper presented at the The 2nd Global Tourism & Hospitality Conference, Hong Kong.

Hsu, C. H. C., & Song, H. (2012). Projected images of major Chinese outbound destinations. *Asia Pacific Journal of Tourism Research, 17*, 577–593.

Huang, S., & Hsu, C. H. C. (2005). Mainland Chinese residents' perceptions and motivations of visiting Hong Kong: Evidence from focus group interviews. *Asia Pacific Journal of Tourism Research, 10*, 191–205.

Lam, T., & Hsu, C. H. C. (2004). Theory of planned behavior: Potential travelers from China. *Journal of Hospitality and Tourism Research, 28*, 463–482.

Lam, T., & Hsu, C. H. C. (2006). Predicting behavioral intention of choosing a travel destination. *Tourism Management, 27*, 589–599.

Li, X., Hsu, C. H. C., & Lawton, L. (2015). Understanding residents' perception changes toward a mega-event through a dual-theory lens. *Journal of Travel Research, 54*, 396–410.

Oh, H., & Hsu, C. H. C. (2001). Volitional degrees of gambling behaviors. *Annals of Tourism Research, 28*, 618–637.

Weber, K., Hsu, C. H. C., & Sparks, B. A. (2014). Consumer responses to service failure: The influence of acculturation. *Cornell Hospitality Quarterly, 55*, 300–313.

Charles R. (Chuck) Goeldner: a profile of service and contribution to the tourism research community

Richard R. Perdue

Academic background

It is my honour and privilege to have been asked to write this profile of Charles R. (Chuck) Goeldner. Over the past 30 years, Chuck has fundamentally altered and helped shape my career, creating for me untold opportunities and experiences. He has done the same for countless others. The following is both an attempt to profile his many contributions to tourism research and a small effort to say "Thank You!" to my friend and mentor.

As with most academic profiles, I could use the following space to talk about the Chuck's service to our field. Table 1 lists just a few of the professional service responsibilities he accepted and continues to accept. While Chuck is perhaps best known as the founding editor of the *Journal of Travel Research* (JTR), Table 2 provides a list of other journal editorial, publisher, and contributor contributions he has made to our scholarship. Combined, these two tables reflect a career of dedicated service and contribution; suffice it to say, it is hard to imagine another tourism academic who has given so freely, broadly, and willingly of his time to our benefit. I could also use this space to talk about the diversity of accolades, recognitions, and honours bestowed on him by both the tourism academic field and the tourism industry. Table 3 provides a bit of those data. Still, the range and diversity of honours inadequately reflect his impact on our field. Finally, I could talk facts; how this Iowa farm boy completed his BA, MA, and PhD at the University of Iowa, served the US Army as a training officer in Germany, served as a Marketing Professor and Business Research Center Director at California State University, Northridge, for eight years, then joined the Marketing faculty in the Leeds School of Business at the University of Colorado (CU), Boulder, where, over the years, he served as a Professor, Journal Editor and Publisher, Chair of the Marketing Division, Director of the Business Research Division, Associate Dean for Undergraduate Programs, Associate Dean for Graduate Programs, and Executive Assistant to the Dean and where today he continues to serve as a Professor Emeritus. I could even talk about the hundreds of articles and reports he published over the years and, of course, THE BOOK. For as long as I have known Chuck, he has been working on THE BOOK and its 12th, soon to be 13th, editions.

None of these data points talk about the essence of Chuck and his many contributions to our field; none would be a full and complete profile. Following are six short "stories" which I hope will help do that. In truth, they are not about his contributions, but rather about his character, which is, as it is for each of us, the foundation of his contributions and the best measure of his true impact on each of us and on our field.

Table 1. Charles R. Goeldner: professional service appointments and elected roles.

Chairman of the Board, Travel and Tourism Research Association
President, Travel and Tourism Research Association
First Vice President, Travel and Tourism Research Association
Second Vice President, Travel and Tourism Research Association
Board of Directors of the International Society of Travel and Tourism Educators
Board of Directors, Travel Industry Association of America
Board of Directors, Travel and Tourism Research Association
Board of Directors, National Tour Association Foundation
Board of Directors, Association for University Business and Economic Research
Board of Directors, Society of Travel and Tourism Educators
Board of Directors, Western Marketing Educators Association
World Travel and Tourism Council Taxation Policy Taskforce
Co-Chair, Travel, Tourism and Hospitality Special Interest Group, American Marketing
Association,
Treasurer, International Academy for the Study of Tourism
Secretary, US Travel Data Center
Trustee, United States Travel Data Center
National Tour Foundation's Research Advisory Council
Academic Council, Institute of Certified Travel Agents
President, Mountain States Chapter of the Travel and Tourism Research Association
President, Association of Directors of Doctoral Programs in Business
Vice President, Western Council for Travel Research
Advisor and Reviewer, President's Commission on Americans Outdoors
President, Association for University Business and Economic Research
Vice President, Association for University Business and Economic Research
Secretary-Treasurer, Association for University Business and Economic Research

Table 2. Charles R. Goeldner: journal and research editorial service appointments.

Founder and Editor, *Journal of Travel Research*
Editor, *Colorado Business Review*
Resource Editor, *Annals of Tourism Research*
Editorial Board, *Journal of Travel and Tourism Marketing*
Editorial Board, *Journal of Sustainable Tourism*
Editorial Board, *Tourism Economics*
Editorial Board, *Tourism Analysis*
Editorial Board, *Turizam*
Editorial Advisory Board, *Anatolia*
Editorial Advisory Board, *World Travel and Tourism Review*
Editorial Advisory Board, *The Successful Hotel Marketer*
Editorial Policy Board, *Leisure Sciences*
Charter Advisory Board, *Journal of International Hospitality Leisure and Tourism Management*
International Editorial Advisory Board, *Issues in Tourism*
Publications Council, CHRIE
Projects and Research Committee, CHRIE
Permanent Collaborator, *The Tourist Review*
Advisory Editor, *Tourism Recreation Research,* Centre for Tourism Research, Lucknow, India
Panel of Experts, *Thomas Cook Business Traveler*
Publisher, *Journal of Marketing Education*
Publisher, *Journal of Macromarketing*

Table 3.   Charles R. Goeldner: awards and recognitions.

World Conference for Graduate Research in Tourism, Hospitality and Leisure designated its best paper award as the "Charles R. Goeldner Recognition Award"
The International Society of Travel and Tourism Educators Martin Opperman Memorial Award for Lifetime Contribution to Tourism Education
Travel and Research Association designated its annual *Journal of Travel Research* best article of the year award as the "Charles R. Goeldner Article of Excellence Award"
National Tour Foundation created the Charles R. Goeldner Research Scholarship
Marketing Educator of the Year by the Western Marketing Educators Association
Inducted into the Travel Industry Association of America Industry Hall of Leaders
Elected Fellow in the International Academy of Hospitality Research
Elected Fellow in the International Academy for the Study of Tourism
Certificate of Merit, United Ski Industries Association
Travel and Tourism Research Association Lifetime Achievement Award
Awarded Honorary Life Membership in Association for University Business and Economic Research
Awarded Lifetime Membership in the Travel and Tourism Research Association
Society of Travel and Tourism Educators Achievement Award
Colorado Tourism Board's Individual Tourism Achievement Award
The Travel Research Association Meritorious Service Award

Legendary work ethic

I joined the CU faculty in 1990 and worked across the hall from Chuck for the next 15 years. I had always thought of myself as somebody that worked hard, but quickly learned just how much harder and longer Chuck worked. For those 15 years (and the years before and since), Chuck easily averaged more than 80 hours per week in the office. He would be there close to 8:00 AM and work until 5:00 PM, go home for dinner, then be back at the office from 7:00 PM to midnight pretty much every workday. Moreover, on weekends, it was rare to walk through the building and not find Chuck in his office. His weekends were always his "catch-up time". Chuck "retired" while I was still at CU, but even today more than 10 years later, when I visit Boulder to see Chuck I go to his university office and almost always find him there working. At his retirement reception, every single speaker spoke about his work ethic and the countless hours he had spent in his office and, in the process, how he had made all of our life better and easier.

Commitment to quality

It is hard to think about Chuck and not think about commitment and focus. I will provide just three of the many, many examples. First, Chuck was the founding editor of JTR. He served in that capacity from 1967 to 2003, an unbelievable 36 years. I served as co-editor for 2002 and 2003, then became editor in 2003. I can speak from personal experience about the time commitment necessary to maintain and grow the Journal. Moreover, Chuck did it before the invention of electronic submission, email, the online journal management systems, and when JTR was published by the University of Colorado, which means that Chuck served the dramatically heavier workload of being both editor and publisher. It is only because of Chuck's commitment and focus on growing the content and quality of JTR that we enjoy its benefits and contributions today.

Second, there is THE BOOK. *Tourism: Principles, Practices and Philosophies* is currently in its 12th edition; the 13th edition is at the publisher. There are thousands of hours of work and a fundamental commitment to continuous improvement behind every edition. For each of those editions, Chuck and his co-authors, initially Robert McIntosh and more recently J.R. Brent Ritchie, have gone through each page of each and every chapter, revising and updating the content, the figures and tables, and instructor resources. As a result, THE BOOK has been the top selling introduction to tourism book as long as I can remember. It is the standard against which all other tourism introductory texts are measured.

Third, Chuck is Mr. TTRA. In 1972, the Eastern Travel Council and the Western Travel Council merged to become the Travel and Tourism Research Association. Chuck was on the first Board of Directors. He is still there! He has served continuously on the TTRA Board for 41 years. During that time, he has served in every capacity imaginable, including not only the various TTRA executive and board positions, but most importantly as the official photographer and historian. I cannot begin to imagine the number of photographs he has taken at TTRA conferences; I do know that he has worn out at least 10 cameras. As he is quick to tell you, he is the only person who has attended every (45) TTRA conference; I suspect he has taken an average of 400 to 500 photographs per conference. Generations of TTRA presidents, including me, have learned to listen very carefully when Chuck, in his self-deprecating way, offers a suggestion or idea. TTRA board members and presidents come and go. Over the years, we have recycled virtually every idea or concept imaginable. Chuck is the constant! He can tell us how our idea worked the last three times TTRA implemented it.

The quiet facilitator

The best way to illustrate this point is to talk of when I first met Chuck. It was the early 1980s at my first TTRA conference in Philadelphia. I knew nobody at the conference, had just begun to do tourism research, and just before the conference received the letter of acceptance for my first article in JTR. I was standing by myself at the side of the room doing my best to work up the courage to try to meet some people; all of a sudden there was a person taking my photograph, talking to me, asking me how I was enjoying the conference, making me feel welcome and included. Next, he introduced himself as Chuck Goeldner. I was surprised when he knew my name and remembered my manuscript. Next thing I know, he is introducing me to, among others, John Hunt, Brent Ritchie, and Don Holocek, people whose research I had been reading and were truly the leaders of our field; again he was making me feel welcome and included, a part of TTRA. Over the years, I have watched Chuck do exactly the same thing to countless other young researchers and first time TTRA attendees. I have come to realize that Chuck is actually quite a shy person and that the camera is his way of breaking the ice and engaging with people. It is his tool to be the ultimate ambassador for TTRA, welcoming generations of TTRA members, and helping those new members begin the process of growing the professional networks and relationships we all seek. I cannot begin to imagine the number of both academic and industry tourism researchers who have been helped along the way to success through his efforts to be welcoming and engaging.

Loyalty and organizational commitment: the Colorado experience part I

Chuck is of a bygone generation, the employee that is fundamentally loyal and committed to an organization. Over the 15 years that I worked with Chuck at the CU, I slowly realized that if the College of Business had a difficult, time-consuming service project that needed to be done, it was given to Chuck. Whether it be the periodic AACSB Accreditation Self

Study, the various assessments, strategic plans, and reviews mandated by all university administrators, or some kind of study or review either requested or mandated by the Colorado legislature or Commission on Higher Education, they all seemed to end up on Chuck's desk. These are the projects that nobody wants, that can take hundreds of hours to effectively complete, for which there are few thank you's and even fewer rewards, but are a critical part of the academic world. Generations of CU Business Deans and Administrators depended on Chuck to accept such projects, get them done both correctly and on time, and not expect much in return. The idea of strategic failure is just not in his lexicon! Many of us wondered why he accepted all of these responsibilities. Over time, I realized it was just in his character. If asked to do something, he seldom says no and always does his best work. Chuck does not know the meaning of selfish or, to be more politically correct, self-protection.

Respect and impact: the Colorado experience part II

It is my observation that, over the years, academics have become increasingly narrow in how we judge each other's quality and contribution, our "impact". Today, all we can seem to talk about is the latest such convolution, the "H-Index". It is so convenient to reduce all measures of contribution to such a simple number. We complain bitterly when university administrators do it, but we do it to ourselves all the time. When I was at CU, there was an unspoken, but very real pecking order among the faculty largely based on one's number of publications in the top tier business research journals. The "Stars" were those who had published the most "top tier articles" (or convinced their colleagues that their one or two articles were of "exceptional" quality). Chuck was not one of the "Stars", primarily because he was busy being a journal editor and doing all the service projects that protected time for the "Stars" to do their research. He was never given the respect, recognition or rewards he so richly deserved. Yet, that did not make him bitter or deter him from being who he was, accepting the service responsibilities, and truly making an impact on the future of the College. I am embarrassed to say that I too once was so naïve as to subscribe to this thinking. I have since come to realize the many different ways in which faculty contribute to organizational success. Never again will I be guilty of thinking we can so narrowly measure one's impact and contributions. I have previously privately apologized to Chuck and now do so publicly.

When I became the JTR Editor

I have purposively saved what I consider the best, most telling story about Chuck for last. First, consider the context; as noted earlier, Chuck was the founder of JTR and served as its Editor for 36 years. It was his professional baby, the culmination of tens of thousands of hours of work. He took JTR from concept to wide acceptance as one of the very best journals in our field. This is what I inherited when I became editor. In the 10 years I have been editor, he has never once either publicly or privately criticized my work as editor and, please trust me, there are any number of places where he could have justifiably done so. Moreover, he has publicly supported me on a number of occasions when it would have been easier to not do so. Perhaps, the best example is one from the very beginning of my tenure as editor. Soon after my appointment, I made a number of changes in the editorial board; one of those changes was to discontinue the appointment of a previous TTRA president. This individual wrote an incendiary letter to Chuck, copied to a number of other former TTRA presidents, questioning both my appointment and my qualifications. When

Chuck showed me the letter, I asked for his advice and would have willingly reversed the decision if he had requested I do so. His response was to do what I considered best for the Journal; he refused to prescribe what he thought that might be. For the past 10 years, he has always been available for advice and counsel, but has never once questioned a decision. When I step away from being editor, I hope to be as magnanimous, supportive, and helpful to my successor.

Conclusion

So, how best to conclude this profile? Most importantly, please join me in thanking Chuck for all that he has done to grow and support tourism research and education. His relentless work ethic, commitment to quality, and quiet efforts to facilitate and support each of us have truly made a difference both in our field and in many of our individual careers. As a former TTRA President and currently the Board Chairman, I want to also thank Chuck for all that he has done to help TTRA be successful, to provide a professional network for both the industry and academic tourism research community, and to continue to advocate for our field. As a scholar, I want to thank Chuck for creating JTR, for supporting the development of many other tourism research journals, and for enhancing the quality of our scholarship. As an individual, I want to personally and sincerely thank Chuck for all that he has done for me as a mentor, colleague, and friend. Finally, I have one more little story to tell. For the naïve, it is sometimes hard to know when Chuck is being really serious, but I know his "tell". When he is being really serious on something important, he rubs his thumbs and forefingers together! If he does that while talking to you, pay attention! It is a learning opportunity!

Chris Cooper: a quit, gentle and humble person

Noel Scott

Introduction

This article provides a portrait of Christopher Paul Cooper, a scholar who has influenced the development of the tourism field of study over almost three decades. Chris Cooper has chaired the United Nations World Tourism Organization Education Council, the peak body for tourism education throughout the world, from 2005 to 2007 and was awarded the United Nations World Tourism Organization Ulysses Prize for contributions to tourism policy and education in 2009. Chris is Pro Vice-Chancellor, Dean of the Faculty of Business, and Professor at Oxford Brookes University and has special responsibility for internationalization. Chris was previously Director of the Christel DeHaan Tourism and Travel Research Centre at the University of Nottingham Business School, and before that Head of the School of Tourism at the University of Queensland, Australia.

Discussing the career, academic works, and contribution of a scholar such as Prof. Chris Cooper is a difficult task, both in collecting suitable and relevant information as well as in analysing it in a way that avoids imposing my own opinion which is equally problematic. In order to avoid these problems, I have sought information from Chris directly, from a number of his doctoral students, many now with successful careers of their own, from a number of his colleagues who have worked with him, as well as from my own experiences of Chris as a Ph.D. supervisor, Head of School, co-researcher, and co-editor, and as a mentor over 14 years. From my work with Chris, I am also familiar with his academic papers and contributions. I would like to thank those who have provided information and their opinions and have included verbatim quotes from emails received to provide a more rounded view of Chris and his work.

However, before beginning to discuss Chris's career and contribution, I would like to consider why such a portrait is both important and necessary. One reason is that learning how a person developed a successful career may be useful as an example for other aspiring to similar positions. A second is that knowledge of an author's career may help to better understand their work and enable that work to be seen in context. In Chris's career, I also perceive that his academic development and success reflects to some extent the development of the field of tourism as a whole from a niche area primarily studied by geographers to a diverse field taught in universities around the world.

Career

Chris was born in Scarborough, North Yorkshire – the first coastal resort in the UK – a fact which may have inclined him towards a career in tourism. He went to Scarborough Boys High School and began his studies in the UK at University College, London and completed his Bachelor of Science (Honours) Geography in 1973. In Britain, the 1960s and 1970s witnessed the establishment of a number of new universities. These were created in response to population growth, increasing national economic prosperity, rapid technological innovation with accompanying losses of industrial and agricultural jobs, and the need for a more educated workforce. For academic administrators of the time, social science degree courses such as tourism were attractive as they required relatively little capital investment and it was easier to recruit staff compared with laboratory-based subjects or medicine.

The 1970s then saw the beginning of a remarkable growth in the field of tourism and more recently, events along with establishment of the more established hotel and hospitality fields at degree level. The first tourism research journals such as *Journal of Travel Research* (first published in 1962) and *Annals of Tourism Research* (1973), and many international conferences were also established during this period. A number of universities established tourism schools in the 1970s, and by the 1980s a steady supply of tourism specialists (mainly with Masters Degrees or tourism management experience) were being recruited to teach a range of (mainly) undergraduate courses. As may be expected, the establishment of new tourism courses required the importing of skills from other disciplines and Chris is a geographer by training. Therefore, it may be logical to think that he went directly into a Ph.D. and then into teaching.

However, Chris decided to work in the tourism industry at the same time as completing his Ph.D. This is was a formative decision that led to an appreciation of tourism as a business and industry sector and helps in part to explain his latter interests in knowledge management and work at the United Nations World Tourism Organization, work that was both academic and practical in nature. This practical experience gave him insight into the nuts and bolts of tour operation and just how competitive it is. While completing his doctoral studies, Chris worked as a market planning and research executive for Thomson Travel Ltd, UK (now TUI) and Grattan Ltd, UK, a British catalogue clothing retailer. He completed his Ph.D. in geography in 1978 on the topic of the spatial and temporal behaviour of tourists on the island of Jersey.

After completing his studies, Chris felt a strong pull to academic life, and moved into the rapidly developing higher education sector, firstly at the Liverpool College of Higher Education from 1979 to 1982 as a Lecturer II in Geography and then as a Senior Lecturer in Tourism Studies at the Dorset Institute of Higher Education from 1982 to 1985. During this time, Chris published a number of papers in geography journals, his first being from his Ph.D. thesis (Cooper, 1981).

He moved to the University of Surrey as a Lecturer in Tourism Management in 1986 and was appointed a Senior Lecturer in Tourism Management in 1992. The Head at Surrey then was Brian Archer and was very supportive of Chris's move. His transition to the University of Surrey anticipates a dramatic expansion in the number of students in the UK studying tourism around 1988 (Cooper, Ruhanen, & Scott, 2004). Also, Chris joined the University of Surrey in the same year that the UK introduced its Research Assessment Exercise (RAE). This has been repeated at five yearly intervals and the results used in decisions concerning the funding of universities and also by universities for schools' budgets as well as individual academic promotion. Research activity is defined by publications and Ph.D.s awarded and therefore directs attention to these areas. Chris, employed at the University of Surrey, was in a good position to capitalise on this emphasis on academic training and scholarship in tourism and related topics (events, hospitality, marketing, and so on). Zhao and Ritchie (2007, p. 481) commenting on their analysis of tourism research authorship in the period 1985–2004 in the eight leading tourism journals found a very strong correlation between doctoral training and academic leadership. In this study, Chris is listed as the 28th most published author in eight tourism journals.

Chris, along with John Westlake and John Fletcher, moved to Bournemouth University in 1996 and was appointed as a Professor of Tourism. This move was partly in response to the appointment of a new Vice Chancellor at the University of Surrey who wanted a mainstream business school and not to specialise so much in tourism and hospitality. Chris, John Westlake, and John Fletcher joined Steve Wanhill who was already at Bournemouth, to form a strong group. They set up the *International Centre for Tourism and Hospitality Research* and drew in research contracts and international students under John Fletcher as Head.

Chris then moved to Brisbane, Australia to become the Foundation Professor of Tourism and Head of the School of Tourism at the University of Queensland from 1999 to 2007. The School of Tourism began in 1974 as part of the Queensland Agricultural College outside Brisbane (now part of The University of Queensland). Its tourism programmes evolved from earlier sub-degree programmes in hospitality. Like the UK, in the 1970s and 1980s there was a binary system of higher education in Australia with Colleges of Advanced Education focusing on vocationally applied degree programmes and universities focusing on more theoretically focused degree programmes (Breakey & Craig-Smith, 2011). This industry and vocationally focused tourism programme did not fit well with the research intensive University of Queensland, and in 1999 Chris's appointment signalled the university's intention to improve the research output of the School.

I joined Chris at The University of Queensland in 2002 after my Ph.D. supervisor at Griffith University, Prof. Bill Faulkner, then Director of the Cooperative Research Centre for Sustainable Tourism (RCST), met his cruel and untimely death from cancer. By that time, most of the staff at the School of Tourism were undertaking or had completed their doctoral studies and were beginning to increase their research output. Chris also established links with a number of universities in China especially Sun Yat Sen University in Guangzhou which led to a joint degree in Events Management established in 2005. During this time, he was heavily involved in the CRCST both as a researcher and as Editor in Chief for the CRCST's publications from 2002 to 2008.

In 2007, Chris moved back to the UK to become Director of the Christel DeHaan Tourism and Travel Research Centre of the University of Nottingham. He now works at the Oxford Brookes University, as Dean of the Business Faculty and Pro Vice-Chancellor. A list of Chris's appointments is given in Table 1.

Academic supervision

In my opinion, one of the most rewarding parts of an academic's job is that of supervising research students at Honours, Masters, and Ph.D. level, and that much about a supervisor's personality and interests can be understood through their management and interaction with their students. Chris has supervised 23 graduate students to completion and I consider myself fortunate to be one. Most of his students have gone on to have an academic career including his first student Dimitrios Buhalis who completed his doctorate from the University of Surrey in 1995 and is now Professor at Bournemouth University. Carlos Costa is Head of the Department and Professor at the University of Aveiro, Portugal; Atsuko Hashimoto is Associate Professor at Brock University, Canada; Gui Santana is Professor at Universidade do Vale do Itajaí, Brasil; Dr Dimitrios Diamantis is at Les Roches Hotel School, Switzerland; Associate Professor Eman Helmy is at Helwan

Table 1.   Chris Cooper's career appointments.

1976–1977	Market Planning Executive, Thomson Travel Ltd, UK
1977–1979	Marketing Planning Executive, Grattan Ltd, UK
1979–1982	Lecturer II in Geography, Liverpool College of Higher Education, UK
1982–1985	Senior Lecturer in Tourism Studies, Dorset Institute of Higher Education, UK
1986–1992	Lecturer in Tourism Management, University of Surrey, UK
1992–1996	Senior Lecturer in Tourism Management, University of Surrey, UK
1996–1999	Professor of Tourism, Bournemouth University, UK
1999–2007	Foundation Professor of Tourism and Head of School School of Tourism, The University of Queensland, Australia
2007–2009	Director, Christel DeHaan Tourism and Travel Research Centre,
2009–2010	Dean, Business School, Oxford Brookes University, UK
2010–to date	Pro Vice-Chancellor and Dean, Business Faculty, Oxford Brookes University, UK

University; Dr Paul Barron is a Reader at Edinburgh Napier University; Drs Michelle Whitford and Sasha Reid are at Griffith University, Australia; David Solnet, Lisa Ruhanen, and Noel Scott are at The University of Queensland Australia; Norain Othman is Deputy Dean (Research & Industry Linkages), Universiti Teknologi MARA, Malaysia; Dr Mary Hollick is at the University of Ballarat; Dr Shi Na Li is at Leeds Metropolitan; Dr Vanessa Gowreesunkar is at the University of Technology, Mauritius; and Dr Rodolfo Baggio is at Boccioni University, Italy.

As part of my preparation for this portrait, I asked several of these past Ph.D. students to write about Chris's supervisory style and their recollections of him from their doctoral studies. In reading through their responses, I am struck by a number of similar themes. The first concerns his strategic and "laid back" style. For example, Paul Barron writes that Chris was:

> very hands off and this allowed me to focus the study on what I felt was important rather than having him impose any strong personal feelings or thoughts that he might have had concerning the topic. This was something I really appreciated as it made the study much more of a personal issue for me. (personal communication, 2014)

Similarly Dimitrios Buhalis talks of being given the *freedom and space to develop his ideas.* (personal communication, 2014)

In his personality, Chris is described by his students as quiet, gentle, and humble with a strong sense of responsibility to his students. Atsuko Hashimoto sees him as typically British and recollects fondly his concern over her adding milk to her tea. All his students respected his knowledge, expertise, and approachability. Rodolfo Baggio writes:

> He has the incredible capacity of being always available for a discussion, a chat or simply for answering a question without being haunting or stressing with regard to what one is doing. His quiet and gentle way of handling any possible issue is one of the characteristics I have most appreciated. (personal communication, 2014)

Chris also operated as a mentor for his students during and after their studies and as Carlos Costa says has *left his foot-print on us.* Dimitrios Buhalis writes: Chris *always treated me as a colleague and an apprentice, making sure that he will show me the tricks of the trade and open doors and avenues for me.* In this way, one of Chris's lasting contributions is in helping to develop a new generation of tourism scholars.

Scholarly writing

As mentioned earlier, the field of tourism has developed into a significant area of university education during Chris's career. Along with this goes a need for textbooks and development of curriculum and pedological pracrtices. This is an area where Chris has made a significant contribution by writing a number of leading textbooks, including *Worldwide Destinations – The Geography of Travel and Tourism* (along with B. Boniface and R. Cooper), *Tourism Principles and Practice* (along with Alan Fyall, John Fletcher, David Gilbert, and Stephen Wanhill), and *Contemporary Tourism – An International Approach* (with Michael Hall). In particular, *Tourism: Principles and Practice* has been a key tourism textbooks during its many editions between 1993 and 2013. In these books, Chris has helped to provide the theoretical and conceptual basis for the study of tourism. Chris is also the Series Editor for Aspects of Tourism, Channelview Publications and for Contemporary Tourism Reviews, Goodfellow Publishers.

Another issue for the development of an academic field such as tourism is the availability of journals as these encourage publications from scholars. Chris founded and co-edited the journal *Progress in Tourism, Recreation and Hospitality Research* (1989– 1994), which transformed into *Progress in Tourism and Hospitality Research* (1994– 1998) and then *International Journal of Tourism Research* (editor 1998–2000) as well as *Tourism and Hospitality Research* (1994–1998); he is now co-editor (with Michael Hall) of *Current Issues in Tourism* (2000 – to date). He is also an editorial board member of 24 journals including *Tourism, Culture & Communication, Tourism Analysis, Journal of Tourism Studies, Journal of Hospitality and Tourism Management, Tourism Recreation Research, Journal of Ecotourism, China Tourism Research, Journal of Policy Research in Tourism, Leisure and Events*, and *International Journal of Hospitality Knowledge Management*.

İn addition to these contributions to the development of scholarship in tourism, Chris has also published a number of his own research articles. His early papers have a distinctive geographical flavour examining tourism development on the Isle of Man and developing the concept of the destination lifecycle (Cooper & Jackson, 1989). He also began publishing on a topic around the same time that has continued throughout his career – tourism education (Cooper & Westlake, 1989). In the early 2000s, he became interested in knowledge management (Cooper, 2002, 2006). He has also published with his students on topics such as tourism network analysis (Scott, Cooper, & Baggio, 2008), sustainable tourism planning (Helmy & Cooper, 2002), and computable general equilibrium modelling (Li, Blake, & Cooper, 2010).

In summary, I can only agree with the comments from his doctoral student and now Associate Professor Atsuko Hashimoto:

> As for Chris' contribution to scholarship, I believe we, tourism scholars today, owe a great deal to Chris and his generation of scholars who expanded the multidisciplinary platform of tourism studies. I do not know how Chris managed it, but his numerous contributions in the form of journal articles, books, editing books and journals, guest lectures and consultancy have all touched us at one point in our scholarly life. (personal communication, 2014)

Within the academic sector, Chris's contributions have been recognized through his membership of the prestigious International Academy for the Study of Tourism. He is also a Member of the United Kingdom Research Excellence Framework Sub-Panel for Sport, Exercise Science and Tourism and a Fellow of the Royal Society for the Arts.

Industry leadership

Perhaps because of his early experience in the industry, Chris has often worked outside purely academic circles. This manifested early in his career in numerous visitor studies and strategy reports. He also worked extensively on education visits to attractions in the UK and has extensive experience in providing executive education for managers and practicioners. Chris has provided leadership to the tourism sector at an international level through his work for the UNWTO. One of his main contributions that started during his time at the Universty of Surrey was work on tourism education with the UNWTO. As part of this involvement, he ran road shows on training the educators around the world along with Eduardo Fayos Sola. Chris has worked for the UNWTO as a Senior Special Advisor – Human Resources, and as a member of the Leadership Forum, Market Panel of Experts and the TEDQUAL Assessment Committee. He was Chairman of the UNWTO Education Council from 2005 to 2007. In 2009, he was awarded the UNWTO Ulysses Prize for contributions to tourism policy and education. Today, he works with the European Union, the International Labour Organization, the Organization for Economic Cooperation and Development (OECD), and the Association of South East Asian Nations (ASEAN). In these roles, Chris has promoted improvements in the standards of training of tourism and hospitality staff, development of education standards at tertiary level in tourism and hospitality, and better utilization of tourism knowledge through improved dissemination of information.

Contribution

If we look back over the material presented earlier, we may see a dedicated academic who has made a real contribution to the academic scholarship and international leadership of tourism. Tourism is an important and vibrant field of study that aspires to be a discipline and a newly recognized sector of the economy that contributes significantly to the economy of many countries. Examining the rapid development of tourism, we may consider that this was an inevitable outcome of technological, social, and economic changes from the 1960s onwards. However, while these megatrends provide the drivers for the development of tourism, they do not create the present conditions, and instead it is the actions of individuals that have tangible consequences. The independent academic field of study and research of tourism has arguably only began in the later quarter of the twentieth century (Pearce, 2005). Chris has been central to the development of tourism scholarship through his involvement in founding of new journals, training of Ph.D. students, his own papers especially on knowledge management, and his work with the UNWTO and other industry bodies. In the sense that a discipline is a group of academics sharing a common interest, Chris Cooper is central to the evolution of tourism to disciplinary status due to his efforts at creating a body of knowledge and future academics (through his Ph.D. teaching). As Dimitrios Diamantis writes:

> Chris is an outstanding scholar to say the least. He not only was concerned for and guided all his PhD students but also he managed us as future educators where eventually most of us become ones, Professor Dimitrios Buhalis, Professor Carlos Costa, Professor Noel Scott and many others. In short, Chris contribution to scholarship has been thought provoking from its early work on TALC in late 1980s, to the educating the educators' contributions in the 1990s and to the knowledge creation articles in 2000s. He has been one of the academics that have sharpened and shaped the tourism body of knowledge, a name that always reflects a postmodernism with syntagmatic dimensions. (personal communication, 2014)

Conclusion

At the beginning of Chris's career in the 1970s, tourism was a growth sector for academia. Today in some countries, student enrolments are falling and it may be that tourism will revert back to a field where academics from other subjects and disciplines work. There does seem to be a strong movement in Australia for tourism and hospitality to be combined into business schools and taught as a major rather than as a standalone degree. However, through the work of Chris Cooper and other pioneering scholars, there is now a strong academic research community supported by texts, monographs, and journals that can provide a centre for the study of tourism.

It appears evident from this portrait that Chris has made a major contribution to tourism scholarship and in addition, his career provides some lessons for aspiring academics. Chris benefited from a grounding in the business of tourism, developed a network of colleagues through his doctoral training, and worked with international organizations to mutual benefit. A colleague once told me that his opinion was if an academic had only completed their Ph. D., then they "ain't done much". Chris has done far more in his career to date than just getting a Ph.D. and provides inspiration for those scholars with their new doctoral certificates who aspire to do more.

References

Breakey, N., & Craig-Smith, S. J. (2011). *Trends and issues in tourism and hospitality degree education in Australia – will the bubble burst?* Paper presented at the 2011 CAUTHE National Conference, Tourism: Creating a brilliant blend, Adelaide.

Cooper, C. (1981). Spatial and temporal patterns of tourist behaviour. *Regional Studies, 15*, 359–371.

Cooper, C. (2002). Knowledge management and research commercialisation agendas. *Current Issues in Tourism, 5*, 375–377.

Cooper, C. (2006). Knowledge management and tourism. *Annals of Tourism Research, 33*, 47–64.

Cooper, C., & Jackson, S. (1989). Destination life cycle: The Isle of Man case study. *Annals of Tourism Research, 16*, 377–398.

Cooper, C., Ruhanen, L., & Scott, N. (2004). *Globalization and knowledge management.* Paper presented at the Tourism Symposium, Abha, Saudi Arabia.

Cooper, C., & Westlake, J. (1989). Tourism teaching into the 1990s. *Tourism Management, 10*, 69–73.

Helmy, E., & Cooper, C. (2002). An assessment of sustainable tourism planning for the archaeological heritage: The case of Egypt. *Journal of Sustainable Tourism, 10*, 514–535.

Li, S., Blake, A., & Cooper, C. (2010). China's tourism in a global financial crisis: A computable general equilibrium approach. *Current Issues in Tourism, 13*, 435–453.

Pearce, P. L. (2005). Professing tourism: Tourism academics as educators, researchers and change leaders. *Journal of Tourism Studies, 16*, 21–33.

Scott, N., Cooper, C., & Baggio, R. (2008). Destination networks: Four Australian cases. *Annals of Tourism Research, 35*, 169–188.

Zhao, W., & Ritchie, J. R. B. (2007). An investigation of academic leadership in tourism research: 1985–2004. *Tourism Management, 28*, 476–490.

Clare Gunn: pioneer, maverick and "founding father" of academic tourism in the USA

John L. Crompton

Introduction

It was the summer of 2014. The 10 students around the table were both curious and excited. They had been told that the legendary man with whom they were about to interact in a lunch-time "brown bag" seminar was 98 years old, and were unsure what to expect. As Clare Gunn walked briskly into the room using a cane only for balance, if they had not known his age they probably would have guessed "early 70s". With a twinkle in his eye and infectious enthusiasm, he regaled his audience for over an hour with testimony on the challenges and opportunities that came with championing tourism as a legitimate field of study in the decades immediately following World War II.

Gunn is arguably the "founding father" of scholarly tourism studies in the academy. His principles of planning and design were so innovative and they violated the popular notions of what tourism was all about. His early articulation of the symbiotic relationship between business and the environment was extremely iconoclastic, and it took 60 years for this to begin to change. His extraordinary pioneering career opened multiple doors for those of us who came after. The following pioneering milestones framed his career and contributions:

- A six-week camping trip of 8575 miles with his family in a Model A Ford on the primitive roads of 1929 from Michigan throughout the West that aroused his interest in tourism. This is described in his book, *Western Tourism: Can Paradise be Regained?* (2004) He called this his "soap box book" because it is filled with his advocacy for halting tourism's erosion of the environment.
- The first academic appointment in the USA in tourism when he was hired by Michigan State University Extension Service in 1945 to provide technical information for new and existing tourism businesses.
- His Ph.D. from the University of Michigan in landscape architecture, the first Ph.D. awarded in that field in the USA.
- When he joined the faculty of the Travel Industry Management Programme at the University of Hawaii, its focus was exclusively on hotels and restaurants. Gunn's classes on "tourism planning" were the first to be taught at a U.S. University.
- In 1970, the only books on "tourism" were anecdotal narratives and travel guides. Gunn's *Vacationscape* was arguably the world's first text book on tourism.
- His leadership and long tenure at Texas A&M University resulted in the first comprehensive tourism curriculum and faculty in the USA that went beyond "add-on" tourism classes at hotel management programmes.

It is an extraordinary career of leadership that because of its pioneering context is unlikely to be matched in the field in the future.

The early years

Clare Gunn was born in 1916 in Grandville, a few miles west of Grand Rapids, Michigan. In high school, he was class president, founder of the school newspaper, and his artistic talents for drawing, sketching, and playing the violin were widely recognized. His father's insatiable desire to travel in the family's 1921 Model T Ford led to frequent family trips to Lake Michigan, parks and other places of educational interest, highlighted by the 1929 six-week tent camping trip through the West. Clare recalled, "Because we were traveling West long before roads were capable of handling the 'modern' cars, we had 29 flat tires and wore out a set of brakes. But this and other camping trips enabled us to drink in the wonders of nature."

The war years

Gunn's artistic talent and love of nature made landscape architecture an obvious course of study when he headed for college first at Grand Rapids Junior College and subsequently at Michigan State College from which he graduated Cum Laude in 1940. He commented: "I felt ready to take on the world. I knew I could replace all the ugliness of the landscape with pleasurable beauty." But the world milieu dictated otherwise, at least for the time being, because the Second World War intervened. He married in 1941 (a partnership that has now endured for 73 years). A brief experience teaching landscape architecture at the University of Massachusetts reinforced his belief that this was the right career choice, but the war economy stalled his career plans. He was rejected for military service because of a history in high school of vision and medical problems, but contributed to the war effort by working as an engineering draftsman in an aircraft manufacturing plant. It was only after the war ended that Gunn could launch his professional career.

Extension specialist in tourism and resorts

In 1945, the Michigan legislature funded a new Extension programme at Michigan State, in anticipation of a post-war travel boom. Clare Gunn was hired as Extension Specialist in Tourism and Resorts, and so became the first academic appointed to a specialist tourism position in the USA. In this role, he travelled through the state for 20 years, interacting with operators of resorts, cabin courts, and food services, observing their physical plants, learning about their experiences, and developing publications which disseminated information on best practices. There were no precedents to guide his role, so he was free to control his own agenda. The extent of his actions and influence can be informed from his 1950 Annual Report which documented: "75 days of field work, 971 letters, distributed 35,031 pieces of literature, 189 field visits, 223 office visits, 13 meetings, and 13,000 visitors to the exhibit" of a one room log cabin he constructed in a campus building basement. This state-of-the-art exhibit illustrated rustic furniture; compact bath facilities; kitchen unit with refrigerator, stove, sink, and cupboards; a 5 gallon electric water heater under a lavatory; and a tip-up bed.

Clare Gunn became the "go-to guy" for all tourism operators in Michigan. However, he gradually recognized that focus on "nuts and bolts" topics was limiting; there were macro-issues that needed to be addressed for tourism to flourish. He observed:

- The focus of tourism was almost exclusively on promotion. Gunn recognized that research, planning, visitor impacts, and relationship of tourism to the natural environment were of at least equal importance.
- The impact of macro-decision on policies made by public agencies on issues such as highways, parks, and conservation, employee rights, school vacations, shifts in political philosophy, zoning, and so on had as much influence on the success of tourism businesses as decisions made at the micro-level by the owners of those businesses.
- There was minimal interaction between those working in parks and recreation, and those in tourism, even though parks were probably the primary destination for the first post-war tourists. He observed,

> The park functioned as a major attraction for visitors and the community offered the needed and desired visitor services, clearly a compatible relationship. I saw this as a logical and fundamental planning principle. However I found many who criticized me severely for such an iconoclastic statement of principle. Park advocates and staff believed that commercialization near parks was a desecration, a carbuncle on the pristine landscapes of parks.

Clare Gunn saw the need for public–private partnerships and interactions, but it took two or three decades for his insights to become conventional wisdom.

- There was no scientific literature addressing any of these large macro-issues.

These themes became the foundation platform upon which he launched the case for tourism as an academic field of study. Clare Gunn provided the road map, but for many years he was a lone voice receiving little support from any of the potential stakeholders.

A pioneering dissertation

For 20 years, he effectively pioneered and developed the Tourism and Resort Services Extension programme at Michigan State. However, an administrative reorganization shifted the programme from Agricultural Extension to the College of Business, which had no tradition of extension and no interest in tourism. The result was the gradual demise of the programme. Clare Gunn's response was to take a sabbatical leave to the University of Michigan to develop his knowledge base, thinking and vision through the medium of a Ph.D. in landscape architecture.

It was the first such degree awarded in the USA. Again, he was in a pioneering role with no precedents, so the experience was as challenging and confusing for the faculty as it was for him. His dissertation "*A Concept for the Design of a Tourism-Recreation Region*" was published under the title, *Guidance for Tourism-Recreation in Michigan's Upper Peninsular*. It was the first major regional tourism plan in the USA and perhaps in the world. Aided by a US$50,000 grant from the federal Economic Development Administration, it integrated substantial field work; user surveys; comparison of market desires and supply base; geographical analysis; extensive stakeholder involvement; and creative project design concepts. It was unprecedented in scope and vision. Because of its pioneering nature, it received widespread publicity and helped to bring Gunn's ideas to a wider audience beyond Michigan.

A temporary sojourn in Hawaii

In 1966, Gunn left his institutionally inhospitable position in Michigan State for a one year visiting professorship in the Department of Travel Industry Management at the University of Hawaii. Inevitably, its focus was on hotel and resort management, but for the first time in his life, and probably for the first time at any academic institution, he taught courses in tourism planning and development. Hawaii was an extraordinarily rich field context in which to study tourism. The experience confirmed that the ideas he had nurtured in Michigan were generalizable. It stimulated him to start work on a book, *Vacationscape: Designing Tourist Regions* (1972), since at this time no books had been published on tourism development.

Developing the tourism field in the academy at Texas A&M

Before embarking on his Hawaiian adventure, Gunn had been persuaded by another former Michigan State faculty member, Leslie M. Reid, to join a multidisciplinary faculty in a new Recreation and Parks Department he was creating and developing at Texas A&M University. Reid intentionally hired specialists from the separate disciplines he believed were important to recreation and parks – economics, forestry, conservatism, planning, sociology, geography, and public service. Contrary to typical departmental structures, his first faculty had national reputations and were all appointed at the full professor rank. This facilitated the immediate launching of both masters and doctoral programmes.

At Texas, A&M Clare Gunn's national reputation was extended to international audiences as he undertook pioneering tourism planning studies in Venezuela, Nova Scotia, Yugoslavia, and Guatemala. Soon after he arrived in Texas, the 10-chapter *Vacationscape* book was completed. Its content was derived solely from his rich experiences and observations, because there was virtually no literature available. When the manuscript was submitted to publishers, it was repeatedly rejected. Since there were no courses in tourism, publishers evaluated its sales potential on likely professional interest. Reviewers of the manuscript indicated that it did not address the "nuts and bolts" issues of interest to businesses. Further, he was criticized by some reviewers for been too conservation oriented to be of interest to tourism businesses, while others said it was too commercial to interest conservationists.

Ultimately, a casual comment at a social event to the Director of the Bureau of Business based at the University of Texas led to that organization publishing it. As the world's first book on tourism, the 3000 printed copies sold quickly. Subsequently, Gunn extended and expanded upon *Vacationscape* in his *Tourism Planning* (1979) text. Google Scholar reports that these two books have been cited almost 1500 and 2500 times, respectively. Clearly, they are classic foundation pieces of the tourism literature. For example, the fourth edition of the *Tourism Planning* (2005) text was translated into Chinese by Professor Wu Bihn of Beijing University, and is widely used in the hundreds of tourism academic programmes offered in China.

Gunn had complete freedom to establish a direction for tourism at Texas A&M. The multidisciplinary faculty meant his colleagues viewed the world through different lenses, and the resultant constructive critical dialogue helped expand and refine his thinking. Gradually his persistent writings and numerous presentations on the symbiosis of conservation and commercial services, and broadening vision of tourism beyond promotion, permeated conventional wisdom and gained credence and traction.

Among his Texas A&M colleagues, this led to awareness of the need to greatly expand the range of tourism classes that were offered, especially at the graduate level. Accordingly, new faculty were hired with tourism expertise in areas such as business planning, cultural anthropology, popular culture, cultural heritage, and visitor impacts.

This was consistent with Gunn's belief that "tourism is not a discipline; it draws upon many disciplines." The expansion attracted high caliber graduate students from around the globe, and resulted in the Department being recognized as the leading research institution in tourism in the world (Jogaratnam, Chou, McCleary, Mena, & Yoo, 2005). This was perhaps the apogee of Gunn's long campaign. The growth of tourism at Texas A&M was reflective of that in the whole field, and it represented validation of the persistent vision Clare Gunn had articulated as a lonely, almost solitary voice, in the post-World War II decades.

In 1974–1975, Gunn was tempted to leave Texas A&M, by the opportunity to re-engage with his professional roots, so he joined the School of Landscape Architecture at the University of Guelph in Ontario, Canada. The department's commitment was to expand into tourism. However, it proved to be a vacuous promise and after a year he returned to Texas A&M.

When he officially retired from Texas A&M in 1985, Gunn responded to the freedom from academic responsibilities by immersing himself in multiple major consulting projects in the USA and elsewhere. These continued to inform his frequent conference presentations and writings. In 1995, he delivered the keynote address at the 32nd Congress of the International Federation of Landscape Architects in Bangkok, Thailand. He described this as

> the greatest and most rewarding highlight of my career. It was a thrill to address the assembly of over 400 landscape architects from around the world, focusing for the first time on the theme of tourism. All tourism development takes place on the land so this profession is better qualified to deal with tourism land issues than any other, but why has it taken so long?

Conclusion

The world changed profoundly during Clare Gunn's remarkable 60-year career. Those changes resulted in the extraordinarily rapid evolution of tourism. He anticipated this exponential growth and prepared the field for it by providing the concepts and tools to accommodate it. The field was slow to respond, but eventually recognized the merits of this "prophet in the wilderness" and embraced his work and ideas. Clare Gunn summarized his career in these terms:

> During the early years of my career I was plagued with frustration and even disappointment. It seemed that the challenges that were stimulating me to study and search for new concepts were not shared by others in tourism and landscape architecture, my professional foundations. I even wondered if I should change the direction of my career. However, it turned out to be tremendously fulfilling. My life has been a long, wonderful and fascinating journey – from oil lamps to electric lights; from news only by newspaper to radio, television and then the internet; from horse-and-buggy transportation to automobiles, planes, and space travel; from a dominating rural population to urban; and from no scholarly journals in tourism to almost 100 of them.

Clare Gunn's work will always be cited in the future because the starting point for every scholar who aspires to understand contemporary state-of-the-art tourism planning to add to its knowledge base has to be Gunn's work. His remarkable lengthy and maverick career will endure because the principles he pioneered have transferred to become part of the tourism field's conventional wisdom.

It should be noted that Gunn's entire collection of books, professional writings, artwork, documentary photographs, and other career records have been stored in perpetuity in Michigan State University Archives and Historical Collections.

References

Gunn, C. A. (1972). *Vacationscape: Designing tourist regions.* Austin: University of Texas, Bureau of Business Research.

Gunn, C. A. (1979). *Tourism planning.* New York, NY: Crane Russak.

Gunn, C. A. (2004). *Western Tourism: Can Paradise be regained?* New York, NY: Cognizant Communication Corporation.

Gunn, C. A. (2005). *Tourism planning* (W. Bihn, Trans.) (4th ed.). Beijing: Beijing University.

Jogaratnam, G., Chou, K., McCleary, K., Mena, M., & Yoo, J. (2005). An analysis of institutional contributors to three major academic tourism journals. *Tourism Management, 26,* 641–648.

Claude Kaspar: a life devoted to tourism and transport – moving theory into practice

Norbert Vanhove

Introduction

My first contact with Claude Kaspar was in Budapest in 1965. It was on the occasion of the 16th AIEST congress that took place in the famous Gillért hotel, a noble hotel situated on the Danube riverbank, at the foot of Gellért Hill. It was and still is an impressive Art-Nouveau building with large, light corridors, and lots of character. It shares its building with the famous Gellért Spa, one of the city's most beautiful thermal bath.

It was my first visit to a communist country. I do not have happy memories of that congress. At that time travelling in an Eastern European country was not easy. One had the permanent feeling of being checked and supervised. We were told that all the rooms in the Gellért hotel were provided with monitoring equipment. Furthermore, the congress was not good. The German Professor Sauermann was very upset and made a speech of one hour to express his dissatisfaction. His proposal was to drop the letter "S" from the acronym AIEST. His intervention was debatable, but he was right.

Claude Kaspar presented a paper with the title "L'expansion des transports touristiques" [The growth of tourism transport]. In this title we find two key words in the career of Claude Kaspar: transport and tourism two fields, which were inseparable in his life. Taking into account the objective of this publication, we focus this "portrait" on his career in the tourism industry.

The St. Gallen boy studied at Bern University

Claude Kaspar, was born in St. Gallen (Romansh speaking Switzerland) in 24 May 1931. After his primary and secondary school (1938–1951), he studied economics at the universities of Bern and Köln (1951–1956). In 1956, he obtained a Doctoral degree Dr rer. pol. at Bern University with his dissertation on "Die Betriebs- und Tarifgestaltung der Elektrizitätswirtschaft und der Eisenbahnen als Träger öffentlicher Dienste" [Modes of operations and tariffs of electricity suppliers and railway companies as part of the public sector].

In 1957, Kaspar came back to his "Ostschweizer Heimat" [his homeland East Switzerland]. From the very beginning of his career, he combined transport and tourism. But he also combined academic activities and praxis. These double combinations characterized his whole career. In 1957, he became the secretary to the Director of a local railway company at the Swiss part of Lake Constance (Bodensee–Toggenburg–Bahn). At the same time, he started his activities in the Seminar für Fremdenverkehr und

Verkehrspolitik [Seminar for tourism and transport policy at the Handelshochschule St. Gallen, HSG]. His first work was a job as academic assistant. At the same time he was responsible for the library. In the early1990s, HSG explicitly became a part of the University of St. Gallen, a university with a limited number of disciplines such as economics, social sciences, and law.

His first teaching task started in the winter semester of 1963/1964. Meanwhile, he prepared a Ph.D. thesis that he presented in 1964. The theme of the Ph.D. thesis was "Die touristische Verkehrsleistung, der Einfluss des Fremdenverkehrs auf die Personentarife öffentlicher Verkehrsmittel". A free translation could be "the touristic transport service, the influence of tourism on the tariffs of public transport modes". This title is once again an illustration of his interest in transport (policy) and tourism. In the same year, he became as the director of the Association for Shipping on Rhine and Lake Constance in North-Eastern Switzerland "Nordostscheizerischen Verbandes für Schiffahrt Rhein-Bodensee". Very important was his decision, in 1967, to go for a fulltime job at the HSG firstly as replacement director of the "Institut für Fremdenverkehr und Verkehrswirtschaft" – IFV [Institute of Tourism and Transport Economics], and later in 1969, as the director-president of the Institut für Tourismus und Verkehrswirtschaft, ITV [Institute for tourism and transport economics].

Professor Kaspar

In 1973, he was nominated as full ordinary professor. His teaching tasks were focussed on the topic of "Verkehrs- und Fremdenverkehrswirtschaftlehre" [Economics of transport and tourism]. Two years later, he became Abteilungsvorstand [dean/department head] of the Business Department of the HSG. His management capabilities lead to his appointment as vice-rector of the University of St. Gallen in 1978. In 1982, he was re-elected as the vice-rector for another 4 years.

Former students of Kaspar appreciate very much about his teaching capacity. Here we bring a testimony of two of his former scholars. The first testimony is from Christian Laesser, professor at the University of St. Gallen, the director of Institut für Systemisches Management und Public Governance and also Secretary General of AIEST (see infra): "Claude was not only a good teacher, contributing to our critical thinking as students, but also a great colleague and friend, fostering a number of successful professional careers". The second testimony is from Tanja Mihalic, professor at the University of Ljubljana, who prepared her Ph.D. thesis under his direction and published together with Claude Kaspar the book "Umweltökonomie im Tourismus" [Environmental economics and tourism]: "He has given me advice on everything from how to gather more sources for my dissertation and how to enter a tourism scientific community. He was a great mentor and truly cosmopolitan."

In 1997, he became emeritus of the University of St. Gallen and at the same time he retired as the president-director of the "Institut für Tourismus und Verkehrswirtschaft". A Festschrift [memorial book] was offered to Claude Kaspar. Prof. Dr Georges Fischer and Dr Christian Laesser (eds.) prepared the "Festschrift Claude Kaspar" with the title of "Theorie und Praxis der Tourismus- und Verkehrswirtschaft im Wertewandel". G. Fischer was at that moment the rector of the University of St. Gallen and at the same time president of the board of directors of the Institute for Tourism and Transport. Christian Laesser was a scientific collaborator at ITV. Very typical for this publication are the two distinguished parts. The first part relates to tourism, with contributions of W. Ender, P. Keller, J. Mazanec, H. Müller, H. Schmidhauser, K. Socher, K. Weiermair, A Würzl, and others.

The second part of the book is dealing with topics on the transport world: G. Aberle, M. Crippa, G. Heimerl, and others. Up to the end of his career tourism and transport were inseparable. In his last lecture at the University of St. Gallen, Kaspar analysed the interactions between politics and science in the field of transport and tourism, based on the example of Switzerland. It is highly recommendable to read his interesting contribution.

In St. Gallen "Hochschulnachrichten" (Fischer, 1996), G. Fischer, rector at that time, underlined the great engagement of Kaspar towards the HSG. His friendliness, charm, and level-headed control [Gelassenheit] were very much appreciated by colleagues, students, and board members. Even on the occasion of the sudden death of his teenage son, although he was full of sadness, I noticed, a few weeks after his son passed away, on the occasion of the annual AIEST congress in Kenya, a remarkable level-headed control with Claude and his intelligent and charming wife Helen Kaspar. The engagement went further than the university. Claude and Helen, both demonstrated a social engagement; Claude was very often an advisor in tourism and transport matters for the national and regional governments. Helen Kaspar was for a long period member of the government of Canton St. Gallen.

Other important functions in the academic and the business world

On top of his teaching and research activities Claude Kaspar was, during his career, very active in the academic and business world as a member of several national or regional commissions in Switzerland. The most important were:

- 1986–1989: president of Hochschulplanungskommission [Federal Committee on Higher Education],
- 1980–1995: member of Nationalstrassen-Überprüfungskommission, NUP [Commission on Swiss Federal Road Network]. Expertenkommission NEAT (Commission of experts for the New Railway Link through the Alps NRLA or Neue Eisenbahn-Alpentransversale, NEAT), Expertenkommission Schweizerische Bundesbahnen SBB (Commission of experts for the Swiss Federal Railways reflexion group), and Strassenforschungskommission [Road Transport Research Commission],
- 1990–2001; president of the Schweizerische Verkehrswissenschatliche Gesellschaft SVWG [Swiss Association of Transport Sciences], and
- 1981–1997: board member of Schweizerische Gesellschaft für Hotelkredit SGH [Swiss Association for Hotel Loans].

In the 1990s, he directed tourist-related development in the Eastern European countries supported by the Swiss Government. He considered his work as an UN expert to reorganize the Hungarian spa-tourism as one of the most challenging tasks in his career. This expertise lasted for 4 years (Die Studentenzeitschrift de Universität St. Gallen, n° 236, 1996). He was honoured for his various international activities by different universities. In 1992, he became an honorary professor at the Technische Universität (TU) in Dresden, Germany and in 1995 Professor h.c. at the Hochschule für Handel, Gastronomie und Tourismus in Budapest, Hungary. In 2000, he was awarded an honorary doctorate degree by the University of Matej Bel in Banska Bystrica, Slovakia.

Kaspar and The Institute of Tourism and Transport Economy

Claude Kaspar is also linked to the Institute of Tourism and Transport Economy. The name of the institute changed several times. Originally it was named as "Seminar für Fremdenverkehr". Later on the name changed successively into:

- Institut für Fremdenverkehr und Verkehrswirtschaft,
- Institut für Tourismus und Verkehrswirtschaft,
- Institut für Öffentliche Dienstleistungen und Tourismus, and
- Institut für Systemisches Management und Public Governance.

The origin of IFV goes back to 1941. The first directors were Prof. Dr Walter Hunziker and Prof. Dr Walter Fischer. In that respect Switzerland was a leader in Europe and in the World. In 1969, he became the director-president of ITV and at the same time extraordinary professor at HSG. Under his leadership together with Dr H.P. Schmidhauser, ITV got a national and international reputation. In his contribution Kaspar (1983), Claude Kasper defined the aims of ITV as follows:

- scientific research of economic problems in tourism and transport economy,
- promotion of training for future managers in tourism and transport, in connection with the St. Gallen Graduate School of Economics,
- post-graduate education for the middle and top level personnel by means of lectures, courses and other training procedures, and
- collection of documentation and literature for research and for teaching.

In the early 1980s, the institute attaches particular importance to the promotion of research in tourism and transport economy. In addition to assignments coming from the tourist and transport industries, which tend to be concerned with economic and managerial problems, the institute has its own internal research program. The focus is on applied research: "For financial reasons there is a preference at the St. Gallen Institute for Applied Research. Thus, although fundamental research is sometimes subsidized, the amount of this work at the institute has had to be restricted. However, applied research has the advantage of keeping the institute and its courses in constant contact with the practical problems of tourism and transport economics". The close contacts with the praxis always were a red line in his career.

The editor of Tourism and Hospitality Research (Volume 5, number 4, p. 374) wrote is his obituary of Prof. Kaspar:

> At that time, the beginning of Claude Kaspar's research activities in tourism and transport were characterized by questions on definition and technical topics. He gave a new inspired dimension through the application of system theory to the research fields of tourism and transport through his research projects at the University of St Gallen. These manifested themselves through an integrated vision of the development of tourist regions, the study of the function of establishments in the destinations, and the exploration of transport networks, combined with an explanation of the effects of tourism and transport on the natural and social environment, all enabled through the application of system theory.

Thomas Bieger, his successor and since 2011 as the Rector of St. Gallen University, characterizes Kaspar as follows:

> His teaching helped hundreds of graduate students to enter demanding positions of leadership. As professor, director and fellow man he generously provided stability and straightforwardness. He did not only have people on his side because of his technical brilliance, but also because of his charm. Tolerance and conscientiousness were always important values to him. His various historical and technical interests made him an inspiring conversational partner. He was still working in an academic environment long after most others have retired, and in the summer of 2004 he presented lectures at the TU in Dresden, Germany.

He passed away on 18 November 2004, after a short, severe illness at the age of 73. Besides his very active academic career, Kaspar took the responsibility to succeed Walter Hunziker as the president of AIEST. This is the topic of the next section of this contribution.

Claude Kaspar – an outstanding AIEST President (1974–1994)

First of all a few words about AIEST would be provided. The acronym AIEST (Association Internationale d'Experts Scientifiques du Tourisme) finds its origin in an initiative of the Heads of the two Swiss Tourism Research Institutes founded at the Universities of St. Gallen and Bern in 1941, Walter Hunziker and Kurt Krapf. After the end of the WWII, both felt the need to make known the fruits of their scientific work to a wider circle of colleagues, and to resume the broken threads of international scientific relations in tourism, in order to develop them as well as the scientific work related to tourism itself. The inaugural meeting of AIEST took place in Rome on 31 May 1951. AIEST is as such the oldest scientific organisation in tourism. Its counterpart in the USA is TTRA, founded in 1970. Under Kaspar's chairmanship, the AIEST had 400 members in 50 countries all over the world. As such, AIEST is a genuine international scientific society. AIEST is an interdisciplinary network of experts, whose members include specialists from different disciplines (economics, business administration, geography, sociology, and other) who have a particular interest in tourism. In accordance with the bylaws the association endeavours to:

- foster friendly relations among its members,
- promote scientific activity on the part of its members, in particular by developing personal contacts, providing documentation and facilitating exchange of views and experience,
- support the activity of scientific institutes of tourism, or other centres of research and education specializing in tourism, and to develop relations between them, as well as between them and the members of the association, and
- organize and co-operate in congresses and other meetings and courses on tourism of a scientific nature.

Therefore, AIEST may be considered as being the international catalyst of scientific activities in tourism. The association does not itself directly engage in tourism research and education, but it endeavours to foster them as much as possible within the limits of its possibilities and those of existing institutions. As a result of strict observance of its scientific character and the intensification of research and education in tourism, AIEST has been able to develop in a most gratifying way and has acquired a position of respect. Four focal points mark its activities and development: the annual congress, the "Tourism Review" as a long-standing tourism journal, the documentation, and the network of experts.

Claude Kaspar devoted a part of his career to the good functioning of AIEST. After the air accident in 1962 in which the late Prof. K. Krapf died, Claude Kaspar was appointed as the Secretary General of AIEST. He was very much appreciated by the AIEST members. It was logical he should succeed Walter Hunziker, after his death in 1974, as the president of AIEST. He was the natural dauphin of Walter Hunziker. Kaspar was the president of AIEST during a period of 20 years (1974–1994). In his last term (1990–1994) as the president, I became a member of the AIEST Committee and had closer contact with Claude Kaspar. Then you become aware that being AIEST president is a part time job. The AIEST was in that time also acting as the editor of "The Tourism Review". He was the president of the editorial committee. He could profit from the support of a very devoted new AIEST Secretary General, Hanspeter Schmidhaiser, and a number of well-known committee members (A. Koch, L. Merlo, V. Planque, B. Ritchie, J. Vila Fradera, etc.). Kaspar was a great AIEST president. I fully agree with Thomas Bieger where he writes: "through his diplomatic skills he succeeded in furthering the development of the organization despite the conflicts at that time between the various research cultures (three to four working languages) and research approaches" (see T. Bieger, Pionier de Systemtheorie in Tourismus und Verkehr, IDT Blickpunkte, Bieger, 2004).

At many AIEST committee meetings and AIEST congresses, he emphasized the necessity of an interdisciplinary approach. The choice of the congress themes under his chairmanship is an illustration of his interdisciplinary concern. On the occasion of the 44th AIEST congress in Wien, one of the most famous AIEST congresses ever, Claude Kaspar handed the torch over to his dauphin Peter Keller. Although Keller was his dauphin, the president elections were not without animosity. The French member L. Michaud was his opponent. The animosity between Keller and Michaud continued for another 4 years.

Tourist Research Centre

On the occasion of the 25th Tourist Research Centre (TRC) meeting in Bruges, in 1990, Rik Medlik wrote on the history of the young TRC. From his text I quote (Vanhove, 2015):

> TRC was formed in the mid 1960s by a small group of researchers who felt the need to meet and exchange experience of research in tourism. Their decision at the time was to a great extent a reaction to larger organizations and their conferences, in which participants tended to talk at each other from the platform rather confer and discuss.

Rik was very polite. The origin of TRC was to a certain extent a discontent with the AIEST working in the beginning of the 1960s (see introduction). A number of AIEST members were of the opinion that AIEST was not the ideal platform to discuss in depth the methodological aspects of tourism research. The reactionaries were René Baretje (Aix-en-Provence), Paul Bernecker (Wien), Alfred Koch (München), Jozef Ramaker (the Netherlands), Maurits Tideman, and Olivier Vanneste (Brugge). All the six were involved in tourism research.

Walter Hunziker, the AIEST President at that time, was not pleased with the idea of starting with a new association. In 1964, on the occasion of the annual AIEST congress in Bregenz, the opposition of Hunziker was less pronounced. The so-called rebels decided to start the following year with TRC. The TRC founders were not against AIEST but were of the opinion that close to or within AIEST, there was a need for an annual exchange of research. This exchange of research is very difficult in a congress with 100–200 participants. I read in the original bylaws "The Tourist research Centre was formed in 1965 to promote exchange of research experience and other forms of co-operation among its members." The first meeting took place in 1965 in Bruges and was organized by Vanneste, Director WES and myself, at that time head of WES tourism research department.

In the late 1960s, an agreement was made with the president of the AIEST. Prof. Hunziker could live with the existence of TRC on condition that TRC members should be member of AIEST. At that time, I was one of The TRC delegation, and we could all agree with that condition. For me, even 45 years later, a word is a word. This agreement opened the possibility for the "Institut für Fremdenverkehr und Verkehrswirtschaft" – IFV [Institute of Tourism and Transport Economics] to join TRC. Claude Kaspar became a member in 1969 and was a very active member in the 1970s and 1980s. He attended 15 meeting very often accompanied with Dr Hanspeter Schmidhauser and later on succeeded by professors Thomas Bieger and Christian Laesser.

Kaspar's scientific work

Kaspar was not only a brilliant professor, a straightforward manager but also a producer of a long list of publications – books and many scientific articles. Not only is the length of the publication list but also especially the quality is impressive. There was no place for nonsense contributions. His most well-known publication is undoubtedly "Die Tourismuslehre im Grundriss" [Principles of theory of tourism], the first publication in the series "St. Galler Beitrage zum Tourismus und der Verkehrswirtschaft" [St. Gallen Series "Contributions to tourism and transport economics"]. In 1996, the fifth edition of that handbook was published. In the same series Kaspar published:

- Kaspar (1976). Die Schweizerische Verkehrspolitik im Rückblick. [The federal transport policy in Switzerland].
- Kaspar (1977). Verkehrswirtschaftslehre im Grundriss. [Introduction into transport economics].
- Kaspar (1994). Management im Tourismus. Eine Grundlage für das Management von Tourismusunternehmungen und -organisationen. [Tourism management – An introduction into management of tourism enterprises].
- Kaspar and Fehrlin (1984). together with P. Fehrlin, Marketingkonzeption für Heilbäderkurorte – Ein Handbuch. [Handbook of management of spa destinations].
- Kaspar (1992, als Herausgeber). Standort und Chancen des Tourismus. [State and chances of tourism].
- Kaspar and Scherly (1991). together with F. Scherly, Einführung in das touristische Management. [Introduction into tourism management].
- Kaspar and Mihalic (1996). together with T. Mihalic: Umweltökonomie im Tourismus. [Environmental economics in tourism].

Three other books, not published in the above-mentioned series, are

- Kaspar, C., G. Haedrich, H. Kleinert, & K. Klemm (1983). Tourismus-Management, Tourismus-Marketing und Fremdenverkehrsplanung, Berlin. [Planning, management and marketing in tourism].
- Kaspar C, P. Bernecker, & J. Mazanec (1984). Zur Entwicklung der Fremdenverkehrsforschung und -lehre der letzten Jahre, Wien. [The state of research and teaching in tourism].
- Kaspar, C. & F. Scherly (1992). Introduction au management touristique, Paul Haupt, Berne [French issue of Introduction into tourism management, 1991].

In this "portrait" we have no place to analyse his economic thinking. But two features are important. First, he believed 100% in the free market economy. Second, he had a special attention to management and system analysis in tourism and transport economics.

Conclusion

There is no better sentence which synthesises the professional work of Claude Kaspar than the one written by Thomas Bieger in his obituary: "a pioneer in system theory in tourism and transport and an intermediary between theory and practice". Claude's friend Claudio Vela describes very well "the man" behind the tourism and transport economist. In the "Festschrift Prof. Dr Claude Kaspar" (Theorie und Praxis der Tourismus- und Verkehrwirtschaft im Wertewandel 1996), Vela characterizes Kaspar as as the "cultivierte Romand" (the cultural man of "romansh speaking Switzerland") and he finishes his laudation as follows:

Schaut man sich das gesamte Erscheinungsbild von Claude Kaspar an, wäre man geneigt, in ihm einen Repräsentanten der Renaissance zu sehen: Wissenschaft, Geist, aufgeklärte Religion, Kultur, Kunst, Natur, alles gepaart mit Menschlichkeit und Charme. Und genau dieses letzte Wort - Charme – prägt den Unterschied: Claude Kaspar is kein alter Golem sondern ein froher, humorvoller, warmer Mensch mit Herz, den man einfach lieb haben muss.

When one looks at the overall picture of Claude Kaspar, one is inclined to consider him as a representative of the Renaissance: science, intelligence, rational religion, culture, art, nature, all this combined with humanity and charm. It is particularly that last word, "charm" that makes the difference. Kaspar is a man with sense of humour, a personality with a warm heart, who we simply should love (a free translation)

We have chosen "Claude Kaspar: a life devoted to tourism and transport – moving theory into practice" as the title of this contribution. In fact, this title is a conclusion of this portrait. But above all he was a leader with a warm personality.

Disclosure statement

No potential conflict of interest was reported by the author.

References

Bieger, T. (2004). *Pionier de Systemtheorie in Tourismus und Verkehr* (Vol. *11*). St. Galen: IDT Blickpunkte.
Fischer, G. (1996). *Grosses engagement für die HSG* (Vol. *123*). St. Galler: Hochschulnachrichten.
Fischer, G., & Laesser, C. (Eds.). (1996). *Theorie und Praxis der Tourismus- und Verkehrswirtschaft im Wertewandel.* Bern: Festschrift zur Emitierung von Prof. Dr. Claude Kaspar, Paul Haupt.
Kaspar, C. (1976). *Die Schweizerische Verkehrspolitik im Rückblick* (Vol. *6*). St. Galler: Beitrage zum Tourismus und der Verkehrswirtschaft.
Kaspar, C. (1977). *Verkehrswirtschaftslehre im Grundriss* (Vol. *7*). St. Galler: Beitrage zum Tourismus und der Verkehrswirtschaft.
Kaspar, C. (1983). Training and research in Switzerland. *Tourism Management, 4*, 219–220. doi:10. 1016/0261-5177(83)90068-7
Kaspar, C. (1992, als Herausgeber). *Standort und Chancen des Tourismus* (Vol. *20*). St. Galler: Beitrage zum Tourismus und der Verkehrswirtschaft.
Kaspar, C. (1996). *Die Tourismuslehre im Grundriss – St. Galler Beitrage zum Tourismus und der Verkehrswirtschaft* (5th ed.). Bern: Verlag Paul Haupt.
Kaspar, C. (1994). *Management im Tourismus. Eine Grundlage für das Management von Tourismusunternehmungen und -Organisationen* (Vol. *13*). St. Galler: Beitrage zum Tourismus und der Verkehrswirtschaft.
Kaspar, C., Bernecker, P., & Mazanec, J. (1984). *Zur Entwicklung der Fremdenverkehrsforschung und -lehre der letzten Jahre.* Wien.
Kaspar, C., & Fehrlin, P. (1984). *Marketingkonzeption für Heilbäderkurorte – Ein handbu* (Vol. *16*). St. Galler: Beitrage zum Tourismus und der Verkehrswirtschaft.
Kaspar, C., Haedrich, G., Kleinert, H., & Klemm, K. (1983). *Tourismus-Management.* Berlin: Tourismus-Marketing und Fremdenverkehrsplanung.
Kaspar, C., & Mihalic, T. (1996). *Umweltökonomie im Tourismus* (Vol. *27*). St. Galler: Beitrage zum Tourismus und der Verkehrswirtschaft.
Kaspar, C., & Scherly, F. (1991). *Einführung in das Touristische Management* (Vol. *21*). St. Galler: Beitrage zum Tourismus und der Verkehrswirtschaft.
Kaspar, C., & Scherly, F. (1992). *Introduction au management touristique.* Berne: Paul Haupt.
Kaspar, C. (1996). Von der Trendwende zum Quantensprung in Verkehr und Tourismus. *The Tourist Review, 4*.
Prof. Dr. Claude Kaspar, Die Studentenzeitschrift der Universität St. Gallen, N° 236, 1996.
Vanhove, N. (2015). Tourist Research Centre (TRC): Short history. *Anatolia: An International Journal of Tourism and Hospitality Research.* doi:10.1080/13032917.2013.872873

Daniel R. Fesenmaier: an accidental, colourful and quintessential scholar

Dan Wang and Bing Pan

Introduction

Daniel R. Fesenmaier is currently Professor and Director of the Eric Friedheim Tourism Institute in the Department of Tourism, Recreation and Sport Management at the University of Florida, USA. In his 40-year academic career, his numerous publications – along with those of his students – have shaped the landscape of tourism research, especially in the areas of tourism and information technology.

Fesenmaier has held positions in several academic institutions in North America. Many of his former Ph.D. students are now established scholars at institutions in North America, the United Kingdom, Europe and East Asia. His colourful personality, language and hairstyle have contributed to his legendary status. His official curriculum vitae boasts a long list of achievements, including many journal articles, books, monographs, research awards and membership in the International Academy of the Study of Tourism. However, when one of the authors interviewed him at a party in Vienna in November 2017, asking him about his contribution to tourism knowledge, he mumbled, "I don't know."

The authors have chosen to compose a portrait of Fesenmaier because he has been talking about his retirement for some time. Thus, it might be the time to summarise his career and academic milestones. In addition, given many of his contemporary colleagues' portraits in Anatolia, it seems fitting for him to receive the same recognition. As many scholars in the tourism community can attest, he is often misunderstood due to his direct interaction style and sharp-edged personality, so this portrait also presents an opportunity to provide a clearer picture of Fesenmaier. Hereafter, Fesenmaier will be shortened as Dr. Fez, as his students and colleagues have called him.

For the purpose to present Dr. Fez in a more comprehensive and objective way, the two authors have interviewed 12 people. Among them, nine are his colleagues and past students, one is Dr. Fez himself, and the other two are authors themselves. Each interview was conducted according to a semi-structured script, including inquiries about his contributions to the academic community, his style as an advisor and collaborator, and anecdotes about him.

After reading through all the transcribed interviews, three adjectives come to mind: accidental (his own words), colourful (Dr. Iis Tussyadiah's) and quintessential (Dr. Pauline Sheldon's). We hope to illustrate these three aspects of his career and personality in the rest of this portrait.

Short biography

Dr. Fez was born and raised in Minneapolis, Minnesota, USA (1951). He started his college education with a major in forestry. However, after 2 years, he found his true interest and talent in mathematics and statistics. In his junior year at the University of Minnesota, he casually took a postgraduate biostatistics course and got an A. Afterward, he changed his focus to mathematical ecology and graduated in 1975 with a bachelor's degree in ecology and plant geography. With a passion to be an urban planner, he started a master's programme in economic geography at Southern Illinois University, Carbondale.

In that programme, he met his first important mentor, Dr. Stan Lieber, who guided him in learning advanced quantitative methods in demand estimation. Dr. Fez worked as a research assistant for Lieber for a project on forecasting recreation demand in Illinois. At the end of his master's programme in 1977, he was recommended to join Professor Michael Goodchild's group to continue his Ph.D. study at the University of Western Ontario, Canada. Dr. Fez has attested that his 3-year Ph.D. journey (1978–1980) with Goodchild's group shaped his later philosophy and approach, including his views on research, training postgraduate students, and developing research group culture.

On the first day of the programme, in the late 1970s, Goodchild showed him how to programme 3-D map objects, which Dr. Fez described as "the coolest thing in the world." During his 3 years of Ph.D. study, Dr. Fez also collaborated with two other Ph.D. students in the group to publish 16 high-quality journal papers. In addition, he experienced the "Friday celebration culture" in his Ph.D. study group. "We went out every Friday late afternoon to talk and celebrate what we had done in the past week," said Fesenmaier. "We talked about ideas and trends, and I think this is a good way to produce the best Ph.D. students."

In 1980, Dr. Fez officially embarked on a journey as a scholar and teacher in higher education, which has lasted through four decades to the present. By observing his career path, two unique points stand out. First, during his career, Dr. Fez has worked for six institutions, including the University of Oklahoma (1980–1983), Texas A&M University (1983–1988), Indiana University (1988–1991), the University of Illinois (1992–2003), Temple University (2003–2014), and the University of Florida (2014-present), all in the United States. He attested, "From a quality of life point of view, I wish I had been more stable. However, by moving around, you learn along with it. From a professional point of view, I had a fantastic life. I am glad I did that." Second, he held multiple positions at the University of Illinois and Temple University, where he spent more than a decade each. At the University of Illinois, in addition to a position in the Department of Leisure Studies, he served as an adjunct professor in the Department of Geography and Department of Advertising. At Temple University, beyond a position in the School of Tourism and Hospitality Management, he served as an adjunct professor in the Department of Management Information Systems at the Fox School of Business. He enjoyed working on interdisciplinary projects and collaborations with scholars from other fields. His Ph.D. students were also encouraged and granted chances to take courses in other disciplines, and many participated in research projects in other fields.

Another highlight in his career was serving as a director for the National Laboratory for Tourism & eCommerce (NLTeC), which Dr. Fez established in 1995 at the University of Illinois. He created NLTeC for better collaboration with destination marketing organizations in Illinois and other states. The NLTeC turned out to be an innovation centre for experimenting with ideas in tourism and information science, eCommerce and online marketing. He worked with his postgraduate students and hired programmers for government and industry projects, and he maintained a self-sustained lab. Meanwhile, he and his students explored research questions that contributed to the field theoretically and practically. The output of the lab included academic papers, consultancy reports, information systems and computer applications. In the past two decades, a total of 23 Ph.D. students and 24 master's students graduated while working at NLTeC, and 150 projects were completed with a total of US$ 6.8 million in funding. He labelled the spirit of NLTeC, "Innovation, Creativity, & Fun". In 2004, NLTeC was moved to Temple University and is now housed at the University of Florida.

Dr. fez and his academic accomplishments

During his 40-year scholarly career, Dr. Fez published one book, six edited books, three monographs and 276 articles 132 of those in refereed journals. Many of his works have been widely cited. According to Google Scholar statistics, his research profile has logged 16,719 citations with an i10-index 173 as of January, 2018. The research work he and his students published substantially influenced research in tourism experience, travellers' online behaviour and the impact of information technology on tourism.

Along the way, Dr. Fez's research evolved to focus on three areas. Figure 1 highlights his seminal papers in the three areas along with his scholarship journey from 1980 to 2017. The first area is travel advertising and demand analysis, focusing on: (1) the nature of decision making in pleasure travel (1980–2000); (2) the nature and role of information used by travellers to guide trip-related decisions (2000–2012) and (3) the application of travel demand modelling in tourism planning (2012–present). Influenced by the learning tracks in his master's and Ph.D. programmes, he had a strong interest in conducting research quantitatively. In his first several years at Texas A&M University, he and his colleagues created an information system to profile visitors' information in Texas, called "TTRIP" (Texas Tourism & Recreation Information Program). His early research in the 1980s focused on measuring and modelling people's leisure behaviour. For instance, a series of papers published by Dr. Fez and Dr. Lieber investigated people's recreation expenditure and provided important implications for recreation planning. Later, in the 1990s, his research interests turned to tourists and destination marketing. Working with scholars such as John Crompton and his colleague at Texas A&M, and his students, including Wesley Roehl, Jame Bigley, Christine Vogt, Kelly MacKay, Jiann-min Jeng and Lan Xia, Dr. Fez investigated tourists' decision making, planning behaviour and use of travel information. As a result, he and his group

Figure 1. Professor Daniel Fesenmaier's three main research areas and important works.

made a substantial contribution to the understanding of tourist information consumption behaviour and decision making.

Dr. Fez's second research focus is tourism marketing and information technology. The four sub-areas are: (1) the use of Internet technology by travellers in the travel planning process; (2) the design of web-based systems for marketing tourism products; (3) emerging technologies for use in tourism marketing; (4) competitive strategies for marketing tourism destinations (including the branding of tourism destinations) and (5) market information systems. In the late 1990s, he observed the enormous potential of information technology and particularly the Internet on traveller behaviour and the tourism industry. With Ulrike Gretzel and Yu-Lan Yuan, he published a paper that highlighted the challenges and changes the Internet created for destination marketing organizations (Gretzel, Yuan, & Fesenmaier, 2000). Since then, Dr. Fez and his students, such as Gretzel, Bing Pan, Yuan, Zheng Xiang, Yeong-Hyeon Hwang, Youcheng Wang, Florian Zach, Sangwon Park and Dan Wang, developed several research streams. These include research on tourism recommendation systems, online travel communities, website design and destination marketing, travel planning on the Internet, search behaviour for online travel information, Internet-mediated travel experience and the impact of smartphones on travel. He and his group are prolific in this area, and their impact has grown quickly with the proliferation of researchers of information technology and tourism-related topics.

In recent years, Dr. Fez turned his research interest to experience design. This area includes: (1) mapping experiences in tourism and hospitality; (2) assessing the role of stories and communication in the tourist experience; (3) application of service dominant logic within the travel experience and (4) identifying emerging metrics for modelling travel experiences. He attested that research efforts in the latter two areas, during past decades, laid a foundation for him to step into the area of experience design. Perceiving that information technology is becoming the invisible hands powering business processes and people's lives in different respects, he believes that what we do with IT platforms is most important. Working with his students, such as Jeongmi (Jamie) Kim, Yeongbae Choe and Jason Stienmetz, he has started to focus on developing IT-based innovative methods to measure tourism experience from multiple dimensions.

Dr. fez and academic communities

Dr. Fez has been actively involved in several academic communities, including the Tourism Education Futures Initiative (TEFI), International Federation for IT and Travel & Tourism (IFITT) and the Travel & Tourism Research Association (TTRA). In fact, he is a co-founder and the inspiration behind TEFI together with Pauline Sheldon.

TEFI was born in 2006–2007 as a result of discussions on the "seismic changes" taking place in higher education. At a meeting in Vienna in 2006, a few tourism educators and industry leaders recognized these industrial changes in terms of scale, diversity and the increasing impact of many divergent factors on the future of tourism and hospitality education. These new challenges called out for a new paradigm in tourism education, so TEFI was formed with the following initial mission: "TEFI seeks to provide vision, knowledge and a framework for tourism education programs to promote global citizenship and optimism for a better world." TEFI now identifies itself as a new and inclusive tourism academy. It is a social movement comprised of people (educators, researchers, industry actors and community members), who seek to progress an alternative type of tourism that is sustainable and just, that delivers blended social, economic and environmental value, and that promotes vibrant flourishing communities.

Dan Fesenmaier and Pauline Sheldon from the University of Hawaii convened the first TEFI conference at Modul University, Vienna, in 2007 with Dr. Karl Woeber. Over the ensuing decade (2007–2017), TEFI gained momentum and held nine annual conferences in eight countries. The frameworks, guidelines and white papers published by TEFI have substantially influenced the development of tourism and hospitality education programmes in many countries (Sheldon,

Fesenmaier, & Tribe, 2011). These days, as the tourism industry faces the challenges of self-service technology, robotics and changing consumer values, the vision of early "TEFI-ites" is worthy of more appreciation.

IFITT is the leading global community encouraging knowledge and experience sharing for a group of practitioners and academics with a true passion for information and communications technology (ICT) in travel and tourism. Dr. Fez attended ENTER, the annual conference of this community, in the second year after its establishment in 1993. Over 20 years, he and his students contributed approximately 40 papers to ENTER conferences, and eight papers were ranked among the top-three best papers in specific years. He and his group brought a sociological perspective to understanding the mutual impact of IT and travellers, which is an important contribution to a community dominated by technology-oriented research streams. Dr. Fez worked in the ENTER programme committee for 18 years. He was awarded the Hannes Werthner Tourism and Technology Lifetime Achievement Award and the 20 Years ENTER Paper Contribution Award by IFITT in 2013 in Innsbruck, Austria.

Besides TEFI and IFITT, Dr. Fez has been active in serving the Travel and Tourism Research Association (TTRA), a nonprofit association dedicated to enhancing the quality, value, effectiveness and use of research in travel marketing, planning and development. He and his students have contributed over 30 papers to the annual TTRA conference since 1992. He also worked with the Journal of Travel Research, TTRA's affiliated journal, to publish a series of invited papers for tourism research foundations from 2012 to 2015. He was also awarded the International Travel and Tourism Research Association (TTRA) Lifetime Achievement Award in 2013.

Dr. Fez's other contributions to tourism studies include being the co-founding editor of Tourism Analysis, the past Editor-in-Chief of the Journal of Information Technology and Tourism, and Editor of the Foundations in Tourism Research Series in the Journal of Travel Research. Among his other achievements, he is a Fellow in the International Academy for the Study of Tourism. He has also been honoured by receiving the Michael D. Olsen Research Award from the University of Delaware (2010), and the Medal of Exceptional Scholarly Achievement (CPTHL, 2007).

Dr. fez and his anecdotal stories

The 12 interviews conducted for this article revealed similar colours and hues of Dr. Fez's personality and character, but each revealed different aspects as well. The common keywords were many, such as "brilliant," "innovative," "creative," and "forward-thinking." In addition, many scholars remembered him with stories that reinforced the type of scholar and colleague he is.

Dr. Fez is described as innovative and creative, as always learning and pushing the frontier forward. He is always looking for the next new idea in understanding travel planning and decision making, advertising, demand analysis, online marketing and experience design. He is also a strong believer in making unique and meaningful contributions to the field, not being repetitive and not publishing merely for the sake of publication.

Dr. Fez has a strong sense of responsibility as a scholar and educator. He has strongly influenced people around him to have a similar sense of obligation. This includes responsibility towards both graduate and undergraduate students and the younger generation; responsibility towards the tourism research community and responsibility towards greater society. Thus, he strongly advocates emphasizing the greater good rather than petty personal gains.

In the interviews about Dr. Fez, there were many stories told by his students, colleagues and collaborators. The authors present here 10 anecdotal stories:

(1) Friday afternoons, or whenever a paper is accepted, are fun times with Dr. Fez. Both authors vividly remembered his research group's happy hours in a pub or bar, whether these occurred in downtown Philadelphia, PA or Champaign, Illinois. Thanksgiving dinner is an annual tradition, with Dr. Fez hosting his entire research group at his home, whether he was living in Champaign, Philadelphia or Gainesville, Florida.

(2) Dr. Fez is a great conversationalist. He can have a conversation with anyone on any topic and make it interesting. Once he drove with Dr. Joe O'Leary from Champaign, Illinois to Montreal for an ENTER conference and he did not stop talking during the all-night trip.

(3) However, his comments and critiques during a conference presentation are always sharp, challenging and to-the-point. The last thing he can stand is intellectual laziness.

(4) Dr. Fez is an early riser: he goes to bed very early and usually arrives at the office prior to 6 o'clock every morning. Sunday morning is also his usual work time.

(5) Dr. Fez reads one book every week (or at least tries to do so).

(6) Dr. Fez is very generous towards his students and friends. On one occasion, he gave his personal credit card to one of his Ph.D. students to book hotels and transportation in Europe, so the student could have some personal fun time beyond the time spent at a conference. He also loaned his car to one of his visiting scholars during another conference.

(7) From time to time, Dr. Fez can "*kick his graduate students' butts*" (Pauline Sheldon's words), too; interestingly, none of his past students mentioned this.

(8) Dr. Fez may be the only person who could cross the European Union border from Switzerland to Italy without a passport. During one of his trips in Europe, he forgot his passport but somehow happened to have his driver's license stuck in his jean pocket. He charmed the border guard into letting him through. In a more unfortunate case, he was sent back on a return flight from San Paulo when he forgot he needed a visa to enter Brazil. Of course, he also missed his keynote speech.

(9) Dr. Fez drinks Diet Coke at every meal, even at breakfast.

(10) Dr. Fez drinks cognac, too – the expensive type – but only with good friends. He can drink cognac all night long but still manage to wake up to give an inspiring speech in the early morning.

The 10 anecdotal stories reflect Dr. Fez as an atypical mentor and advisor in that he always blends work, study and fun. When asked why he has the drive, energy and motivation to push forward all the time, he simply said, "*It's fun.*"

Conclusion

Dr. Fez is an accidental tourism scholar who never intended to be a scholar at the beginning of his college career. He moved from forestry and ecology to geography, recreation, decision making, tourism marketing and ultimately to tourism and information technology. He is colourful in his personality, language, personal interaction and hairstyle, though many misunderstand his direct and challenging communication style. He is also a quintessential scholar: he contributed much to the tourism academy and helped build the community of tourism research. The landscape of tourism research would have been different – and definitely a lot more boring – without him. As Dr. Fez famously proclaimed at several Ph.D. workshops in ENTER conferences: "*research is better than sex!*". For him, research has never been about work; he is always having fun with his research and continues to do so, and he enjoys having creative people around him. Recently, he stopped talking about his upcoming retirement, so this portrait might be pre-mature. Perhaps he will continue to have new ideas and new plans every day and venture into a new territory of research. In his words, that would be "*fantastic!*"

Acknowledgements

To portray a broader picture of Professor Daniel Fesenmaier, the authors had conversations with some of his colleagues, collaborators and former students. The authors would like to thank the following scholars who shared their perspectives for this portrait: Dr. Ulrike Gretzel, Dr. Yunpeng Li, Dr. Sangwon Park, Professor Pauline Sheldon, Dr. Jason Stienmetz, Dr. Iis Tussyadiah, Professor Hannes Werthner, Professor Karl Wöber, Dr. Zheng (Phil) Xiang and Dr. Florian Zach.

Disclosure statement

No potential conflict of interest was reported by the authors.

References

Choe, Y., Kim, J., & Fesenmaier, D. R. (2017). Use of social media across the trip experience: An application of latent transition analysis. *Journal of Travel & Tourism Marketing*, *34*(4), 431–443.

Choe, Y., Stienmetz, J. L., & Fesenmaier, D. R. (2017). Measuring destination marketing: Comparing four models of advertising conversion. *Journal of Travel Research*, *56*(2), 143–157.

Fesenmaier, D. R. (1985a). On modelling aggregation impact in spatially distributed data. *Quality and Quantity*, *19*, 71–82.

Fesenmaier, D. R. (1985b). Modeling variation in destination patronage for outdoor recreation activity. *Journal of Travel Research*, *24*(2), 17–22.

Fesenmaier, D. R., Goodchild, M. F., & Lieber, S. R. (1980). The correlates of day-hiking: The effect of aggregation. *Journal of Leisure Research*, *12*, 213–228.

Fesenmaier, D. R., Goodchild, M. F., & Lieber, S. R. (1981). The importance of urban milieu in predicting recreation participation: The case of day-hiking. *Leisure Sciences*, *4*(4), 459–476.

Fesenmaier, D. R., & Jeng, J. (2000). Assessing structure in the pleasure trip planning process. *Tourism Analysis*, *5*(3), 13–28.

Fesenmaier, D. R., & Xiang, Z. (2017). *Design Science in Tourism: Foundations of Destination Management (Co-Editors)*. Vienna: Springer.

Gretzel, U., Yuan, Y., & Fesenmaier, D. R. (2000). Preparing for the new economy: Advertising and change in destination marketing organizations. *Journal of Travel Research*, *39*(2), 146–156.

Hwang, Y. H., Gretzel, U., & Fesenmaier, D. R. (2006). Multi-city trip patterns of international travelers to the U.S.: An analysis of trip structures. *Annals of Tourism Research*, *33*(4), 1057–1078.

Kim, J., & Fesenmaier, D. R. (2015). Measuring emotion in real time: Implications for tourism design. *Journal of Travel Research*, *54*(4), 419–429.

Kim, J., & Fesenmaier, D. R. (2017). Sharing tourism experiences: The posttrip experience. *Journal of Travel Research*, *56*(1), 28–40.

Lue, C., Crompton, J. L., & Fesenmaier, D. R. (1992). Conceptualizing the role and structure of multi-destination pleasure trips. *Annals of Tourism Research*, *20*, 289–301.

MacKay, K. J., & Fesenmaier, D. R. (1997). Pictorial element of destination promotion in image formation. *Annals of Tourism Research*, *24*(3), 537–565.

MacKay, K. J., & Fesenmaier, D. R. (2000). Travel information search and tourist behavior. *Journal of Travel Research*, *38*(4), 417–423.

Pan, B., & Fesenmaier, D. R. (2006). Exploring the structure of travel planning on the Internet. *Annals of Tourism Research*, *33*(3), 809–832.

Pan, B., Zheng, X., Law, R., & Fesenmaier, D. R. (2011). The dynamics of search engine marketing for tourism destinations. *Journal of Travel Research*, *50*(4), 365–377.

Park, S., Nicolau, J. C., & Fesenmaier, D. R. (2012). Assessing destination advertising using a hierarchical decision model. *Annals of Tourism Research, 40*(1), 260–282.

Roehl, W., & Fesenmaier, D. R. (1992). Risk perceptions and pleasure travel: An exploratory analysis. *Journal of Travel Research, 30*(4), 17–26.

Sheldon, P. J., Fesenmaier, D. R., & Tribe, J. (2011). The tourism education futures initiative (TEFI): Activating change in tourism education. *Journal of Teaching in Travel & Tourism, 11*(1), 2–23.

Vogt, C., & Fesenmaier, D. R. (1998). Expanding the functional tourism information search model: Incorporating aesthetic, hedonic, innovation and sign dimensions. *Annals of Tourism Research, 25*(3), 551–579.

Wang, D., Park, S., & Fesenmaier, D. R. (2012). The role of smartphones in mediating the touristic experience. *Journal of Travel Research, 51*(4), 371–387.

Wang, Y., & Fesenmaier, D. R. (2004a). Modeling participation in an online travel community. *Journal of Travel Research, 42*(3), 261–270.

Wang, Y., & Fesenmaier, D. R. (2004b). Towards understanding the needs and motivations for contributing to an online travel community: An integrated model. *Tourism Management, 25*, 709–722.

Xiang, Z., & Fesenmaier, D. R. (2017). *Analytics in SMART Tourism Design: Concepts and Methods (Co-Editors)*. Vienna: Springer.

Xiang, Z., Gretzel, U., & Fesenmaier, D. R. (2009). Semantic representation of tourism on the Internet. *Journal of Travel Research, 47*(2), 137–150.

Index